Mitchell Masterpieces

AN ILLUSTRATED HISTORY OF PAINT JOBS ON B-25s IN FOREIGN SERVICE

VOLUME 2

Mitchell Masterpieces

An illustrated history of paint jobs on B-25s in foreign service

Volume 2

Wim Nijenhuis

Violaero

A masterpiece of camouflage at Melsbroek, Belgium. A hangar especially built and camouflaged by the German Luftwaffe to look like a row of village houses. The German forces constructed the fake facade around the hangar in a bid to protect Luftwaffe aircraft prior to their retreat from the area. After the Normandy Invasion, three B-25 Mitchell squadrons of the 2nd Tactical Air Force of the RAF were stationed at Melsbroek. One of the Mitchells is parked in this former German hangar with the text "Rauchen Verboten" (No Smoking) written on the back wall. (RAF)

ISBN: 978-90-8616-237-6

NUGI: 465
1st print, October 2019

© Copyright 2019
Lanasta, Odoorn

Design: Jantinus Mulder

www.lanasta.com

All correspondence regarding copyrights, translation or any other matter can be directed to: Lanasta, Oude Kampenweg 29, 7873 AG Odoorn, the Netherlands.

Contents

FOREWORD

By Dave Poissant,
Burlington, Ontario

Chairman, 2nd Tactical Air Force Medium Bombers Association Canada
B-25 History Project Historian

When young men at war are concentrated far from loved ones and home, their thoughts, discussions and dreams inevitably turn to the folks back home and, especially, the wives and girlfriends still there. Nowhere is that more evident than in the Air Force. What better a 'canvas' than the large expanse of metal on the nose of an aircraft? Perfect for illustrating the affection for a pilot's wife, girlfriend or daughter or perhaps a crew's agreed-upon yearning for an unattainable celebrity; or even a piece of fictional whimsy.

American airmen were, arguably, the originators of nose art and became very proficient at it, as well-documented in Wim Nijenhuis' Mitchell Masterpieces Volume 1. The incredible detailing on some of USAAF nose art points to frustrated commercial artists and sign painters serving in the air force. It's easy to imagine a Mitchell crew readying for another mission as they gently pat their nose art for luck, connecting with home in hope of safe return. When U.S. Army Air Forces dispersed throughout WWII's various theatres, the new art form was quickly taken up by host air forces, evidenced by the photos and descriptions we see in this volume, thanks to Wim's extensive research and ever-widening contacts within the B-25 community.

In these pages we see nose art as simple as a girl's name: "Yvonne" or "Carol"; we also see references to a favourite tipple c/w accompanying artwork: "Beer is Best" or "Ouwe Jongens". In No. 98 Squadron RAF, where my Dad served as an RCAF Pilot, an early Squadron Leader, R.D. Pitcairn, came up with the idea of naming his Mitchell after

My Dad and his crew in September 1944 at RAF Dunsfold.
From left they are: Cyrille 'Cy' Poissant (Pilot), Peter 'Doc' Ryan (Observer), Fred 'Bing' Bing (Wireless Op/Air Gunner) and George 'Ole' Olson (Air Gunner). (Photo David Poissant)

the fictional "Snow White" and other Mitchells of his flight could be named for dwarfs; to date, we've documented "Grumpy"' and "Sneezy". My Dad piloted "Grumpy" on four operations. "Snow White" was felled by FW190s on 21 September, 1943 with no survivors; "Grumpy" and "Sneezy" survived the war with 125 and 113 ops respectively, to be struck off charge (SOC) and scrapped. Wim records the paint for "Grumpy" and "Sneezy" herein; no records of "Snow White's" markings have yet surfaced.

Along with nose art, Wim also explains the various national and squadron markings used to enable quick identification differentiating friend and foe in the melee that is often air warfare.

Wim Nijenhuis has authored three authoritative books on Mitchells:
- *B-25 Factory Times*
- *Mitchell Masterpieces Volume 1*
- *Mitchell Masterpieces Volume 2*

If you're a B-25 Mitchell fan, all deserve homes in your library.

Dave.

A B-25 warbird with the nose art of "Grumpy", photographed at Duxford in October 1989. (Wim Nijenhuis)

ACKNOWLEDGEMENTS

This book would not have been possible without the generous help of other people. Many sources were consulted and individuals or organisations allowed me the use of their photographs or other material.

Special thanks goes to David Poissant from Ontario, Canada. David is Chairman/Editor of the 2nd Tactical Air Force Medium Bombers Association. I have met David during the gathering of B-25s for the 75th Doolittle Anniversary in April 2017 at Grimes Field and Dayton, Ohio, and get to know him as a warm and competent personality. David wrote a beautiful and catchy foreword and has provided me with some interesting photos of RAF Mitchells.

I would like to thank the following individuals or organisations (in alphabetical order) who have helped me, in the past or recently, for their time and effort for providing information or pictures that could be used in this book.

★ Almer Regter	Netherlands
★ Australian War Memorial	Australia
★ Bureau Maritieme Historie	Netherlands
★ Carl Geust	Finland
★ Coert Munk	Netherlands
★ Dan Desko	U.S.A.
★ Dan Hagedorn	U.S.A.
★ Danilo Villarroel Canga	Chile
★ Gene Boswell	U.S.A.
★ Gerben Tornij	Netherlands
★ Imperial War Museum	United Kingdom
★ Ilya Grinberg	U.S.A.
★ Kasia Ptak	Netherlands
★ Musée de L'Air	France
★ Nationaal Archief	Netherlands
★ Norman L. Avery	U.S.A.
★ (former) North American Rockwell	U.S.A.
★ Paco Andreu	Spain
★ Ronald Jeurissen	Netherlands
★ Royal Air Force	United Kingdom
★ Royal Canadian Air Force	Canada
★ Royal Netherlands Air Force	Netherlands
★ U.S. National Archives	U.S.A.
★ Wilko Jonker	Netherlands

Finally, I want to thank Rob van Oosterzee, for his great and conscientious help with the linguistic issues of the manuscript, and for providing some very useful suggestions.

Photo courtesy: Where known, the photos are listed with their sources.

INTRODUCTION

This is the second volume about paint jobs on the North American B-25 Mitchell. Volume 1 dealt with the B-25s in service with the U.S. Armed Forces. This Volume 2 covers the B-25s in service with the foreign military forces.

The B-25 was the most widely used allied medium bomber of the Second World War. After the produced airplanes left the factories, they served in the armed forces of the United States as well as other allied countries during and after the war. During the war, especially the United Kingdom and the Soviet Union were the major users of the B-25. During and after the war, relatively large numbers of B-25s were used by the Netherlands, Canada, China, Brazil and Venezuela. But also other countries used the B-25 after the war, whether or not in military conflicts. Most countries then just started using the B-25 in their air forces.

This book focuses on the B-25s used in the military forces of the countries outside the U.S.A. A brief history of the units is given, in particular limited to what is related to the use of the B-25 bomber. Initially, the airplanes were mostly painted in standard camouflage colours in the factories. But by 1944, more and more airplanes were delivered uncamouflaged. Therefore, we see that most B-25s that served after the war were natural aluminium finished. Also, war decorations with the famous nose art disappeared. But nevertheless, the shiny aluminium airplanes with their colourful markings were also really masterpieces. Often in this book reference is made to the U.S. colour schemes. Detailed information about the U.S. colour schemes on the B-25 is given in the book *"Mitchell Masterpieces Volume 1"*.
By no means this book pretends to be complete. The subject is by far too complex and detailed to be described in full here. Therefore, this book should serve only as a general view of services, colours and markings. Like Volume 1, a choice has been made of the most relevant units and the individual airplanes. Many examples are shown. These include several pictures that are less known or even completely unknown. Pictures of specific armed forces with B-25s are very rare. Although some of the pictures are un-fortunately of a poor quality, they are nevertheless interesting in the context of the subject.

The development of the factories and the production of the B-25 bombers are extensively described and illustrated in my previous book *"B-25 Factory Times"*. Together with *"B-25 Factory Times"* and *"Mitchell Masterpieces Vol. 1"*, this book is a thorough continuation of the production and deployment history of the B-25 Mitchell. A masterpiece from North American Aviation Inc.

Wim Nijenhuis

Nose art in the RAF was less exuberant than in the USAAF. The well known British Avro Lancaster "S for Sugar" was not decorated with a nice painting but with a quote. "No enemy aircraft will fly over the Reich territory" was said by Hermann Göring, head of the Luftwaffe at the start of WWII. This famous Lancaster Mk. I with registration number R5868 and squadron code PO-S, was in service with No. 467 Squadron. In total she flew 137 operational sorties. Preserved following the war, she was transferred to RAF Wroughton where it was from 1947 to 1958 in moth-balls. She was the gate guard at RAF Scampton from 1958 until 1970 and then transferred to RAF Bicester where she was restored between 1970 and 1972. Finally, she was taking her place at the RAF Museum in London in 1972, where it remains to the present day. (Life magazine)

CAMOUFLAGE AND NOSE ART

Like all other military powers in World War II, the U.S. used camouflage paint schemes for their aircraft, including the B-25. The B-25 remained in production throughout the war, so there were many variations in the paint finish. The airplanes were generally painted at the factories in accordance with the requirements of the U.S. Army Air Corps and later Army Air Forces. In the early 1940s, the standard colour of bombers was matt Dark Olive Drab No. 41 and matt Neutral Grey No. 43. But gradually the colour numbers changed and by 1944, the USAAF had decided that it no longer required camouflage on the majority of its combat airplanes. Mostly, these schemes were also implemented for the B-25s that were delivered to other countries. In the operational field, the aircraft were often provided with additional markings and other paintings such as nose art and squadron characters. The development of the U.S. camouflage schemes and nose art is extensively described in the book *"Mitchell Masterpieces Volume I"*.

In the world of airplane nose art, especially the Americans are well-known. However, the British Royal Air Force also knew many forms of art. This includes Canada, New Zealand, Australia, Netherlands, Poland, France and South Africa. These countries had units that operated within the RAF. Although considerably less, many British airplanes had artwork often located at the nose area,

but it could also be found on an aircraft's tail or fuselage. Bombers and fighters featured art on aircraft and ranged from cartoon characters to stylised portraits of the aircrew's sweethearts and simple squadron badges. Like the Americans, the practice of painting distinctive art on aircraft in the RAF reached a peak during the Second World War. It begun almost as soon as war was declared in September 1939. Initially, nose art was limited in a small size, even on fighter aircraft, and scarcely visible on the large four-engine bombers. As losses mounted, nose art was seen as a morale-booster for the crews who flew over enemy territory almost nightly and size limits were allowed to expand on most bombers. If a bomber crew was assigned a particular aircraft, they were sometimes able to choose the name and artwork and this enabled a powerful bond between the men and the machine. Often, but not always, the name and the artwork were directly related to the letter designation for the particular aircraft within the squadron. The majority of the RAF-crews were in their very early twenties and many even flew wartime operations while in their teens. So, like the U.S. forces, the majority of the nose art reflects their interest in "pin-up" girls of the day and other images related to their interest in the opposite sex. However the Disney cartoon characters were popular subjects as well.

In the Pacific region, not only the allied air forces of the U.S. had nose art or other paintings, but also those of Australia and the Netherlands. At the beginning of World War Two, the Royal Australian Air Force was not at full strength and rapidly developed its forces. This included a major involvement in Europe through RAF Bomber Command and in the Mediterranean area. Of course, the RAAF was also very active in the defence of Australia and participation in the Pacific campaign. The Netherlands was also active in the South West Pacific Theatre. They were active with her Royal Netherlands East Indies Army Air Force. The RNEIAAF was the air arm of the Royal Netherlands East Indies Army in the Dutch East Indies. It was an entirely separate organisation from the Dutch Air Force. During the war, the RNEIAAF was operated from bases in Australia and the Dutch East Indies. Nose art of both countries were not as prolific as those of the U.S.

On the eastern front, the Soviet Air Force also decorated their airplanes. The method of nose-art on Soviet airplanes was substantially different from that of the United States or the UK. Although in principle the purpose was the same. Nose art was also a morale booster and the art on the airplane identified it and made it unique from all of the aircraft in their unit or on their base. The Soviet Air Force decorated their airplanes with historical images, mythical beasts, and patriotic slogans. Often it consisted of squadron emblems with a coloured text. The patriotic slogans were frequently painted on the side of the fuselage together with awards and kills. This was applied to both own manufactured airplanes as the Lend-Lease airplanes. The Soviets hardly knew paintings in the form of pin-ups, movie stars and cartoon characters.

After termination of the war, most of the airplanes were scrapped. Airplanes that survived were often converted to accommodate new military roles or were sold to other countries or the civilian market. It meant at least the end of the large-scale "nose art industry". Nevertheless, special paintings and nose art still existed. Although on a smaller scale, but still. In some Latin American countries which had just switched to buying the former war airplanes, the airplanes had sometimes a form of art. That was also the case with the Royal Netherlands East Indies Army Air Force that still military action conducted in the Dutch East Indies, later Indonesia, to 1950.

Soviet nose-art on a Lend-Lease Douglas A-20G Boston of the Soviet Air Force. Lend-Lease was the program of supplying vast amounts of war material between the United States and other Allied nations during WWII. This airplane is the regiment commander's airplane of the 3rd squadron of the Baltic Fleet Air Force of the 51st MTAP (Mine-Torpedo Air Regiment). The airplane is standard U.S. Olive Drab with Neutral Grey. This command airplane has Soviet medals and the inscription "Tallinskiy Ap" (Tallinn Air Regiment). (Bundesarchive)

A B-25J of the Fuerza Aérea Mexicana (FAM) at the end of her career in Mexico. (Collection Wim Nijenhuis)

THE B-25 IN FOREIGN SERVICE

New Olive Drab/Neutral Grey camouflaged B-25s at the flight line of North American Aviation at Inglewood, California. The airplanes are intended for four of the main operators of the B-25. From front to rear: the Soviet Union, the Netherlands, the United Kingdom and the United States. (North American Rockwell)

The B-25 was a successful product from North American Aviation Inc. In the period from 1941 until 1945, a total of 9,889 B-25 airplanes were produced in two factories, one at Inglewood, California, and one in Kansas City, Kansas. After the produced airplanes left the factories, most of them served in the armed forces of the United States during the Second World War. The B-25s accepted by the Army Air Forces were mainly used by the U.S. Army Air Forces and the U.S. Navy. During the war, about 2,200 B-25s were supplied to the military forces of other countries in small or large numbers. Particularly, the United Kingdom and the Soviet Union were the largest users with nearly 900 B-25 bombers each. But also reasonably large numbers were used by the Netherlands, Canada, Australia, China and Brazil.

At the end of the war, many aircraft were scrapped in the operational theatres. But also from 1945, thousands of American aircraft began arriving back in the United States. The country had a huge surplus of aircraft including the B-25. Many remained in military service and were used for post-war military roles, mainly in the United States. But also other countries used the B-25 after the war, whether or not in military conflicts. Some countries then just started to take over B-25s for their military forces. These were mostly surplus B-25s from the U.S., the United Kingdom and the Netherlands. Especially Canada, Indonesia, Brazil and Venezuela used significant numbers after the war. Smaller numbers were bought in particular by Latin American countries.

Foreign service

The military operators of the B-25 Mitchell outside the United States (in alphabetical order).

- **Australia**
  - *Royal Australian Air Force*
- **Biafra**
  - *Biafran Air Force*
- **Bolivia**
  - *Bolivian Air Force*
- **Brazil**
  - *Brazilian Air Force*
- **Canada**
  - *Royal Canadian Air Force*
- **China**
  - *Chinese Nationalist Air Force*
  - *People's Liberation Army Air Force*
- **Chile**
  - *Chilean Air Force*
- **Colombia**
  - *Colombian Air Force*
- **Cuba**
  - *Cuban Air Force*
- **Dominican Republic**
  - *Dominican Air Force*
- **Ecuador**
  - *Ecuadorian Air Force*
- **France**
  - *Free French Air Force*
- **Haïti**
  - *Haitian Air Force*
- **Indonesia**
  - *Indonesian Air Force*
- **Mexico**
  - *Mexican Air Force*
- **Netherlands**
  - *Royal Netherlands East Indies Army Air Force*
  - *Royal Netherlands Military Flying School*
  - *Naval Air Service*
- **Peru**
  - *Peruvian Air Force*
- **Soviet Union**
  - *Soviet Air Force*
- **Spain**
  - *Spanish Air Force*
- **United Kingdom**
  - *Royal Air Force*
- **Uruguay**
  - *Uruguayan Air Force*
- **Venezuela**
  - *Venezuelan Air Force*

During the first years of the war, the B-25s were generally painted at the factory in accordance with the requirements of the U.S. Army Air Corps and later Army Air Forces. The most common colours of the bombers were Olive Drab upper surfaces with Neutral Grey undersurfaces. By January 1944, most airplanes coming off the production line were not painted. Instead, they received a wax coating or were oversprayed with a lightweight clear coat. The new airplanes would only have national insignia, squadron and airplane number markings. Therefore, late B-25H and J models left the plants in a natural aluminium finish. Older aircraft generally retained their camouflage paint until such time as the aircraft required a major overhaul. The anti-glare panels of natural aluminium finished aircraft were typically Olive Drab or Flat Black.

Because the post-war B-25s were mostly of the later models, they were therefore substantially uncamouflaged. We see that most post-war B-25s of foreign countries were natural aluminium finished with only their own national markings. Sometimes they had additional markings or colours and in some cases they were still colourful airplanes. In the Second World War, primarily nose art was very popular. While many nations decorated their airplanes with nose art, United States Air Force pilots were unique in their penchant for painting pretty girls on the sides of their planes. But not only girls, also stars from the Hol-

lywood movie industry and many cartoon characters dominated the noses of bombers. The Second World War turned nose art into a major industry. It was to become the golden age of airplane nose art. But this was not the case for the other countries during the war. We see many examples of nose art in the U.K., Soviet Union, the Netherlands and Australia. Here they also had fine nose art, but this still did not have the scope of

the American art. With the end of the war, the nose art industry also ended. Only in a few cases after the war we see beautiful nose art or other paintings. But anyway, the sometimes mirror-like aluminium Mitchells remain masterpieces. The countries outside the U.S. which have flown with the B-25 for military use are described hereinafter. They are mainly grouped by continent.

Many of the post-war B-25s of foreign countries were overall natural aluminium finished with only their own national markings. This is a very clean and shining B-25 of the PVA (Photo Reconnaissance Department) of the Royal Netherlands East Indies Army Air Force in 1947. (Collection Gerben Tornij)

LEND-LEASE

In this book several times reference is made to the Lend-Lease programme of the United States. Therefore, I will give a brief explanation about this programme.

During World War II, the United States began to provide significant military supplies and other assistance to the Allies in September 1940, even though the United States did not enter the war until December 1941. The Lend-Lease Act of 11 March, 1941, was the principal means for providing U.S. military aid to foreign nations during World War II. The Act authorized the President to transfer defence materials for which Congress appropriated money to the government of any country whose defence the President deems vital to the defence of the United States. The materials included military hardware such as airplanes, ships, tanks, small arms, machine tools, equipment for building roads and air strips, industrial chemicals, and communications equipment. The U.S. also sent clothing and foodstuffs such as evaporated milk, flour, starch, dried beans, canned meat and fish, and concentrated orange juice. After the Act was signed, the new Office of Lend-Lease Administration shipped supplies from U.S. ports to the United Kingdom which, by late April, was receiving vast

September 1942, Ladd Army Airfield, Alaska, twelve B-25s with A-20s and P-39s along the runway. Ladd Army Airfield was the military airfield located just east of Fairbanks. It was originally called Fairbanks Air Base, but was renamed Ladd Field on 1 December, 1939. Beginning in 1942, Ladd Field became the centre of the ALSIB-route, through which nearly 8,000 military aircraft from the United States were transferred to the Soviets. (USAF)

quantities of food and war materials. Shipments of food and military supplies grew steadily every month and more countries were added to the list of aid recipients. By the end of 1942, the list included the Soviet Union, China, Australia, New Zealand, and the governments-in-exile of Poland, the Netherlands, and Norway. Later, the Free French and new Latin American allies, including Paraguay, Brazil, and Peru, received supplies. The airplanes delivered through Lend-Lease were flown from the U.S. to the different countries via several Air Ferry Routes, including the North Atlantic Route, South Atlantic Route and South Pacific Route. One of the primary routes was the northern ALSIB-route (Alaska-Siberia). This was the air route between Alaska and the former USSR. The Lend-Lease programme ended in September 1945. In general, the aid was free, although some hardware, such as airplanes and ships, were returned after the war. In return, the U.S. was given leases on army and naval bases in Allied territory during the war. Over the course of the war, the United States contracted Lend-Lease agreements with more than 30 countries, dispensing some $50 billion in assistance.

According to a War Department report of 31 December, 1946, the B-25 Lend-Lease shipments were as listed in the following table. However, it does not mean that they actually correspond with the real numbers that have served in those countries.

	Total	UK	Sovjet Union	China	Brazil	Canada	Netherlands
B-25 bombers	2,085	807	865	131	29	4	249
B-25 engines	1,031	296	633	44	16	3	39
B-25 propellers	932	337	534	43	15	3	

The ALSIB-route was a logistic masterpiece. This picture of 10 September, 1944, symbolizes the delivery of the 5,000th aircraft to the Soviet Union through the ALSIB-route. However, the Soviet officer looks not too happy with this ceremony. In 1943, about 10 to 20 machines per month were transferred to Krasnoyarsk airfield in Siberia. The peak was observed in September 1943, when 26 bombers flew from Fairbanks to Krasnoyarsk. (USAF)

UNITED KINGDOM

flew with No. 681 and No. 684 Squadron at RAF Dum Dum near Calcutta, India, respectively.

The first true British B-25s were 23 B-25B models which were designated Mitchell Mk.I and used for training. They had the RAF serials FK161 through FK183 and were delivered from May 1942, to No. 111 Operational Training Unit based at Nassau in the Bahamas. These bombers were used exclusively for training and familiarisation. This OTU was intended primarily to train

The Royal Air Force (RAF) was one of the largest users of the B-25 outside the USAAF. During the Second World War, the RAF was the only air force to use the B-25 on raids against Europe from bases in the United Kingdom. Most B-25s went to Britain via the North Atlantic air ferry route under the Lend-Lease programme. The North Atlantic air ferry route was a series of Air Routes over the North Atlantic Ocean through which airplanes were ferried from the United States and Canada to Great Britain.

At the start of the war, the RAF in the Far East operated five former Dutch B-25Cs used by the Photographic Reconnaissance Unit No. 5 (PRU). In March 1942, they arrived at Bangalore. These Netherlands East Indies B-25s were converted for camera work and transferred to the RAF. The airplanes later

Two of the first Mitchells delivered to RAF Bomber Command in 1942. They belonged to the three Mk.Is that arrived in England for testing. At left, FK161, a B–25B with US-AAF serial number 40–2341 with yellow prototype markings and camouflaged Dark Green with Dark Earth on the upper surfaces and Sky on the undersurfaces. At right, FK165, a B–25B s/n 40-2339, camouflaged in Olive Drab and Neutral Grey. Both airplanes went to the Aeroplane and Armament Experimental Establishment based at Boscombe Down, Wiltshire. (Collection Wim Nijenhuis)

crews on American airplanes. It continued to function with the Mitchell until August 1945. However, three of the Mk.Is arrived in England for testing during May 1942. The RAF received about 540 B-25Cs and B-25Ds, which were designated as Mk.II. Between June and August 1942, the Mk.IIs arrived in batches in the U.K. and thereafter in a steady flow. The RAF Mitchells generally retained the retractable ventral turret, since protection from below was absolutely

Rare pictures of FR209, one of the two B-25G models delivered to the RAF. This Mitchell coded "F", USAAF s/n 42-64823, was photographed at Hendon on 15 September, 1945. She was flown by A&AEE (Aeroplane and Armament Experimental Establishment), the Empire Central Flying School, and the Met Research Flight before becoming an instructional airframe 6891M at Dyce, Scotland. It was the longest surviving Mitchell of the RAF. She was converted to a Mk.II with glass nose and served until September 1951. **Above:** *The post-war converted FR209. The camouflage paint has gone and the ship is natural aluminium finished. (Collection Wim Nijenhuis)*

essential for medium-altitude operations over Europe. The RAF received two B-25G models. Both airplanes, FR208 and FR209, were used for experimental work by the Aeroplane and Armament Experimental Establishment (A&AEE). There was still another B-25G. This was s/n *42-65094*, and was 'acquired' in the Middle East and used as a transport for high-ranking officers. It was seen around the Middle East and Arabia in 1945/1946. It was transferred to the UK, but it was never given a UK serial. The B-25J was designated as Mk.III and the RAF was allocated over 310 Mk.IIIs. Deliveries took place between August 1944 and August of 1945.

Most of the British B-25s flew with the 2nd Tactical Air Force (2nd TAF). They played a very important role there. This air force was formed in June 1943 from No. 2 Group from Bomber Command and was organised into squadrons, servicing echelons and airfields. Squadrons comprised only aircraft and aircrew. Usually, a squadron had thirty aircraft and thirty crews, of which twenty four were active and six were reserve. Wings were initially formed with three squadrons each, although from late July 1944, they usually had four squadrons each. Usually, a wing contained only one type of aircraft and was based at one airfield. Relating to the Mitchells, in June 1944, the 2nd TAF comprised of

A 2nd TAF original Victory in Europe card from 8 May, 1945. On the front, are the flags of the Allies coming together on the German swastika. In the lower right corner is the emblem of the 2nd TAF. On the back of the card was a message from Air Marshall Sir Arthur Coningham.

(Collection Wim Nijenhuis)

the following wings and squadrons:
- 137 Wing, No. 226 Squadron and No. 342 (Lorraine) Squadron
- 138 Wing, No. 305 (Polish) Squadron
- 139 Wing, No. 98 Squadron, No. 180 Squadron and No. 320 (Dutch) Squadron

The servicing echelons served the same squadron more or less permanently and were in any case trained in the servicing of only one type of aircraft. The 2nd TAF attacked airfields, communications centres, railways and bridges before and after D-Day.

A number of Mitchells were delivered to Canada and flew because of the British Commonwealth Air Training Plan (BCATP) in Canadian training units. This was an agreement concluded between Canada, the United Kingdom, Australia and New Zealand. The RAF moved a number of its training schools to Canada. The RAF Mitchells operated in No. 5 Operational Training Unit. This is described in the chapter Canada. In addition to the 2nd TAF, some B-25s were used by various second-line RAF units in the UK and abroad. After the war, most of the British B-25s were returned to the U.S. or scrapped after being struck off charge. A few remained as instructional airframes and in communication or training roles until 1951.

One of the few Mitchells used by a second-line unit was this B–25J–1 with s/n 43-27774. In the period 1945 to 1947, it was used as a VIP transport by the Mediterranean and Middle East Communications Squadron based in Egypt. The airplane is overall natural aluminium finished with the RAF roundels and fin-flash, but still with the U.S. serial on the vertical tails. Note the modified tail end. (RAF)

HD373 was a Mk.III with U.S. s/n 43-28001. This Olive Drab/Neutral Grey ship remained as a test aircraft with the A&AEE at Boscombe Down until 1947. (Collection Wim Nijenhuis)

This is one of the ex-Dutch Mitchells transferred to the RAF in the Far East. They operated with No. 5 (PRU). In March 1942, they arrived at Bangalore and were converted for camera work. The airplanes were painted overall PRU Blue with a large aircraft code letter in Sky on the rear fuselage. This is N5-144, a B-25C with s/n 41-12495, still in the Dutch camouflage and markings but already with a small British aircraft code letter C painted on her vertical stabiliser. (Collection Wim Nijenhuis)

CAMOUFLAGE AND MARKINGS

The most common colours for British bombers during World War Two, were Dark Green with Dark Earth upper surfaces and Matt Black lower surfaces. But that was not for the British Mitchells. A few early British Mitchells were painted Dark Green with Medium Grey or Dark Green/Dark Earth with Sky lower surfaces. The ex-Dutch Mitchells in the Far East were overall PRU blue.

The standard colour for the Mitchell was Dark Olive Drab over Neutral Grey because the airplanes were generally painted at the factory in accordance with the requirements of the U.S. Army Air Corps and later Army Air Forces. In 1940, the U.S. standard colour of bombers was matt Dark Olive Drab No. 41 and matt Neutral Grey No. 43. But in June 1943, the Army-Navy Aircraft Camouflage Standard Colours was adopted and the new ANA colour names were 603 Sea Gray (Neutral) and 613 Olive Drab. This is described in detail in the book *"Mitchell Masterpieces Vol. 1"*. The RAF agreed to receive aircraft painted following U.S. standards. Dark Olive Drab was considered close to the Dark Green then in use on aircraft used by the RAF in Europe. Therefore, most of the British Mitchells were also painted in these colours. After maintenance some Mitchells were painted Dark Green on upper surfaces and Dark Sea Grey on the lower surfaces. Areas of the former USAAF markings were painted out. These were the roundels on the fuselage and wings, and the serial number on the tail. Sometimes a large patch of dark-

Type A.1

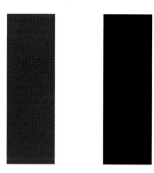

Fin flash Type A

SEAC

British national markings on some early RAF Mitchells.

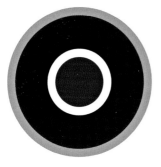

Type C.1

Type B

Fin flash Type C

Common British national markings on RAF Mitchells.

*On top of both wings the common roundel was of the Type B as on the aircraft EV-W. But from the end of 1944, also the Type C.1 was used as can be seen in the screen shot **below** from the RAF film "Rhine Barrier Smashed". (Collection Wim Nijenhuis, RAF)*

er colour was visible on the spot where the previous marking had been painted over. Sometimes the airplanes showed darker or lighter variations in shades depending on the place where the aircraft were operated or after repairs.

From 1940 onwards, most operational airplanes of the RAF displayed a prominent three-letter code on the fuselage. The two-letter group designates the squadron and the third letter the call-sign for the individual airplane. In general, when an airplane was lost or withdrawn from use, its call sign was applied to its replacement or another

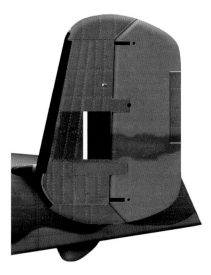

A well known but nevertheless masterful picture of the tail sections of British Mk.II Mitchells at Melsbroek, Belgium in 1944. Both airplanes show invasion stripes around the fuselages and fin flashes on the vertical stabilisers. The British Mitchells were normally always provided with de-icer boots on the wings and vertical stabilisers. (Maritieme Historie)

airplane. Therefore, we see the same call-sign letter several times on different aircraft within a squadron. The squadron code letters were normally painted Dull Red on the fuselage behind the wings. For bomber aircraft, the aircraft letter was painted in Dull Red on both sides of the nose. However, some airplanes had all these letters Medium Sea Grey. The RAF serial number was painted black on the rear fuselage. Serial numbers are used to identify the individual

aircraft and display a unique serial number. The RAF Mitchells had a serial number of two letters and three numbers. The red, white and blue fin flash Type C was applied on the inside and outside of both vertical stabilisers. The common roundel on the rear fuselage was of the Type C.1. On top of both wings the roundel was of the Type B. By the end of 1944, airplanes also had Type C.1 roundels on the wing upper surfaces. The colours were Identification Red (Dull),

Identification Blue (Dull) and Chrome Yellow. Some very early delivered Mitchells carried Type A.1 roundels and Type A fin flashes. The ex-Dutch Mitchells in Asia used the SEAC (South East Asia Command) roundel on the wing upper surfaces.

From the beginning of June 1944, many of the Mitchells were painted with the so-called invasion stripes in connection with the imminent Allied landing operations in

Fine example of nose art on a British B-25 from the RAF. In this case a Mk.II of No. 320 (Dutch) Squadron at Melsbroek, Belgium, in March 1945. "Riding High" was Mitchell FR202, with squadron code NO-G. The detail picture is from a later date given the larger number of bomb symbols. (Collection Wim Nijenhuis)

Normandy. These were intended for recognition for the allied air and ground forces and consisted of two showy black stripes and three white stripes around the fuselage and the wings. After June 1944, often the invasion stripes were crudely scrubbed out to halfway down the fuselage side. Many of the Mitchells which had taken part in D-Day still retained their lower wing stripes, but the upper wing stripes were removed. By the end of the war, the stripes disappeared gradually, but some airplanes still flew with the stripes until the end of the war.

At the beginning of the war, British aircraft hardly had any nose art, artistic or other private images. But as the war progressed and the Americans in England also operated with their bomber squadrons, more and more British aircraft were also adorned with a form of nose art. The Americans were very pronounced in this respect, but the British did it in a more modest way. Although later in the war, British airplanes also showed larger and sometimes bold nose art. But this was mainly on the heavy bombers such as the Lancaster, Halifax and Stirling. On the Mitchells, nose art was applied only on a modest scale. However, they were mostly provided with bomb symbols for accomplished missions. These were often made with a template in white, yellow or sometimes red colour.

Painting white mission symbols around the black bordered orange triangle on the noses of Mk.II Mitchells of No. 320 (Dutch) Squadron. (NIMH, Collection Wim Nijenhuis)

No. 13 Operational Training Unit

In the RAF and RCAF, the road to a Mitchell squadron usually led through No. 13 Operational Training Unit (OTU). Pilots at No. 13 OTU normally received about three hours of dual instruction on Mitchells, followed by 27 hours flying in sole control. About a third of the flying hours consisted of formation flying. Navigators logged about the same hours or a bit more. No. 13 Operational Training Unit was formed at Bicester on 8 April, 1940. Bicester was an airfield on the outskirts of the English town of Bicester in Oxfordshire. Throughout the war, Bicester was used as a training centre, and became home to No. 13 OTU, under the control of Bomber Command. Due to a

change in RAF policy, No. 104 and No. 108 Squadrons were merged, becoming No. 13 Operational Training Unit (OTU) with 36 Blenheims and 12 Ansons. No. 13 OTU became one of only two major medium bomber training units. By August 1941, the aircraft inventory of No. 13 OTU was 48 Blenheims, 16 Ansons and 2 Lysanders. Initially training Blenheim crews for daylight operations, its role was later extended to include night intruder training. In May 1943, B-25 Mitchells and Douglas Boston bombers were added to the unit strength as well as De Havilland Mosquitoes. By now, No. 13 OTU was sporting a mixed bag of types at Bicester: Albemarles, Ansons, Blenheims,

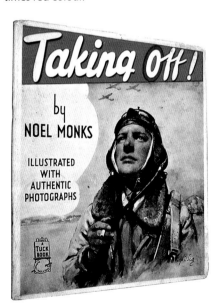

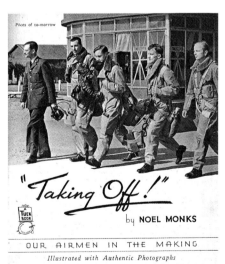

There were various propaganda posters and leaflets that encouraged the young volunteers to join the RAF, promising opportunities, learning a trade and excitement. Noel Monks wrote a 48 page booklet "Taking Off", published by Raphael Tuck & Sons, Ltd., London, ca. 1940. On the title page the sub-title "Our airmen in the making". Well, No. 13 OTU would make many airmen for the RAF B-25 Mitchell squadrons. (Collection Wim Nijenhuis)

The pilots' billet of No. 13 OTU at Bicester.
(Collection Ken Fenton)

Defiants, Martinets, Mosquitoes, Oxfords, a Tiger Moth, Bostons and Mitchells. RAF Bicester was an all-grass airfield and proved unsuited during wet winter periods for the American medium bombers with their tricycle undercarriage and heavy weight. So, a building programme of satellite airfields was set up. At various times these included Finmere, Hinton-in-the-Hedges, Turweston and Weston-on-the-Green. The Mitchells of No. 13 OTU were actually based at Finmere. In June 1943, the unit transferred to Fighter Command. The aircraft inventory in January 1944 comprised 9 Ansons, 7 Bostons, 3 Martinets, 26 Mitchells and 26 Mosquitoes. The build up for the D-Day invasion was now underway and Bicester airfield played its part. It was also used as a glider base. Soldiers of the Glider Pilot Regiment trained at Bicester before setting off for D-Day, Arnhem and, eventually, the Rhine Crossing. In October 1944, the unit moved to Harwell and in June 1945, the Mitchell training ended. In July 1945, the unit moved to Middleton St. George and remained there until 21 April, 1947 when it moved to Leeming, where on 1 May it merged with No. 54 OTU to form No. 228 Operational Conversion Unit.

No. 13 OTU flew with a total of nearly 50 Mk.IIs and nearly 20 Mk.IIIs. The Mitchells had the camouflage pattern described earlier.

Pictures of No. 13 OTU are very rare. Here a Dutch crew in front of their Mitchell of No. 13 Operational Training Unit at Harwell Airfield in 1945. Unfortunately, there is little to be seen of the aircraft, but it seems to be Olive Drab/Neutral Grey camouflaged with the Type C.1 roundel on the rear fuselage. (NIMH)

NO. 111 OPERATIONAL TRAINING UNIT

No.111 Operational Training Unit (OTU) was based at Nassau on a small island of New Providence, one of the many that form the Bahamas. No.111 OTU was established by the Royal Air Force in Nassau to serve as a training location. The unit was set up on 20 August, 1942, as a General Reconnaissance Unit to train crews on U.S. built types, mainly the B-25 Mitchell and B-24 Liberator. The reason that RAF ground and aircrews were posted to this spot, was to have space in which operational flying training could be carried out, without being shot down by incoming German intruders. The training comprised of several levels and was performed by three Wings (Squadrons) in total.

The 1st and 2nd Wings were on Oakes Field and trained on the B-25. Within the 1st Wing only pilots were flying, meanwhile the others (navigators, radio operators and air-gunners) had theory lessons. After finishing this level, the complete crews were moved to the 2nd Wing where they undertook mainly navigation flights. At the 3rd Wing, at Windsor Field, they flew on four- engined B-24 Liberators. Thirteen crews per month were to be inducted, building up to a total capacity of 39 crews in a 12-week course. Training began in November 1942, initially on Mitchells and at the same time the unit flew anti-submarine patrols over the Western Atlantic. On 25 November, 1942, the first flight

A factory fresh ship during a flight near Quebec, Canada, in May 1942. The airplane is flown by a crew of RAF Ferry Command and has the standard Olive Drab/Neutral Grey colours. The fuselage roundel is of the Type A.1 and the fin flash is Type A. This is FK170, a B–25B with U.S. s/n 40-2314. She later served with No. 111 Operational Training Unit. (Public Archives Canada)

of a B-25 (FK164) took place. Training continued until 1945, when in July the unit left for the UK, arriving at Lossiemouth, within No 17 Group on 1 August. On 1 September, 1945, it was transferred to No 18 Group and finally disbanded on 21 May, 1946.

No. 111 OTU flew with 19 Mk.Is, 50 Mk.IIs and 13 Mk.IIIs. The Mitchells had the squadron-code letter F with the addition of an aircraft letter. Both were Sky or Light Grey

Pictures of No. 111 OTU are also rare. Here an example with two Mitchells of the training unit during a training flight near the Bahamas. These bombers were used exclusively for training and familiarisation. In the background is Mitchell Mk.III, KJ583 with aircraft letters JB, and in the foreground a Mk.II with serial number FV954 and aircraft letters FB. (Collection PHDr. Jiri Rajllch)

Left: *February 1944, a crew in training in front of a Mitchell Mk.II with code letters FF at Oakes Field in the Bahamas. In the background another Mk.II airplane with letters FK.* (Archiv Z. Hurta)

coloured. The Dark Earth/Dark Green scheme was applied to a few of the aircraft sent to the Bahamas. But most of the Mitchells here were also painted in the Olive Drab/Neutral Grey scheme.

In February 1944, the Duke of Windsor, Governor of the Bahamas, visited Oakes Fields for an inspection of No. 111 OTU. He inspected the Czechoslovak contingent. The aircraft letters seems to be CF.
(Collection Kudláček)

Airplane FW at Oakes Field. (Collection Wim Nijenhuis)

Right: *Another 1944 picture of crew members in front of a Mitchell at Nassau. The ship in the background has the letters FC.*
(Collection Wim Nijenhuis)

Left: *In 1998, a series of postage stamps was issued in the Bahamas in connection with the 80th Anniversary of the Royal Air Force with an illustration of a Mitchell Mk.III. The airplane, however, has the markings of No. 180 Squadron and, therefore, has no relationship with No. 111 OTU at the Bahamas.* (Collection Wim Nijenhuis)

FV914, VO-A, a Mitchell Mk.II of No. 98 Squadron in action. She is a B-25C-20 with U.S. serial number 42-64636. The airplane has the standard colours of the RAF used on the Mitchells during the Second World War.

(North American Rockwell, via Marc Bongearts)

No. 98 Squadron

No. 98 Squadron was formed at Harlaxton, Lincolnshire, on 30 August, 1917. During the expansion of the RAF in 1936, No. 98 Sqn. was to be found in the Order of Battle. Equipped with Hawker Hinds, the squadron was transformed at Abingdon into a day-bomber squadron. In August of that year it moved to Hucknall and there, in 1938, it was re-equipped with Fairey Battles. For the first nine months of the Second World War, No. 98 Sqn. served as a reserve squadron and during the period April to June 1940, it was based in France. After reorganisation at Gatwick in July 1940, the squadron, still equipped with Battles, moved to Kaldadarness, Iceland, with Coastal Command. It was the first RAF unit to be based there. It was disbanded in July 1941, but on 12 September, 1942, reorganised at West Raynham as a bomber squadron flying the B-25 Mitchell, which it retained until the end of the war.

The new squadron was part of No. 2 Group of Bomber Command, operating against enemy communications and airfields in occupied Europe in preparation for the invasion of Europe. It moved to Foulsham in October 1942. By December 1942, the Squadron was operational but due to troubles with the gun turrets it was confined to air-sea rescue searches. The first bombing raid was on 22 January, 1943, when six Mitchells took off to bomb the oil installations at Terneuzen in

the Netherlands. In August 1943, by which time it was part of the 2nd Tactical Air Force, No. 98 Sqn. moved to Dunsfold, and subsequently took part in pre-invasion attacks on Northern France and on the Noball sites (V-weapon launching sites) located along the French and Belgium coasts. At the end

of March 1944, the Squadron was detached to Swanton Morley, Norfolk, for two weeks for an army exercise and further training. On 5 and 6 June, 1944, Mitchells went off to bomb targets in the Caen area. After D-Day the squadron carried out an increasing number of tactical operations, in support of

This is "Broom", another aircraft with the squadron code VO-A. The airplane is FW189, a B-25D-30 with s/n 43-3395. Her crew is posing in front of the airplane with a nose art that represents a clean sweep. (Fred Halsey via David Poissant)

the advancing Allied armies. From October 1944 onwards, it was based at Melsbroek, Belgium. The squadron came into action, bombing the lanes of communication between the Maas and the Rhine. At the end of April 1945, it moved to Germany, to its new airfield, Achmer near Osnabrück. On 2 May, 1945, the squadron carried out its last operation of the war when six Mitch-

One of the British Mitchells with nose art. This is FL176, VO–B, and nick-named "Grumpy". At right, ground personnel of No. 98 Sqn. gather at the aircraft's nose at Dunsfold, Surrey, as Corporal V. Feast paints the 101st bomb symbol onto its tally of operations. (Australian War Memorial, North American Rockwell)

Grumpy

Grumpy is one of the seven dwarfs in Disney's 1937 film "Snow White and the Seven Dwarfs". He lives in a cottage in the forest with the other dwarfs. The first known accounts of the Snow White story came from the Brothers Grimm, who, during the early years of the 19th century, collected and published a number of old European folktales. The Brothers Grimm published it in 1812 in the first edition of their collection "Grimms' Fairy Tales". Although the most famous version of the tale today is Disney's classic animated film. Disney's variation of Snow White gave the dwarfs names. A wide variety of posters, banners and standees were created for distribution of the film to theatres all over the world. A masterpiece was this enormous 6x2.75 m billboard made up of 12 panels created in Britain for the 1937 release of the film there. The poster itself is based on the work of artist Gustaf Tenggren, a chief illustrator for The Walt Disney Company. The poster was originally printed by W. E. Berry Ltd., Bradford. (RKO Radio Pictures)

ells took off to bomb the railway centre at Itzehoe. The next few months saw the squadron engaged in mostly ferrying duties and conducted tours over the Ruhr. The Mitchells, supplied under Lend-Lease Programme, were gradually withdrawn. After the end of the war No. 98 Sqn. converted to Mosquitoes and remained with the occupation forces.

No. 98 Sqn. had a mixture of Canadian and British personnel in both the flight crew and ground crew and flew with the Mitchell Mk.II and Mk.III. It has flown with over 110 Mk.IIs and about 40 Mk.IIIs. The squadron code letters on the Mitchells during World War Two were VO. The airplanes of No. 98 Sqn. had the standard camouflage and markings as mentioned earlier.

A Mk.II in landing. This is VO-D, FV929, a B-25C with USAAF s/n 42-64742. (IWM/CH11991)

Left: *VO-J in flight.* (Maritieme Historie)

The Mitchells VO-K and VO-F drop their bombs. VO-F was nicknamed "Sneezy". She had the RAF serial FW218 and was a B-25D-30 with the U.S. serial number 43-3538. "Sneezy" joined No. 98 Squadron on 12 April, 1944 and completed 113 operations. She survived the war and was struck off charge 5 June, 1947. "Sneezy" was also one of the seven dwarfs in Disney's 1937 animated film "Snow White and the Seven Dwarfs". (Collection Wim Nijenhuis, Ray Rogerson via David Poissant)

Not the best picture, but nonetheless a nice close-up of VO-F "Hot Gen". Another Mitchell with the airplane letter F. The "Hot Gen" nose art is nowadays painted on a warbird of the Canadian Warplane Museum and is made by artist-illustrator Lance Russwurm at Kitchener-Waterloo, Ontario. Also today, a pinup with red lips steals the show. (Canadian Warplane Heritage Museum, Tahitia)

Left: Nice shot of VO-K at Melsbroek. The airplane is pretty weathered but has no further mission symbols or nose art. (Collection Michael Enright)

An unidentified Mitchell of No. 98 Sqn. with nose art of a stork with a baby and bombs. (Logan Morrison via David Poissant)

A well known but beautiful picture of VO-S, FV985 in flight. The ship with s/n 41-30660 has the belly gun turret extended. It is a D model that clearly shows the short waves in the transition from Olive Drab camouflage to the Neutral Grey underside. A distinctive painting method of the Kansas City factory of North American. On 23 July, 1944 during an attack on the railway yard at Glos/Montfort, France, her bomb load exploded immediately after being jettisoned probably due to intervalometer problems. The entire crew was killed. (Maritieme Historie)

Two airplanes showing well the weathering of the paint and the various dark repainted areas around the roundel and the U.S. serial on the tail. VO-W has the full invasion stripes and on VO-Y, the invasion stripes are disappeared except under the fuselage.
(Collection Wim Nijenhuis)

VO-Z was another machine of No. 98 Squadron.
(Collection Wayne Allen)

~ 33 ~

"Carol" and "Hedy", names on two B-25J models of No. 98 Sqn. Pictures of British B-25Js are generally very little published. "Carol" was named after the daughter of pilot Eric Webb and "Hedy" from the estate of pilot Davey Delparte. (Collection David Poissant)

No. 180 Squadron

This squadron was formed as No. 180 (Bomber) Squadron at West Raynham, Norfolk, on 13 September, 1942, as a light-bomber squadron equipped with Mitchells and as part of No.2 Group, Bomber Command. Early in October it moved to Foulsham. On 22 January, 1943, it flew its first operational mission with six airplanes against oil targets at Terneuzen in the Netherlands. However, there were heavy losses on this first raid. Two planes failed to return, including the airplane with the Commanding Officer Wing Cdr C.C.Hodder AFC. This led to the squadron being removed from further operations until May. At the end of May 1943, the squadron together with No. 98 and No. 320 Sqn. formed No.139 Wing of the 2nd TAF and were all equipped with the Mitchell. It was moved to Dunsfold in August 1943, and was heavily involved in daylight tactical operations in France and Belgium in support of the forthcoming invasion. In April 1944, the squadron moved for two weeks to Swanton Morley. Follow-

A famous guest at the squadron. Ernest Hemingway flew with No. 180 Squadron in Wing Commander Alan Lynn's Mitchell, serial FW118 on the 20 June, 1944 afternoon raid on the Noball site at Moyenville, France. Hemingway (1899-1961) was an American novelist and short-story writer, awarded the Nobel Prize for Literature in 1954. He was noted both for the intense masculinity of his writing and for his adventurous and widely publicized life. Hemingway was also war correspondent and during World War II, he was present at the Normandy landings and the liberation of Paris. (IWM CL198)

Nice view of a Mitchell flying over Dunsfold in 1944. The squadrons No. 98, No. 180 and No. 320 formed No.139 Wing of the 2nd TAF and were all equipped with Mitchells and operated for a while from Dunsfold. (Public Archives Canada)

ing the D-Day landings, it also flew some night intruder missions in support of the push out of Normandy. After supporting the breakout from the Normandy beachhead in June 1944, the squadron moved to Melsbroek, Belgium in October. It resumed operations in support of the main armies and took part in the fighting during the battle of the Bulge. It supported the allied advance across Europe and from April 1945 until the end of the war, it operated from Achmer, Germany. At the end of the war, the squadron remained on the continent, exchanging its Lend-Lease Mitchells for Mosquitoes in September 1945. In March 1946, the squadron moved to the airfield Wahn, Cologne, Germany, to become part of the post-war occupation force, and on 31 March, 1946, it was renumbered as No. 69 Squadron.

No. 180 Sqn. has flown with nearly 100 Mk.IIs and about 40 Mk.IIIs. The squadron code letters on the Mitchells were EV. The airplanes of No. 180 Sqn. had the standard camouflage and markings as mentioned earlier.

Still a modest nose art. Informal group portrait made in July 1944, of RAF ground staff with RAAF and Royal New Zealand Air Force air crew in front of EV-D, named "Daily Delivery". The nose art illustration portrays a stork carrying a large bomb.
(Australian War Memorial)

Everything for Norway

ALT FOR NORGE
ORGAN FOR DEN NASJONALE FRONT

10. september 1941.

"Alt for Norge". Probably the Mitchell crew or one of them, had relationship with Norway. This is the nose art on FL205, EV-G. "Alt for Norge" or "Everything for Norway" is the electoral language or motto King Haakon VII chose when he received the offer of Norway's throne in 1905. At right, a postcard from 1906 with a portrait of King Haakon VII and the "Alt for Norge" election language on a background of Norwegian colours. "Everything for Norway" was also one of the illegal newspapers published during the German occupation of Norway during World War II. (Frank Morgan via David Poissant, Nasjonalbiblioteket)

Two times Mitchells heading to the runway. All airplanes are in the standard RAF camouflage scheme.

__Right:__ Three Mk.IIs with at the end number FL707, EV-Z, taxiing along the perimeter track at Dunsfold, for take off on a cross-Channel bombing sortie in support of Operation Starkey. (IWM/CH11040)

__Left:__ After the Normandy landings Mk.IIIs taxying to the runway at Melsbroek, Belgium, for another daylight bombing sortie in Germany. (IWM/C5016)

Melsbroek, December 1944, a ground crew is parking Mitchell FW206, EV-H, after a raid on canal locks at Zutphen in the Netherlands. (Collection David Poissant)

Middle: *FV916, EV-N, is being refuelled and bombed up at Dunsfold, between cross-Channel sorties in support of Operation Starkey. Operation Starkey was a sham British and Canadian amphibious invasion in August/September 1943 into the Boulogne area of northern France. (IWM/CH11038)*

Melsbroek, Belgium, December 1944. Airplane EV-P is being taken apart into three sections by a repair and salvage unit for use as spares. The fuselage of the B-25 was divided into three major sections: front, centre and the rear section. The front section was the entire fuselage from the nose to the forward end of the bomb bay. The centre section was the main structure of the B-25 and included the bomb bay and the passageway above it. It was built integrally with the wing centre section with the engine nacelles. The rear fuselage section was the entire fuselage aft of the bomb bay to the end of the fuselage. (RAF)

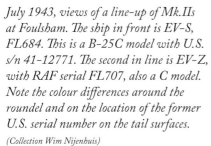

July 1943, views of a line-up of Mk.IIs at Foulsham. The ship in front is EV-S, FL684. This is a B-25C model with U.S. s/n 41-12771. The second in line is EV-Z, with RAF serial FL707, also a C model. Note the colour differences around the roundel and on the location of the former U.S. serial number on the tail surfaces.

(Collection Wim Nijenhuis)

Three Mitchells in flight forma-
tion. The airplane nearest to the
camera is the same FL684.
(Collection Wim Nijenhuis)

Another Mitchell with aircraft letter S.
This is VO-S with serial FL704, return-
ing to its base at Dunsfold, after a sortie
over enemy targets in France in support of
Operation Starkey. (IWM CH11037)

Left: *A great colour picture of ship FL218,*
EV-W, named "Nulli Secundus". This is a
B-25C with U.S. s/n 41-12806. It is pho-
tographed here on 28 July, 1943, during a
line-up of 180 Sqn. Mitchell's at Foulsham
for introduction to the press.

Bottom: *The same ship in flight showing*
the standard but weathered colours. The
words Nulli Secundus on the nose art is
Latin for second to none. On 25 January,
1944, the airplane was hit by flak during
an attack on Zudausques in Northern
France. The pilot managed to get the air-
craft back to within one mile of Hawkinge,
but it went out of control before he could
bail out. The pilot was killed, his crew had
abandoned the plane before the crash.
(Collection Wim Nijenhuis, North American Rockwell)

EV-W, FL-218, is leading a formation of six No. 180 Squadron Mitchells.
(Collection Wim Nijenhuis)

EV-T of No. 180 Sqn. with full invasion stripes. Note the straight division line between the Olive Drab and Neutral Grey colours.
(Collection Ron Dupas)

Mk.IIs parked on the flight line at Melsbroek airfield in Brussels, Belgium, 1944. The invasion stripes are now very weathered. *(Fred Guest)*

A nice winter scene, Melsbroek in the severe winter of 1944-1945. It was cold and hard work to keep the Mitchells operational. The glass surfaces and the engines of Mitchell VO-R are protected from the weather with tarpaulins. *(Collection David Poissant)*

A job for the maintenance crew. Ship KJ574, s/n 44-28762, a Mk.III of No. 180 Sqn. was involved in a ground collision with another Mitchell in early 1945 at Melsbroek. Note the nearly straight division line between the Olive Drab and Neutral Grey colours as usual on J models in the North American factory in Kansas City. *(Ray Rogerson via David Poissant).*

"Jupiter" with lightning and bomb in his hands. This is a Mitchell Mk.III and most likely airplane KJ684 of No 180 Sqn.
(Collection Michael Tabone)

No. 226 Squadron

Preparations for the invasion. Three Mk.IIs of No. 226 Sqn. about to bomb railway yards in Northern France on the evening of 12 May, 1944. The airplanes are MQ-S, FV905 named "Stalingrad", MQ-A, FW130 and MQ-H, FW128. At No. 226 Sqn. we see the aircraft letter was repeated with a small white or light grey letter on the vertical tail surfaces. (IWM/CH13071)

Below: *A close up of "Stalingrad".*

(George Kozoriz via David Poissant)

No. 226 Squadron was originally formed in World War I. In March 1937, the squadron was reformed at Upper Heyford as No. 226 (Bomber) Squadron under the RAF Expansion Scheme. It flew with Hawker Audaxes, a variant of the Hawker Hart biplane light bomber. In October 1937, it was re-equipped with Fairey Battles. In September 1939, it moved to Rheims, France, as part of No.72 Wing of the Advanced Air Striking Force. Its first operational mission in World War Two was on 9 September, when three Battles reconnoitred the Thionville area in France. The Battles suffered very heavy losses during the Battle of France and the squadron was forced to retreat west, and had to be evacuated from Brest in mid-June 1940. Later that month, it was reforming at Sydenham near Belfast. It flew regular dawn and dusk patrols along the coast of Northern Ireland as a precaution against possible landings by enemy agents. In May 1941, it moved to Wattisham, Suffolk, and the squadron converted to Bristol Blenheims. It was involved in daylight attacks against coastal targets and enemy shipping. In No-

After the invasion. Two great pictures of invasion coloured Mitchell Mk.IIs on their way to bomb the 21st Panzer Division, dispersed in the Forêt de Grimbosq south of Caen. All airplanes have full invasion stripes and on both wings the roundel Type B. At left, MQ-A, FW130, flies over an Allied convoy bound for France and at right, the airplanes are dropping 500-lb MC bombs over the target in the evening of 12 June, 1944. The airplanes are MQ-A and in the background MQ-V. (IWM/CL106, IWM/CL107)

A close up of "Honeymoon Express". This airplane MQ-F, was decorated for the wedding of Squadron Leader Paddy Lyle on 14 June, 1945.
(T.C. Thomas via David Poissant)

MQ-R "Michael 'n Jane" posed with crew at Vitry-en-Artois in France. (Collection David Poissant)

vember the squadron started flying with the Douglas Boston bomber and in December 1941, the squadron was based on Swanton Morley.

During the early summer of 1943, it converted to Mitchells and subsequently took part in pre-invasion attacks on Northern France and on Noball sites in the Pas de Calais. By now No 2 Group had been transferred from Bomber Command to 2nd TAF and the squadrons targets were enemy airfields and lines of communication, both inside and outside the immediate invasion area. In May 1944, it was based on Hartford Bridge in Hampshire. Little known were the "Ginger Flights". These were Special Signals Flights made by No. 226 Sqn. and code-named "Ginger Flight". These operations began on the night of 1 June, 1944, from Hartford Bridge. Mitchell crews were tasked to carry out single aircraft intelligence-gathering missions. These solo missions were flown late at night at 20,000 feet, deep in enemy territory. Information gathered via radio from French resistance forces on these missions frequently resulted in immediate tasking of 2nd TAF fighter-bomber and rocket-carrying Typhoons. In October, as the Allies advanced towards Germany, the squadron moved to Vitry-en-Artois in France, operating in support of the advancing armies till the end of the war. In April 1945, the squadron moved again and this time to Gilze-Ri-

MQ-T in flight with in the background MQ-X. The picture shows clearly the repainted parts of the locations of the American markings. Unfortunately, the nose art is only partially visible. (Public Archives Canada)

jen in the Netherlands. Its last operational mission in WWII was on 2 May, 1945, when 12 Mitchells bombed marshalling yards at the town Itzehoe in Germany. No. 226 Sqn. was disbanded on 20 September, 1945.
The squadron had flown with about 80 Mk.IIs and nearly 30 Mk.IIIs. The squadron code letters on the Mitchells of this squadron were MQ. The airplanes of No. 226 Sqn.

had the standard RAF camouflage and markings as mentioned earlier. However, at this squadron the aircraft letter was repeated with a small letter on the vertical tail surfaces. The colour of this letter was white or light grey.

A daylight attack on the railway bridge over the River IJssel at Deventer in the Netherlands. A Mitchell of No. 226 Sqn. is flying over the target. The airplane has invasion stripes but they have already largely disappeared on the wings. The bridge was bombed several times, but was never hit. Smoke rises from exploded bombs and damaged buildings in the city. At right, a screen shot taken during the Mitchell bombing of 28 October, 1944. The railway bridge is surrounded by bomb craters and the bright flash of light in the centre is a bomb that explodes just beside the bridge. One 26 November 1944, during another attack on the bridge, one of the squadron's Mitchells was shot down and killing the entire crew. *(Collection Wim Nijenhuis, RAF)*

"Shagga" with a kangaroo painted on the nose of this unidentified Mitchell of No. 226 Sqn. (Joe Ouellette via David Poissant)

No. 2803 L. R. V.   Spoorbrug — Deventer.

In April 1945, the railway bridge was finally destroyed by German troops during their retreat. This is a postcard of the bridge shortly before the war. (Collection Wim Nijenhuis)

Tail detail of MQ-X, FW276. It has invasion stripes around the fuselage and the aircraft letter X repeated with a small letter on the vertical stabilisers.

(Collection John Foxton)

Right: *A nice picture of HD378 of No. 226 Sqn. in flight, this is a B-25J-5 s/n 43-28006. It clearly shows the weathering of the lower surfaces.*

(Collection Wim Nijenhuis)

No. 305 (POLISH) SQUADRON

No. 305 Squadron was a bomber squadron that had flown only a few months with the Mitchell. The squadron was formed at Bramcote, Warwickshire, on 29 August, 1940. The majority of its personnel were "French Poles", i.e. those who had served with the French Forces prior to the capitulation of France. In order to assist in the training by British methods, a number of "British Poles", i.e. those trained at Hucknall near Nottingham, were added to the strength. The squadron also had an ancillary establishment of British personnel. It was originally equipped with the Fairey Battle. In November 1940, it began to convert to Vickers Wellingtons and in December it moved and

A red and white coloured Polish checkerboard was applied on the noses of the "Polish" Mitchells. Above it, POLAND was written in small white capital letters.

transferred to Syerston, Nottinghamshire. It started operational flying in April 1941. The first operational mission was on 25/26 April, 1941, when three Wellingtons bombed petrol and fuel oil storage tanks at Rotterdam in the Netherlands. The squadron continued to operate with No. 1 Group until August 1943, and during this period, it was based at Syerston, Lindholme, Hemswell. Between June 1941 and August 1943 the Squadron was based at Ingham, Lincolnshire. It then disposed of its Wellingtons and early in September 1943, without aircraft it moved to Swanton Morley and joined the 2nd TAF.

At Swanton Morley the squadron converted to the Mitchell. After a month of conversion to the new aircraft, the unit returned to operational flying. The first combat mission of four machines was on 5 November, 1943 on V-1 missile launchers in France. Similar flights were repeated and the targets were Noball sites, enemy headquarters and for-

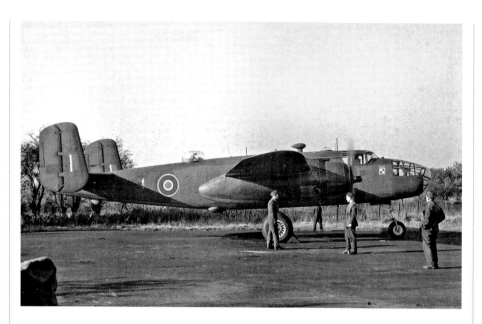

Lasham, November 1943. Airplane SM-B, FL201, is warming up its engines. This is an early B-25C model with s/n 41-12577. Note the different engine exhausts compared to the later models with the individual exhausts for each cylinder.

(Collection Lechosława Musiałkowskiego, via W. Sankowski).

One of the airplanes of No. 305 (Polish) Squadron. At the end of 1943, this squadron flew briefly with the Mitchell.

(Collection Lechosława Musiałkowskiego, via W. Sankowski)

This is SM-E, FV923, another Mk.II, at Lasham. It is a B-25C-25 with U.S. s/n 42-64736, and equipped with the typical Clayton S exhaust system. The airplane was used in three combat missions. (Collection Lechosława Musiałkowskiego, via W. Sankowski).

SM-L, FL192, at Swanton Morley. This early C model was one of the first Mk.IIs delivered to No. 305 Sqn. it had the former U.S. serial 41-12725. The airplane previously served with No. 98 Squadron and the areas of the former code letters are overpainted with probably a slightly different Olive Drab tone or the British equivalent Dark Green. The SM code letters are still to be applied. (Collection Lechosława Musiałkowskiego, via W. Sankowski).

tifications in the Cape Gris Nez region. The biggest change for the squadrons was that the missions were now flown in daytime and with fighter cover. But very few Polish crews flew more than 10 missions on Mitchells. During the brief period of flying the Mitchell, No. 305 Sqn. made 15 sorties in five combat missions and suffered only one loss, when on 14 November aircraft SM-D with serial number *FV941*, crashed during a training flight killing the entire crew. The

squadron was transferred to Lasham on 18 November, 1943. It ceased flying Mitchells in December and began converting to the Mosquito FB.VI. During the remainder of the European war, it operated somewhere on the hazy frontier between light-bomber and fighter-intruder duties with the Mosquito. Throughout 1944, No. 305 Sqn. was stationed at RAF Lasham in England and then briefly at RAF Hartford Bridge before moving to the Epinoy airfield in France in

November 1944. In April 1945, the squadron saw less flying. It flew its last mission exactly four years after their first, in the night from 25 to 26 April 1945. Twelve Mosquitos bombed and/or strafed enemy troops and transport in Northern Germany. After the hostilities ended, the squadron continued to operate in Germany as part of the occupation forces and, after a brief return to England, was finally disbanded formally on 6 January, 1947.

Another Mk.II at Swanton Morley. This is airplane SM-O, FL686, a B-25C with U.S. s/n 41-12572. This airplane is also painted in the standard Olive Drab/ Neutral Grey camouflage with the Type C.1 roundels on the fuselage and the Type B roundels on top of both wings. It has the straight colour division line between the two colours as was used on the early Mitchells produced in the Inglewood factory. (Collection Lechosława Musiałkowskiego, via W. Sankowski).

The squadron has flown with only 12 Mk.IIs. The squadron code letters on the Mitchells of this squadron were SM. The airplanes of No. 305 Sqn. had the standard camouflage and markings as mentioned earlier, supplemented by a Polish checkerboard as a national marking on the nose.

SM-Q, FV948, at Swanton Morley. This Mk.II took part in three combat missions of No. 305 Sqn. This airplane is a B-25D-15 with s/n 41-30477 and has the close wavy colour division line as applied by the Kansas City plant of North American. The airplane later served with No. 226 Squadron. (Collection Lechosława Musiałkowskiego, via W. Sankowski).

No. 320 (Dutch) Squadron

No. 320 (Dutch) Squadron was formed around a number of Fokker T-VIII-w seaplanes that escaped from the Netherlands. When the Germans invaded the Netherlands, several seaplanes of the Royal Netherlands Naval Air Service were evacuated to Britain when their home bases became unavailable. The twin-engined patrol seaplanes were flown to Pembroke Dock and on 1 June, 1940, formed No. 320 Squadron of Coastal Command. For several months the squadron flew patrols until shortage of spares forced the withdrawal of the Fokkers. They were replaced by the Lockheed Hudson. In September 1940, No. 320 Sqn. moved to Leuchars in Scotland for patrols and attacks on enemy shipping in the North Sea. In January 1941, No. 320 Sqn. merged with another Dutch squadron, No. 321 Sqn. and formed a new Dutch No. 320 Squadron. In March 1942, the squadron moved to the east coast to RAF Bircham Newton, where it continued the same duties, now focusing on German shipping.

No. 320 Squadron flew from Dunsfold from February 1944 until October 1944. In April 1944, General Eisenhower visited the Dutch naval squadron at Dunsfold. During the inspection of the Dutch squadron he made a conversation with the Mitchell crews. A moral boost for the troops. (NIMH)

In March 1943, No. 320 Sqn. flew its last operational Hudson-mission and it was for 320 the farewell of Coastal Command. On 15 March, the squadron departed to Methwold and received its first B-25 Mitchells. But already on 30 March, 1943, the squadron moved to RAF Attlebridge and was transferred to No.2 Group of Bomber Command. Here it received in partial deliveries more B-25s. It became a daylight bomber squadron, a role it performed until the end of the war. It began daylight raids on 17 August, attacking enemy communications targets and airfields as part of Second Tactical Air Force. The squadron relocated to Lasham on 30 August, 1943. In December, the attacks on V-1 installations significantly increased. The squadron moved to Dunsfold on 18 February, 1944. The British Mitchell-squadrons No. 98 and No. 180 were also stationed here. The technical department was separately organized as the RAF No. 6320 Servicing Echelon. The month of May was marked by the impending invasion of Normandy. For the invasion, the airplanes were painted with the famous black and white invasion stripes and many bombardment flights were carried out. In October 1944, the squadron moved to Melsbroek in Belgium and flew against targets in Belgium, the Netherlands and Germany, including the Battle of the Bulge and crossing of the Rhine at Wezel. In November 1944, No. 320 Sqn. received the first heavier armed B-25J model, referred to as Mk.III by the British.

In late April 1945, the squadron transferred to Achmer in West Germany, where on 2 May, 1945, its last operational flight of the

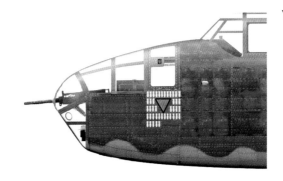

A black bordered orange triangle as Dutch national sign was applied on the noses of the "Dutch" Mitchells.

war was carried out. After that, only some non-operational flights were made and on 2 August, 1945, the squadron retained only its name, but it was transferred to the control of the Royal Netherlands Navy and ceased to be an RAF unit. On the same date, No. 6320 Servicing Echelon was disbanded.

Between 8 and 14 August, the Mitchells were flown back to England and transferred to Fersfield and were soon thereafter preserved at Kirkbride. The further operations of the squadron in Dutch service after the war are described in the chapter Netherlands.

According to RAF regulations, 320 squadron was assigned a so-called squadron code consisting of the letters NO. These appeared on the fuselage sides and in addition, each airplane had an individual letter and an RAF serial number. No. 320 Sqn. has flown with 64 Mitchell Mk.IIs with the RAF serials *FR141* to *FR207* (three were lost in transit). They were originally ordered for the ML-KNIL (Royal Netherlands East Indies Army Air Force) under Lend-Lease, but were transferred to the RAF after the Japanese occupation of the Dutch East Indies. More airplanes were on loan from other British squadrons. The serial numbers of 37 airplanes are known, of these there were 19 Mk.IIs and 18 Mk.IIIs. The airplanes of No. 320 Sqn. had the standard camouflage as mentioned earlier and supplemented by an orange Dutch triangle as a national marking on the nose.

This airplane had an attractive nose-art. It's the FR141 with aircraft code NO-B, a B-25C-10 with s/n 42-32272. It had the nickname "Ouwe Jongens" (Old Boys). Compared to the British squadrons, the average age of the Dutch crews was quite high. Probably therefore this name. The nose art contains a number of typical Dutch elements: a Dutch mill, a fishing boy from Volendam on wooden shoes, a pipe from Gouda and a bottle of Bols Gin. Lucas Bols is an Amsterdam distiller of alcohol and liquor. The company was founded in 1575 and is nowadays the oldest distillery in the world. The first century of their existence, Bols produced especially for the local market. But that changed when son Lucas Bols, a major shareholder of the VOC (Dutch East Indies Company), in 1664 also started distilling gin in addition to liquors. The gins of Bols were soon an international success, and that remained for centuries. The international reputation of Bols continued to grow and the brand was sold a number of times. Nowadays, it is a stock market listed company. (via Marc Bongaerts, Collection Wim Nijenhuis)

Mitchell Mk.IIs lined up at Dunsfold, Surrey. The airplane NO-D has a beautiful nose art of a Volendam woman in traditional costume with bombs in her arms and in a basket instead of fish. Hollandsche Nieuwe (Dutch New) is the Dutch name for the first, young herring of the season that is suitable for consumption. Every year, fish lovers look forward to the first new herring from sea and a lot of money is paid for the first barrel, which is usually auctioned for charities.
(Collection Wim Nijenhuis)

Below: *"Ouwe Jongens" was a very popular airplane to photograph. Many crew members gladly posed in front of the airplane like this picture of March 1944.*
(Collection Wim Nijenhuis)

Dutch pilots in the RAF. In 1943, the RAF dropped cigarette packets into the Netherlands to commemorate Queen Wilhelmina's birthday. The front of the packet shows a Mitchell bomber with the text Nederlandsche Marine Vliegers (Dutch Marine Pilots). The reverse shows three uniformed airmen complete with the RAF badge and the Netherlands pilot's badge. *(Collection David Poissant)*

Airplane FR142, NO-F, was called "Margriet". This was a B-25C-10 with s/n 42-32273. The airplane was one of the first that arrived at Attlebridge. During late March and early April 1943, this airplane was ferried from the U.S. to England. She was personally flown by Prince Bernhard and was named after the little Princess Margriet, born on 19 January, 1943, in Ottawa, Canada. She was the third daughter of Princess Juliana and Prince Bernhard of the Netherlands. (Nationaal Archief)

Prince Bernhard

During his lifetime, Prince Bernhard (1911-2004) has flown in many aircraft. During his long career, he flew with more than 200 different types of military and civil aircraft, including the B-25, B-24 Liberator and the Spitfire. On 2 August, 1945, Prince Bernhard arrived back in the Netherlands at Teuge Airport with (from left to right) the Dutch princesses Beatrix, Irene, Margriet and their mother Princess Juliana who became Queen in September 1948. (ANP photo, NIOD)

Tradition in fishery

A couple in traditional costumes of Volendam at the beginning of the 20th century. Volendam is an old fishing village on the IJsselmeer. It is a popular tourist attraction in the Netherlands, well known for its old fishing boats and the traditional clothing still worn by some residents. Characteristic is especially the women's costume with its high, pointed bonnet which is worn on the head and the red coral necklaces. It is one of the most recognizable of the Dutch traditional costumes, and is often featured on tourist postcards.
(Collection Wim Nijenhuis)

Right and below: *Mitchell FR183 with aircraft code NO-E during a major overhaul in the maintenance hangar. She already has a nice nose art of a pin-up with a snake at her feet. In the other picture the airplane now has 84 mission symbols applied to the nose. The picture is taken after the German surrender. The letters VE are painted below the cockpit.*
(Collection Wim Nijenhuis)

"All for Adolf" was a British-loaned airplane with serial FV970 and code letters NO-K. It was assigned to No. 320 Sqn. on 15 June, 1944. It is a B-25D-15 with s/n 41-30832. The message on the nose is clear. All bombs for the leader of Nazi-Germany.
(Maritieme Historie)

Low pass of Mitchell NO-G in October 1943. This is FR170, a B-25C-15 and one of the three Mitchells No. 320 Sqn. had with the call-sign letter G for the individual airplane. The other two G's were both B-25D models. At right, one of the other G's with a crocodile painted on her nose. This is FR202, a B-25D-25 with s/n 42-87323. (Collection Wim Nijenhuis, Collection David Poissant)

A great action shot of NO-K. This is probably airplane FR181 or FV-970. It has full invasion stripes on the wings and fuselage. The roundels on the wings are of the Type B. She is bombing the SMN steel works, east of Caen, on 22 June, 1944. **Left:** The entrance for employees of the SMN (Société Métallurgique de Normandie) around 1930 with the factory in the background. The SMN was a big steel mill in Colombelles, Caen, Normandy. It opened in 1912 and closed in 1993.

(Maritieme Historie, Rectorat de Caen)

Airplane FR-193 with code NO–L at 10,000 feet. The airplane is photographed during an attack on the bridge at Venlo, Netherlands, on 29 October, 1944. The invasion stripes below the wing have been overpainted. After the war, the ship served with the Dutch Naval Air Service and went finally to the Dutch National War and Resistance Museum at Overloon. *(RAF)*

Lots of rain and snow at Melsbroek in 1944–1945. Poor weather conditions but two very atmospheric pictures of ships with the aircraft letter M.
Above: FR192, a B-25D-15 s/n 41-30791, and at **left** FR199, a B-25D-25 with s/n 42-87261. *(Nederlands Instituut voor Militaire Historie)*

Right FR199 is photographed here at Melsbroek in March 1945. She is now named "Monique Mother" and has a lot more "war experiences" on her nose. *(Collection Wim Nijenhuis)*

Great picture of a Mitchell with aircraft code NO-S during take-off. The airplane is probably FR204. The invasion stripes are clearly visible and the top half of these on the fuselage are already gone.
(Australian War Memorial)

Lasham, October 1943, an impressive line-up of 320 squadron Mitchells in standard RAF colours and markings and the orange Dutch triangle. Ship NO-S with serial FR165 is a B-25C-10 with USAAF serial 42-32351. **Below:** The same airplane second in row. The first one is FR157, NO-X.
(Collection Wim Nijenhuis)

There were also Belgian crews flying with No. 320 Sqn. Here a picture of a Belgian aircrew watching as another Belgian officer adds a pin-up photograph to the bomb-tally on the nose of NO-P at Melsbroek. *(Collection Wim Nijenhuis)*

The NO-U, FR184, a B-25D-15, s/n 41-30804. The airplane has 53 mission symbols painted on her nose. On 4 May, 1944, she was hit by German anti-aircraft fire near Abbeville in France, and ditched at sea. *(via Bert Olsder)*

Another airplane with code letters NO-U. This is most likely FR207 and has female nose art and a large scoreboard of bomb symbols for her completed missions.

(Collections Jean de Norman et d'Audenhove, Michel Moncheur)

Bombing up another Mk.III. This is NO-V, HD346, with U.S. serial 43-3874. It is not entirely sure, but most likely the airplane is nicknamed "Lotsys II" or "Patsys II". At right, the same ship but shortly after the end of the war. She has changed the name and is now called "Pat's Victorie". The paint around the letter V seems relatively new. *(Collection Wim Nijenhuis, Collection Gerben Tornij)*

Two times NO-X with nice detail of the nose. The ships are FR-157 and/or FW-193. The black bordered orange triangle was applied on both sides of the nose in front of the airplane call sign letter.

(Collection Wim Nijenhuis)

This is a Mitchell Mk. III with serial KJ596 and code NO-Z. It is a B-25J-15, s/n 44-28965. She is nicknamed "Blasting Basterd". It has an image of an angry wolf next to that of "Margriet". This last was to replace the loss of the original FR142 "Margriet". (Collection Gerben Tornij)

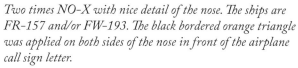

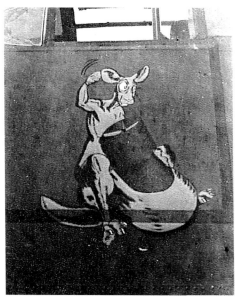

The aircraft letter of this Mitchell is very faded but it looks like an A and makes the word "Ann". In that case, this is HD392 with the U.S. serial 44-28734. It is one of the J-models loaned from the British, who referred to it as the Mitchell Mk.III. The nose art is a painting of a kangaroo with a bomb in her pouch. Maybe someone of the crew had a link with Australia. (Collection Wim Nijenhuis)

No. 342 (Lorraine) Squadron

Just like the Polish 305 squadron, No. 342 squadron flew only a very short time with the Mitchell. This squadron was formed on 7 April, 1943 at West Raynham, Norfolk, around French personnel that had been transferred from the Middle East. They had previously been operating in two units, Escadrilles "Metz" and "Nancy", and A and B Flights in the new squadron took over those titles respectively. No. 342 Sqn. was a French bomber squadron that carried out daylight bombing raids from 1943 and 1944, and then day and night bombing raids to support the invasion of Europe. In May 1943, the squadron was transferred to Sculthorpe, Norfold. Originally, the squadron was part of No. 2 Group RAF of Bomber Command and equipped with Douglas Boston medium bombers. In June 1943, it became a unit of the 2nd TAF and began operations on 12 June, 1943, flying daylight raids against targets in northern France and the Netherlands. On 19 August, the unit moved to the airfield of Hartford Bridge. Early in 1944,

attacks on Noball sites in the Pas-de-Calais began and as the time of the landings in Normandy approached, No.342 took part in an interdiction campaign to isolate the invasion area from the rest of France. Day and night missions were flown against enemy communications targets until the Allied break out and in October 1944, the squadron moved to Vitry-en-Artois in France to get closer to its targets. The Bostons continued to be used until 31 March, 1945. Then the squadron paused to complete conversion to the Mitchell. But the Mitchells were

only used for a short period. The first Mitchell mission was on 8 April, 1945, together with Bostons of No. 226 Sqn. On 22 April, 1945, the Lorraine squadron left Vitry en Artois in two boxes of six aircraft and two Mitchells separately and was stationed at Gilze-Rijen in the Netherlands. After moving to Gilze-Rijen, tactical bombing began on 23 April, but on 2 May operations already ended when the last war mission was flown with 12 Mitchells in an attack on a railway at Itzehoe, Germany. In November 1945, the Lorraine squadron moved to Dijon, flying the De Havilland Mosquito. The squadron was disbanded on 2 December, 1945. Most of the Mitchells were sent back to England

On the nose of most of the "French" Mitchells, a white Cross of Lorraine was added on a red/blue badge. The aircraft letters were Dull Red, however, many of the squadron airplanes had the letters in Medium Sea Grey. The aircraft letters of the squadron often had a small yellow outline.

Two crew members in front of OA-K with a large scoreboard of mission symbols. The insignia is applied without the red/blue badge.
(Collection Wim Nijenhuis)

French flag on rudder outer surfaces

French roundel on fuselage

French roundel on fuselage by May 1945

French roundel on upper/lower wing surfaces

Mitchell Mk.IIIs in flight. No. 342 Sqn. used the common RAF camouflage and markings, but the Mitchells of the squadron had French roundels and the blue, white and red French flag painted over the entire outer surfaces of the rudders. The blue colour was adjacent to the vertical stabiliser.
(Collection Bernard Desbiens)

and at least one remained in French service and was stripped of armament and flew for a short time with the French Armée de l'Air. See chapter France.

The squadron has flown with 7 Mk.IIs and 22 Mk.IIIs. The Mitchells of No. 342 Squadron had the squadron-code letters OA. These letters and the aircraft letter were Dull Red, however, many of the squadron airplanes had the letters in Medium Sea Grey. The bombers of the Free French squadron used the normal RAF camouflage and markings

with some French touches. Because the Mitchells were used late in the war, the British C.1 roundels were replaced with French roundels. The RAF fin-flash was replaced with the blue, white and red French flag painted over the entire outer surfaces of the rudders. On the nose of most of the airplanes, a white Cross of Lorraine was added on a red/blue badge.

In May 1945, Mitchells of the group were decorated with new French markings and each of them was given the name of a town

in Lorraine. The roundels on the fuselage were painted white with a blue cross of Lorraine inside. Just like on top of the wings, the roundels were now also painted on the lower surfaces of both wings. On 10 June, the Mitchells of the squadron took part in a flypast over Frankfurt, organised by the 2nd TAF in honour of General Yukov. On 18 June, during the VE-Day parade over the Champs-Élysées in Paris, they flew in Cross of Lorraine formation.

B-25 Mitchell OA-A with serial KJ 565 in flight. The Lorraine insignia is painted below the cockpit. An appropriate name for the Mitchell of this squadron. The crew of "Lorraine" in front of their aircraft OA-A.
(Collection Louis Pavageau, Icare)

One of the ships of the squadron was "Ville de Lorient II", also called "Thore Ben" (broken mouth). It is OA-R, KJ568. This was a B-25J-15 model with serial number 44-28756. Most likely, it was numbered II because that there had already been a Douglas Boston in the squadron with the same name. The aircraft letters of the squadron often had a small yellow outline. The added name "Thore Ben" is of a later date. *(Collection Wim Nijenhuis, ABSA39-45)*

Left: OA-M of No. 342 Sqn. The aircraft letter M seems to be applied over a freshly repainted part of the nose. The airplane is named "Conflans", painted above the Lorraine insignia.
(Jean-Marc Puech)

Another picture of OA-R, here photographed later in the war at Gilze-Rijen in the Netherlands. She is now named "Nancy". The locations of the former name and Lorraine insignia have been painted over. Next to the Lorraine insignia is the coat of Arms of the city of Nancy. This is a city in France, originated in the 11th century and is the capital of the Department of Meurthe-et-Moselle, in the Lorraine Région. The city is situated on the river Meurthe. *(Collection Odile Rozoy-Kunz)*

Right: This is OA-S, KJ729, a B-25J-20 with U.S. s/n 44-29855, named "Lunéville". This is a commune in the Meurthe-et-Moselle department in North-Eastern France. It is the seat of the arrondissement of Lunéville. *(Christian Guichard)*

Airplane OA-T, KJ630 at Gilze-Rijen. This is a B-25J-20 s/n 44-29159. She is named "Saint-Dié". The dull red aircraft letters of the French have a yellow outline. Saint-Dié-des-Vosges is a commune in the Vosges department in Lorraine in North-Eastern France. Saint-Dié is located southeast of Nancy and Lunéville.

(collection Odile Rozo Kunz)

Another city name on one of the French Mitchells. Épinal is a city in the Vosges department. This airplane is OA-U, KJ678, a B-25J-20 s/n 44-29636. *(Malcolm Laird)*

Collection "Patrie"

Cover of number 37 of the Collection "Patrie" of 1917, published by Frédéric Rouff, Paris. This was a weekly magazine, dealing with events during the First World War, with front cover drawn in colour and black and white drawings between the texts. The magazines were sold between 10 and 30 centimes on small format of 19x14 cm, with 24 pages. *(Collection Wim Nijenhuis)*

"Fort de Vaux" a B-25J-20 s/n 44-29487, in August 1945. This Mk.III has the aircraft code letters OA-V and serial number KJ666. The fort de Vaux located in Vaux-devant-Damloup, near Verdun, France, was built from 1881 to 1884 under the Séré de Rivières system and strengthened in 1888. The battles of Fort Vaux are a part of the battle of Verdun in 1916. Vaux-devant-Damloup is a commune in the Department of the Meuse, in Région Alsace-Champagne-Ardenne-Lorraine. *(Icare no. 176)*

Two Mk.III's in flight. In front is OA-X, KJ687, named "Toul" and further away from the camera OA-B, KJ645. Both are B-25J-20 models with s/n 44-29645 and 44-29377 respectively. Both have the French markings and the aircraft letter also added on the vertical stabilisers. *(Musée de L'Air)*

In May 1945, Mitchells of the group were decorated with French markings for victory flypasts. The RAF roundels on the fuselages were painted white with probably a blue cross of Lorraine and French roundels were also applied on the wing undersurfaces. The top turrets and all the armament are removed and it seems that the airplanes have new camouflage paint. *(Collection Gaubert, Collection Wim Nijenhuis)*

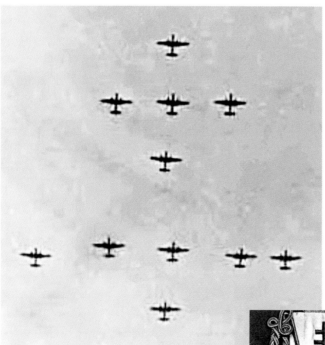

A nice art work on the cover of the French aviation magazine Icare no. 176 from 2001. It shows three Mitchells of No. 342 Squadron in flight. (Collection Wim Nijenhuis)

Unfortunately, a picture from a distance, but nevertheless it shows a masterpiece of a formation. On 18 June, 1945, an impressive parade was organized at the Champs Elysees in Paris. Over the parade twelve Mitchells of No. 342 Squadron were flying in a Cross of Lorraine formation.

(Musée de l'Ordre de la Libération, Collection F. Broche)

NETHERLANDS

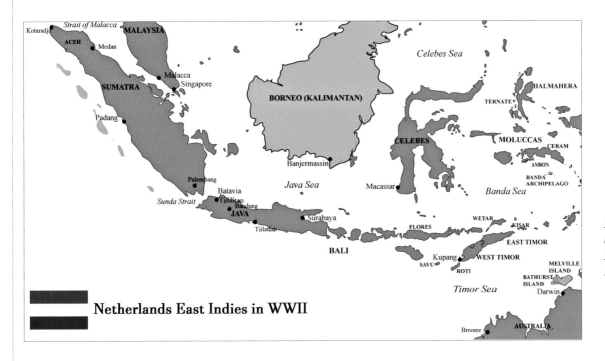

Netherlands East Indies in WWII

Map of the area of the Netherlands East Indies in the Second World War.

ROYAL NETHERLANDS EAST INDIES ARMY AIR FORCE

Outside the United States itself, the Netherlands was, together with the United Kingdom and the Soviet Union, one of the largest customers of the B-25 Mitchell. The B-25 has played an important role in the Dutch military history. Both in and after World War II, the B-25 was used in large numbers by the ML-KNIL (Militaire Luchtvaart - Koninklijk Nederlandsch-Indisch Leger), the military aviation component of the Royal Netherlands East Indies Army, the RNEIAAF. In the war years the B-25 was used in the struggle against the Japanese. This fight started

from Australia where, after an initially difficult start, the B-25s were used increasingly. Hundreds of operational flights were made. After the war, the B-25s were used for more peace-loving operations and to help victims of the Japanese occupation. Also all kinds of transports were a major task for the B-25s. During the police actions in 1947 and 1948, the B-25 got another role of military significance. In the end, after the transfer of sovereignty, a small number of aircraft was handed over to the Indonesian Air Force.

The Netherlands East Indies was a Dutch Colony that comprised an area what is now Indonesia. On 30 May, 1914, the test flight department of the Royal Netherlands East Indies Army was established and on 30 March, 1939, the ML-KNIL was formed as an independent weapon. On 30 June, 1941, the Netherlands Purchasing Commission (NPC) commissioned by the Dutch Government placed an order for 162 B-25s. These B-25s were all of the type C with the factory designation NA-90 and for which the Netherlands East Indies (NEI) serials N5-122 through N5-283 were reserved. With this order, the Netherlands was then the only purchaser of B-25s outside the United States. According to the contract, the aircraft would be delivered at the end of October 1942, directly after the first U.S. contract of 184 airplanes of the types B-25, B-25A, B-25B and 863 B-25Cs. The contract would be completed in April 1943, after the production of the aforementioned airplanes intended for the U.S. However, in view of the rising tension, the NPC asked immediately after placing the order for early delivery. In August 1941, this was consented by General Spaatz and the delivery should take place in phases between September 1942 and February 1943. In the meantime, however, the U.S. was attacked at Pearl Harbor and the original order for 162 aircraft was overtaken by America's entry into the Second World War. The aircraft were not delivered to the RNEIAAF, but went to the USAAF. This direct American involvement

resulted in a message to the NPC, in which they were informed that delivery of the 162 aircraft could be accelerated. The first aircraft could be made available in March 1942, after which the whole order could be completed by the end of 1942. Once again, urgent delivery was asked. This was initially denied, but apparently with a view to the course of the fight around the Philippines, the Americans agreed on 21 January, 1942 with an emergency supply of 60 aircraft to be delivered in several phases. These different assignments, renewed assignments and shipments led to administrative confusion. Therefore, different numbers and dates are circulating about the deliveries of B-25s purchased by the Netherlands. In addition

to these problems around the assignments and deliveries, there were also many problems related to bombsights, drift meters, generators, radios and machine guns.

On 2 March, 1942, the first airplane of the first partial shipment arrived at last at RAAF (Royal Australian Air Force) Station Archerfield, Brisbane, and on 8 March, 1942, the first airplane of five arrived at Bangalore, India. It was the intention of the RNEIAAF to send half of the B-25s to India. But because of the altered situation in the Netherlands East Indies, this was changed on 1 March, 1942. This resulted in the fact that only six B-25s went to Bangalore, one of which directly crashed during the ferry landing at

Two rare pictures of B-25s assigned to the Netherlands East Indies Army Air Force. Both airplanes still have U.S. markings with a Dutch number including the small number on the wing leading edge on either side of the engines. The N5-145, s/n 41-12509, is seen here after her arrival at Bangalore, India, in March 1942. Her markings were quickly replaced with British markings with the aircraft letter B. It was one of the five Dutch B-25s operated by the Photographic Reconnaissance Unit No. 5 (PRU). The N5-149, s/n 41-12499, is photographed in

Australia. It is believed that this picture has been electronically modified with the wrong USAAF serial. The N5-149 had s/n 41-12438 and the N5-157 had s/n 41-12499. Nevertheless, both aircraft were reassigned to the USAAF in Australia.

(Collection Wim Nijenhuis)

The Tjililitan air base was not only used as air base, there were also regular exhibitions for the public and the military. The picture shows an exhibition on 4 and 5 September, 1948. At the air base, different aircraft had been prepared for a visit in one of the hangars. Apart from other aircraft, there are four B–25s including a strafer. They all have a Netherlands East Indies M aircraft number.
(via Bert van Willigenburg)

Accra. The B-25s at Bangalore were later converted for camera work and transferred to the RAF. Afterwards, each time part shipments of B-25Cs and B-25Ds were flown to and received in Australia. From May 1943, the first B-25Js were delivered. In the period from 1942 to 1950, various B-25s have flown in different squadrons under the Dutch flag. Most of the B-25s flew with No. 18 Squadron of the RNEIAAF. In smaller numbers they have served with No. 16 Squadron, the NEITS, the NEI-PEP, the RAPWI, the PVA and finally in some training units.

In 1946, the insecurity in the Netherlands East Indies took alarming proportions. There were countless victims of guerrilla actions by various groups. The Dutch wanted to stop this by a large-scale military action. This military action became known as the first police action. During this first police action from 21 July to 5 August, 1947, B-25s were mainly used for reconnaissance and the bombing of railways and artillery line-ups of the TNI (Tentara Nasional Indonesia). A total of 55 sorties were flown during

the first police action. The Dutch authority seemed restored, but in 1948 the underground struggle flared up again. Plans were made to penetrate to the core of the republican-held areas and to arrest the nationalist leadership. This led to a second police action from 19 December, 1948 until 5 January, 1949. During the second police action, B-25s were stationed at Tjililitan, Semarang, Medan, and Andir (Bandung). It was the intention to support ground troops and defeat the air force of the TNI. During the second police action, a total of 337 sorties were flown. The world opinion, however, took a clear position against the Dutch colonial politics and the military actions had to be terminated. Eventually, this resulted in the independence of Indonesia on 27 December, 1949.

The B-25s have flown until the termination of the RNEIAAF by the Netherlands Government on 26 July, 1950. It is interesting to mention that in 1944, 39 B-25s were transferred from the RNEIAAF to No. 2 Squadron of the RAAF. In May and June 1950, after

the transfer of sovereignty, 42 B-25s were transferred to the AURI (Angkatan Udara Republik Indonesia) and assigned to No. 1 Squadron at Tjililitan.

The RNEIAAF has flown with three different versions of the B-25, the models C, D and J. Both the early and late types of the C and D were used. Therefore, both models with a single engine exhaust and the engines with an exhaust for each cylinder were in service. The J models were both with a glass nose and a solid strafer nose. Basically all airplanes were built and delivered according to the specifications of North American. These were amended from time to time and in any model there were small or larger changes and improvements. As the B-25s of the USAAF, most attacks on ships were made through "shipping". These attacks on mast height were dangerous because of the violent return fire from the target. Therefore, the B-25s needed heavier forward armament and the nose of several airplanes was modified with a package of four fixed .50 machine guns. In addition, two .50 machine guns were added in packs on each side against the fuselage under the cockpit. Later models of the B-25J were equipped with the strafer noses with eight .50 machine guns. Often, the top turret located directly behind the cockpit was removed. There were also several changes as applied in the U.S. forces. Extra machine guns in the tail and in the waist positions of the fuselage, extra sheeting, and so on. Therefore, a wide variety of aircraft flew in the RNEIAAF.

The top turret of a B-25 bomber is being cleaned. On the left upper wing the Dutch red/white/blue flag. (Nationaal Archief)

CAMOUFLAGE AND MARKINGS

As from the date of entering into service, the colours of the RNEIAAF B-25s were painted at the factory in accordance with the requirements of the U.S. Army Air Corps and later Army Air Forces. In 1940, the standard colour of bombers was matt Dark Olive Drab No. 41 and matt Neutral Grey No. 43. In the warm and humid climate however,

result of modifications, repairs and regular maintenance. Metal parts were often left unpainted and fabric covered parts were treated with aluminium-coloured lacquer. But a number of airplanes still have flown for a long time with camouflage colours. Even in 1949/1950, there still flew some camouflaged B-25s with aluminium co-

loured sheeting due to cannibalization by other ships. The aluminium coloured B-25s had black anti-glare panels.

The NEI serials of the aircraft ran from N5-122 to N5-266. In the course of July 1942, the airplanes were re-numbered, probably because of the confusion of the partial deliveries. In the RNEIAAF, the letter N was for North American and the figure 5 was for bomber. The remaining three figures stood for the aircraft number. Until about July 1944, the N5-numbering was in white on the rear part of the fuselage and also in small white numbers on the fuselage just before the wing leading edge. On the first airplanes, it was also repeated in small white figures on the wing leading edge on either side of the engines. The original USAAF-serial was in yellow on both outer vertical tail surfaces. After about July 1944 until the second half of 1947, the N5-number was in white or sometimes in yellow or faded Medium Sea Grey on the fuselage nose.

Early Dutch national marking Practically not used on the Dutch B-25s

Dutch flag in four positions. 1948 fin flash had same shape but was smaller

the olive drab discoloured in various shades of brown to brown-yellow. From mid-1943, the number of the Dark Olive Drab shade 41, was changed to Olive Drab ANA 613 and Neutral Grey shade 43 in Neutral Grey ANA 603. The colour composition hardly underwent any changes. From 1944, the aircraft were gradually stripped of the colours and were natural aluminium finished. During the transition period from camouflage to bare metal, there were various variations in the appearance of the B-25s. This was the

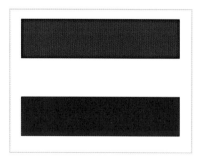

Dutch flag with white border, introduced in September 1945

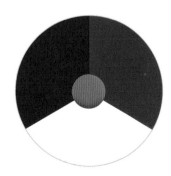

Dutch roundel, introduced in July 1948

The number was also repeated in white or yellow on the tail surfaces instead of the USAAF number. In the autumn of 1947, the N5-numbering was replaced with M-numbers and increased by 200. For example, the N5-264 became M-464. Most airplanes were then natural aluminium finished and the new serial was in black. The letter and number were painted on the vertical tail surfaces. The sequence number only on the nose. From July 1948, the full M-registration was painted in black on the fuselage rear part. In general there was a great variety in colours, places and fonts of the NEI serials. Initially, the national marking was an orange triangle with black border. However, as early as February 1942 this triangle was no longer used, so in practice the Dutch Mitchells have never flown with this marking. The triangle was replaced with the Dutch red/white/blue flag in four positions. On both sides of the rear fuselage and on both lower surfaces of the wings. In September, 1945, these were bordered by a white band. In that period, the flag was applied in more or other positions like below and above the wing, as the USAAF did. Often natural aluminium finished airplanes retained the flag without white band. In July, 1948, the pre-war Dutch roundel was re-introduced and was applied in six positions. The airplanes got a red/white/blue fin-flash on both vertical tail surfaces.

No. 16 Squadron

In November 1946, No. 16 Squadron was established at Palembang from personnel and equipment from No. 18 Squadron. The first two months after its establishment were a relatively quiet period. In early 1947, the situation changed and the squadron flew several operational sorties in short time. The squadron was deployed for reconnaissance, transport and convoy security. It also supported operations by the infantry. Jointly with the Navy, many hours of reconnaissance flights/patrols were carried out above the sea.

During the first police action on 21 July 1947, the squadron bombed the airport of Mandah, provided support for the advance of Dutch troops and performed reconnaissance flights. In total, the squadron flew 77 sorties during this police action. After this first police action, the activities of the

squadron were reduced. One went back to the "normal" work that mainly consisted of providing air support to the ground troops. In that period, the squadron was facing a shortage of personnel and spare equipment. Furthermore, there was a shortage of good quality housing in and around Palembang. For that reason, 16th Squadron moved to Pangkal Pinang on Bangka Island at the end of 1947. Some airplanes remained stationed at Palembang airport. However, in April 1948, it was decided to disband the squadron because of shortage of personnel and material. This decision was effected in August 1948. No. 16 Squadron was merged with No. 18 Squadron and stationed at Tjililitan. Released personnel and B-25s were assigned to No. 18 Squadron. So, No. 16 Squadron has existed for only two years.

A beautiful shot of N5-221 during a flight in May 1947. The natural aluminium finished ship has the No. 16 Squadron insignia prominent on her nose. This was a black dragon on a black bordered yellow circle, a red shield with black figures 16. The top turret has been removed. (Nationaal Archief)

A picture of the N5-240 during an air-show on 18 January, 1947 on the Army Day at Pangkal Pinang on Banka Island. The B-25 was stripped of camouflage and used as transport airplane. It was a B-25J-15 with s/n 44-29033. It has the black number N5-240 painted on her nose and the Dutch national flag without white border as marking in four positions. The plane was assigned to No. 18 Sqn. and in 1947 for a short time assigned to No. 16 Sqn. *(Nationaal Archief)*

B-25s of No.16 Sqn. at Talangbetoetoe airfield, Sumatra. **At right:** The N5-258 is a B-25J-25, s/n 44-30399.
Bottom: In front the N5-221, a B-25J-1 with serial number 43-27688. The second airplane is N5-256, s/n 44-30505 a B-25J-25, and the third is N5-258. The airplanes are still partly Olive Drab/Neutral Grey and partly stripped of the camouflage paint. The national insignias are with and without white borders. *(Collection Max Schep)*

Palembang, May 1947, a magnificent shot of two very low flying B-25s over N5-252 during an inspection by General Kruls. In 1947, N5-252 was assigned to No. 16 Squadron and she was shot down on 21 July, 1947. *(Nationaal Archief)*

Splendid picture of nose art of a woman riding on a bomb. This ship N5-257 was assigned to No. 16 Sqn. in 1947. The fuselage is still Olive Drab and the nose has been stripped of the camouflage paint. *(Nationaal Archief)*

Three other ships of No.16 Squadron. In front is M-458 and in the centre is M-421. Both airplanes are overall natural aluminium finished and equipped with nose art. They have the national markings in six positions. The nose art on M-458 is a dragon. *(Nationaal Archief)*

M-459, a B-25J-30 s/n 44-31201, is still Olive Drab/Neutral Grey, but the nose is already stripped of paint and equipped with nose art. *(Collection Gerben Tornij)*

No. 18 Squadron

After the attack on Pearl Harbor on 7 December, 1941, the Japanese rapidly conquered the Philippines, Singapore, Malacca and the Dutch East Indies. On 8 March, 1942, the Dutch East Indies capitulated and most RNEIAAF personnel got in captivity. Others escaped and spread across India and Australia. On 1 April, 1942, the first B-25, N5-134, arrived at the RAAF air base Fairbairn near Canberra and on 4 April, 1942, No. 18 Squadron was established as part of the RAAF. The available new aircraft arrived between 10 and 12 April. Because these B-25s were immediately passed on to the 3rd Bomb Group of the USAAF upon their arrival in Australia, the newly formed NEI squadron had to improvise with the few available B-25s.

The general tasks of the squadron comprised sea search, ship attacks, bombing raids and photo reconnaissance flights. In December 1942, the squadron was transferred to MacDonald airstrip near Darwin. But on 8 May, 1943, for several operational reasons the squadron soon moved to Batchelor. In the four months that the squadron was stationed at Mc Donald, it made about sixty operational sorties. After the relocation the squadron started operational tasks with reconnaissance sorties, anti-shipping missions and offensive reconnaissance flights. At the end of 1944, it was reported that No. 18 Squadron had to be transferred to the island of New Britain to a base at Jacquinot Bay. Here it would be supportive to ground forces to break the Japanese resistance in and around Rabaul. In the first half of 1945, the first personnel departed. At the

One of the first B-25s intended for No. 18 Squadron. The third airplane in line is a B-25C, s/n 41-12462. The airplane is standing on the ramp of North American Aviation at Inglewood and has orange triangles as national marking in six positions. The U.S. serial 112462 is painted in yellow and the NEI serial N5-126 is white. However, immediately after arrival on Archerfield in the beginning of March 1942, the triangles were removed and replaced with the Dutch red white and blue flag. But that was for a very short time. At the end of March, the airplane had already been transferred to the 3rd BG of the USAAF. (North American Rockwell)

same time, however, the squadron was receiving orders to move to Morotai. But because of the many squadrons and aircraft on Morotai, it was decided that the squadron had to go to Balikpapan on Borneo, where it arrived in July 1945. In the period from early 1943 to mid 1945, the B-25s of No. 18 Squadron flew about 1,000 operational missions and some 2,000 sorties. A sortie was an operational flight of four to six hours on average. In the war period, most missions of the ML-KNIL were carried out by No. 18 Squadron.

With the surrender of Japan on 15 August, 1945, the war ended in the Pacific. In the following months, the squadron searched for prisoners and concentration camps all over the entire archipelago. Food, medicines and other basic necessities were dropped. Internees were also flown to Australia to recover. In January 1946, No. 18 Squadron was stationed at Tjililitan on the North-West coast of Java. This airport was a few kilometres away from Batavia, now Jakarta. In the subsequent turbulent years with the two police actions in July 1947 and December 1948, the squadron played an important role. No. 18 Squadron was disbanded on 26 July, 1950.

On the ferry flight from the U.S. to Australia, some B-25s carried nose art designed by the Disney studios. It consisted of an orange triangle, pointed downwards, with a black outline. Based on this orange triangle, the Walt Disney studios designed the emblem "Shooting gremlin in a wooden shoe". Through the triangle a name was applied of an East Indies base. In these examples "Kalidjati" and "Brastagi". But the emblem was forbidden by the RNEIAAF command in Australia, and removed from the airplanes after their arrival in Australia. Later ferry flights took place without this artwork.

(via Max Schep)

RAAF Base Fairbairn, Canberra, April 1944. Olive Drab/Neutral Grey B-25s with the "Gremlin gunner" emblem are lined up after their ferry flight from the U.S. As can be seen, the emblem was not always applied in the same place on the nose. (Collection Gerben Tornij)

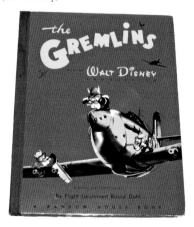

At right, the book "The Gremlins". The term Gremlin denoting a mischievous creature that sabotages aircraft, originates in Royal Air Force slang in the 1920s among the British pilots stationed in Malta, the Middle East, and India. This 1943 book is one of the earliest books on the RAF phenomenon known as Gremlins. It is a children's book, written by the famous Roald Dahl. It was his first children's book. Roald Dahl (1916-1990) was a British novelist, short story writer, poet, screenwriter, and fighter pilot. Dahl served in the Royal Air Force during the Second World War. The book was written while he was still in the RAF. (Collection Wim Nijenhuis)

Another nose art based on a famous character from Walt Disney. Donald Duck with aviator goggles in an eggshell. This is N5-128, s/n 41-12935, a B-25C. In August 1942, the ship arrived in Australia and was assigned to No. 18 Sqn. The airplane was later transferred to the NEI Transport Squadron and the NEI Pool. Donald Duck is a character created by Walt Disney. His short temper and instantly recognizable voice have made him one of the most popular cartoon characters of all time. He made his debut on 9 June, 1934, in the "Silly Symphony" cartoon "The Wise Little Hen" created by Walt Disney. Known for having a fiery temper, humorous "duck" voice and mannerisms and having appeared in cartoons, films, video games, comic books and more, Donald Duck is one of the most iconic Disney characters.

(Australian War Memorial)

Left: *A press photo of Walt Disney with Donald Duck, who celebrates his 50th anniversary in 1984.*

(©MCMLIV Walt Disney Productions).

Animals were often a rewarding subject for airplane nose art. Here an example of animal nose art on a B-25 of No. 18 Sqn. A white eagle on N5-129.

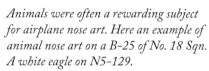

(Collection Gerben Tornij)

1942, a line-up of newly arrived early B-25Cs at Fairbairn. All airplanes are camouflaged Olive Drab/Neutral Grey and have the Dutch red/white/blue flag in four positions. On both sides of the rear fuselage and on both lower surfaces of the wings.

(Collection Wim Nijenhuis)

Popeye

Popeye's creator Elzie Segar in 1935 at the drawing board. The famous cartoon figure and comic character was created by Elzie Crisler Segar (1894-1938) in the year 1929. Popeye is generally known as "Popeye, the sailor man". Popeye is actually sailor with pipe in his mouth and highly toned muscular arms. He munches spinach to get incredible strength so that he can fight out the villainous Bluto to save his fiancée Olive Oyl from the villain. The only thing he loves more than spinach and the sea is his flighty, flirty girlfriend, Olive Oyl. He first appeared in the daily King Features comic strip "Thimble Theatre" on 17 January, 1929. Popeye became the strip's title in later years.

Bottom: Cover of a 1932 Popeye comic book by Sonnet Publishing.

(Collection Wim Nijenhuis)

New B-25s in the hangar of No. 18 Sqn. at Fairbairn. The airplane in front is the second N5-134, s/n 41-12885, a B-25C. The first N5-134, s/n 41-12439, landed at Fairbairn on 1 April, 1942, was renumbered N5-123 and transferred to the USAAF in September 1942. The Olive Drab/Neutral Grey ship has the Dutch flag in four positions and the yellow USAAF serial on her tail. The U.S. roundel on top of the left wing was removed but the place is still clearly visible. The nose was later provided with the cartoon character Popeye the Sailor Man. Apparently, he was O.K.

(Collection Wim Nijenhuis, Collection Gerben Tornij)

A crew member points with his finger to "Popeye" on the second N5-134. This B-25C arrived in August 1942 in Australia and was assigned to No. 18 Sqn.
(Collection Wim Nijenhuis)

Centre, right: *An interesting picture of the same aircraft. The outlines for the design of "Popeye" have been made but not yet painted.* (Colllection Gerben Tornij)

Centre, left: *Again the N5-134 in Canberra, but now photographed with her serial painted on the nose.*
(Gordon L. C. O'Neil)

In accordance with the regulations of 1942, the flags were applied to the fuselage and to the underside of both wings as can be seen in this picture of N5-137. She has the yellow U.S. serial still on her tail surfaces. Later, the airplane was provided with a kangaroo nose art.
(Collection Gerben Tornij)

B-25C N5-139, s/n 41-12913, in flight. On the first B-25s of the RNEIAAF, the NEI serial number was also painted in small white figures on the leading edge of the wing on either side of the engines.
(Collection Wim Nijenhuis)

Right: *Three B-25s of No. 18 Sqn photographed in 1942 or very early in 1943. In front again N5-139 and next to her N5-140, a B-25D. The U.S. roundel on the left wing has been painted over but the U.S. serial numbers are still present.*

(Nationaal Archief)

N5-144 at Batchelor. This was a B-25D with s/n 41-29717. The airplane has Olive Drab upper surfaces and Neutral Grey lower surfaces. The U.S. serial number is yellow and the Dutch serial number is white. From February 1942, the national insignia was a red, white and blue flag in four positions. On both sides of the rear fuselage and on both lower surfaces of the wings. (Royal Netherlands Air Force)

N5-145 was nicknamed "De Vliegende Hollander" (The Flying Dutchman). It was a B-25C, s/n 41-12798, flown by Guus Winckel. At left, flying Dutchman Winckel in the cockpit of his ship. The airplane of No. 18 Sqn. crashed in a downwind landing at Batchelor on 18 October, 1943. "Flying Dutchman" is a name frequently used for Dutch pilots. Originally, the "Flying Dutchman" is a legendary ghost ship that can never make port and is doomed to sail the oceans forever. The myth is likely to have originated from 17th-century nautical folklore and was inspired by the story of a Dutch sea captain named Willem van der Decken who boasted that he could complete the journey around the Cape of Good Hope, the southern tip of Africa. *(Collection Wim Nijenhuis)*

Left: A flying Dutchman recruitment poster for the liberation of the Netherlands East Indies from 1945 by the Dutch Government. (Royal Netherlands Air Force)

Below: *Another airplane of No. 18 Sqn. with a nickname was "De Strietser". This is N5-154, a B-25D-15 s/n 41-30584. Note the added gun package with two .50 machine guns. This ship was later transferred to the NEI-TSM and PVA. (Collection Wim Nijenhuis)*

The first "Lienke" N5-146, s/n 42-32512, in flight. This B-25C-15 of pilot Guus Hagers was nicknamed "Lienke", after the name of his wife. She was held captive in a Japanese prison camp. The NEI flag has been painted over the removed USAAF roundel. The nickname was painted in yellow letters.

(Collection Wim Nijenhuis)

Nose art in the NEI was rarely applied and was quite modest. This is one of the few but also naughtiest. N5-149 was painted in accordance with the U.S. colour scheme Olive Drab and Neutral Grey. The national markings are Dutch flags in four positions on the rear fuselage and on the undersurfaces of the wings. The USAAF-serial 42-32511 was yellow on the outside of both vertical tail surfaces. The registration N5-149 was white behind the flag on the fuselage and in small figures just behind the cockpit. Soon it got the name "De 2 C's". The name was painted in white on both sides of the fuselage below the cockpit. This name refers to the name Corrie Cato, the wife of Jan de Jongh, who was the first pilot on the plane in April 1943.

Far right: The name was later replaced with a bold pin-up with the name "Sarinah" and the Malaysian text "Plesiran 'Neer?". Most likely, that happened during maintenance work after 1944. It is not known how long this nose art remained on the airplane. In the period between 1944 and 1947, the plane was converted into transport airplane and at some point stripped of its camouflage colours and nose art.

(via Guus v. Oorschot, via Gerben Tornij)

One of the transport airplanes of No. 18 Sqn. was N5-160. It was a B-25D-15, s/n 43-30713. In 1944, the airplane was converted to a transporter. Here, ground crew members are working on the nose of the airplane at Tjililitan in February, 1947. Note the special shape of the black letter and numbers. *(Nationaal Archief)*

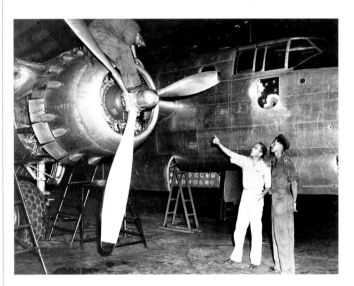

In 1947, N5-160 was renumbered M-360 and the airplane was in use as a VIP-transport for Army Commander General Spoor. Here the airplane in 1948 and 1949, during visits of General Spoor to Java and Sumatra. The airplane is natural aluminium finished with black number M-360 on the fuselage, fin flashes on the vertical tails and the national roundel in six positions. On the nose is the "Zuiderkruis" emblem with night sky and stars of the Cabinet of the Army Commander.

(Collection Wim Nijenhuis, Nationaal Archief)

Four B-25s of No. 18 Sqn. The airplane in front is N5-177 and the second one is N5-188. N5-177 is a B-25D-25, s/n 42-87311, and nicknamed "Old Dutch Cleanser". At right, an unofficial squadron badge.
(Collection Gerben Tornij)

"Mississippi Dream" was the nickname given to N5-161. This B-25D-15, s/n 41-30816, arrived in Australia in September 1943 and was assigned to No. 18 Sqn. Just a few months later, on 8 December, 1943, she crashed during landing at Kalumburu, Western Australia. Judging by the drawing of a woman's head on the nose, the crew was obviously impressed by a beauty in Mississippi during their stay at Jackson.
Left: A 1940s postcard from Jackson.
(Collection Gerben Tornij, Collection Wim Nijenhuis)

N5-180 was a B-25D-25 with s/n 42-87416 painted on her tail. In February 1944, she was assigned to No. 18 Sqn. In August 1944, she was converted for propaganda campaign and nicknamed "Ada".
(Collection H. Blankwaardt via S. Sweers)

"Old Dutch Cleanser" was one of the big brands of pumice-based kitchen cleaners. According to the U.S. Patent and Trademark Office, a trademark for Old Dutch was filed on 15 September, 1905, and registered on 27 March, 1906. The whole trademark is "Old Dutch Cleanser chases dirt, makes everything spick and span." The cleanser emblem was painted on N5-177 but forbidden by higher command. On N5-177 the text was replaced by the name "Gwen". (Collection Gerben Tornij)

Left: A vintage advertisement from "Ladies' Home Journal" of September 1929.

(Collection Wim Nijenhuis)

In the second half of 1944, preparations were made at No. 18 Sqn. to make a number of propaganda flights to Java. The aim was to cover a larger part of West Java with two aircraft, making photographs of the area, and dropping leaflets above the internment camps and the more important towns of the island. The aircraft that were used were N5-180 "Ada" and N5-185 "Lienke". On 4 August, 1944, both aircraft were handed over to the technical department, which prepared the B-25s for these long-distance flights. One of the adaptations was fitting extra large fuel tanks, while all unnecessary equipment was removed. Even all the paint was removed from the undersides of the airplanes. On the fuselage and wings of both planes enormous Dutch red, white and blue flags were painted. These are pictures of "Ada" with the route she flew painted on her nose. The flight on 24 September, 1944, lasted over 12 hours. After this mission the airplane was written off.

(Collections Wim Nijenhuis, Gerben Tornij)

The second "Lienke". This is airplane N5-185, a B-25D-30, s/n 43-3421. In 1944 and 1945, this airplane was used twice for propaganda flights and was, therefore, provided with large Dutch flags on the rear fuselage and under the wings.

Centre: "Lienke" with the route Bandoeng, Garoet, Tasikmalaja painted on her nose.
(Collection Gerben Tornij)

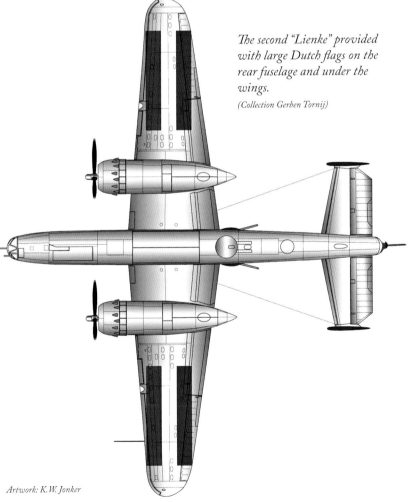

The second "Lienke" provided with large Dutch flags on the rear fuselage and under the wings.
(Collection Gerben Tornij)

Artwork: K.W. Jonker

Four B-25s of No. 18 Sqn. In front
N5-188, s/n 42-87260, a B-25D-25.
The other ships, N5-218, N5-230 and N5-
226, are the newer B-25J models. N5-188
was modified with a tail gun and waist
gun positions and was nicknamed "Pistol
Packing Mama". N5-218 was nicknamed
"Grace".

(Collection Wim Nijenhuis)

Right: Another picture of "Pistol Packing Mama" but still with the U.S. serial
number on her vertical tail.

(Collection Gerben Tornij)

N5-221 was a B-25J-1, s/n
43-27688. On the picture,
the full armed airplane is in
front of a row B-25s. They
are all Olive Drab/Neutral
Grey. In 1947, she was transferred to No. 16 Squadron
and stripped of her cam-
ouflage paint. The national
insignias are without white
borders. (Nationaal Archief)

Left: *Even an Alberto Vargas nose art was not missing on Dutch B-25s. This is N5-223 of No. 18 Sqn., a B-25J-5 with s/n 43-27926. Probably, the woman had a red swimsuit.*
(Collection Wim Nijenhuis)

A well-known but still impressive picture of the heavily armed nose of N5-237 of No. 18 Sqn. The airplane is set up under camouflage nets. She is a B-25J-15 and her U.S. s/n is 44-29030.
(Collection Wim Nijenhuis)

Three very weathered B-25Js in flight. Bottom, N5-228, s/n 43-28182, centre N5-226, s/n 43-27929 and the airplane on top is N5-246, s/n 44-29514. All airplanes are Olive Drab/Neutral Grey, but have a mix of different markings. The N5 numbers were painted on the nose of the airplanes and on the vertical tail surfaces of N5-228. Both other ships have no numbers on their tails. The national insignia on the rear fuselage has a white border, but not the insignias on the left upper wing. The remains of the U.S. roundels on the left upper wings are still clearly visible. (Sectie Luchtmachthistorie KLu)

Rare colour picture of the N5-240 after landing. This is a B-25J-15, s/n 44-29033. It looks like she has a coloured engine cowling ring. This is one of the airplanes that was transferred to the AURI in 1950 and flew up to the mid 1950s.
(Collection Gerben Tornij)

Details and markings of a weathered N5-243, s/n 44-29261, a B-25J-20. Below the right wing the white bordered red, white and blue flag is painted. N5-243 is painted on both sides of the nose. The squadron insignia is painted only on the left side below the cockpit.
Above: *On 28 January, 1947, former Minister C.P.M. Romme visits the airport Manado, Minahasa. He is received by many people, including clergy and officers. In the background N5-243, the airplane with which he travelled through the eastern Netherlands East Indies.*
Right: *Romme in front of the airplane.*
(Nationaal Archief)

Tjililitan 7 August, 1947. Lieutenant-
Colonel R.E. Jessurun receives two
American Awards, the Air Medal and
the Medal of Freedom, from the hands
of consul general dr. Walter C. Foote. The
airplane behind Jessurun is N5-244, a
B-25J-20, s/n 44-29262. The airplane is
unarmed and natural aluminium finished.
On the nose a temporarily emblem from
approximately 1946, in the form of a wing with in the middle a triangular framework pointing upwards, containing the text "18 Sqdn".
Jessurun was squadron commander from 13 June, 1945 to 14 February, 1946. He was later killed in an air crash with the B-25 M-409 at
Kroja, on 14 May, 1949. (Nationaal Archief)

Tjililitan, 29 April, 1947,
memorial service for the
fallen of No. 18 Sqn. Family
members and relations of the
fallen bring a last greeting.
The airplane is N5-246,
s/n 44-29514, a B-25J-20.
She is painted Olive Drab/
Neutral Grey with the white
bordered national marking.
The USAAF serial on the
vertical stabilisers has been
removed and roughly painted
over. The number N5-246 on
the nose of this ship was yellow. (Nationaal Archief)

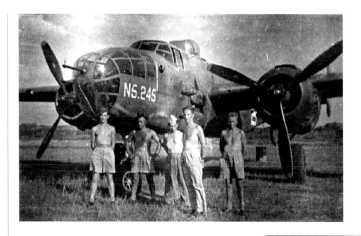

The third and last "Lienke" from Guus
Hagers. This is a B-25J-20, s/n 44-29263,
with the airplane number N5-245. The
Olive Drab/Neutral Grey airplane before
the name "Lienke" was applied on her nose.

(Collection Gerben Tornij, Collection Wim Nijenhuis)

Lienke

Guus Hagers was sent to Australia to pick up a
number of aircraft. While he was waiting for the
aircraft that had not been delivered there yet, the
Dutch East Indies were attacked and occupied by
Japan. For Guus and his fellow fliers it was impossible to return. Lienke stayed behind on Java and
ended up in various Japanese camps. Guus and
Lienke had no contact and did not know if the other
was still alive. Three years long, Guus was fighting
to get a chance to return to Java, to his wife. Every-
thing he did, he did for Lienke. To his dismay, he thereby got entangled in a dirty political game. After the war Guus and Lienke were miraculously reunited. Their story
was written in a book and published in 2014 under the title "Het vergeten verhaal
van een onwankelbare liefde in oorlogstijd" ("The forgotten story of an unwavering
love in wartime"). (De Geus)

During the war and shortly after the
war, aircraft were gradually stripped of
the camouflage paint and were partly or
entirely aluminium-coloured. In the picture
are B-25s at Kemajoran airfield, Batavia,
March 1947. The first three are N5-263,
N5-233 and N5-243. All airplanes are
Olive Drab/Neutral Grey, except N5-
263 in front. This ship has been partially
stripped of her camouflage and has a new
black airplane number. The font of the
airplane number differs from the original
as on the other airplanes. It has also the
temporarily emblem.

(Nationaal Archief)

A good example of the B-25s M-426 and M-456 with partly stripped paint. From 1944, the B-25s were gradually stripped of the camouflage paint and were natural aluminium finished. During the transition period from camouflage to bare metal, there were many variations in the appearance of the B-25s. In the autumn of 1947, the N5-numbering was replaced with M-numbers increased by 200. So, these ships were the former N5-226 and N5-256. In general there was a great variety in colours, places and fonts of the NEI serials.

(Collection Gerben Tornij)

The metamorphosis of an airplane. Two pictures of N5-233, a B-25J-15, s/n 44-29022. **Left:** She has the original glass nose and is painted in the Olive Drab/Neutral Grey scheme. Forty-two bombs and two ships symbolise her completed missions. Note the two Japanese flags on the fuselage below the top turret.

Bottom: Photographed in the late 1940s. The top turret and the paint have removed and the glass nose has been replaced by a solid 8-gun strafer nose. The Dutch roundel is applied in six positions and the airplane has a red/white/blue fin-flash on both vertical tail surfaces. The Dutch serial number has been changed with an M and increased by 200. Now M-433 is painted in black on the natural aluminium finished airplane. The insignia of No. 18 Sqn. is painted on her nose. *(Collection Wim Nijenhuis)*

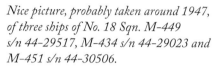

Nice picture, probably taken around 1947, of three ships of No. 18 Sqn. M-449 s/n 44-29517, M-434 s/n 44-29023 and M-451 s/n 44-30506.

The top turrets have been removed as well as the camouflage paint. On the nose the black numbers that were repeated on the vertical tail surfaces but there preceded by an M. The national insignias have a white border. All planes have the orange triangle squadron insignia on the nose. This insignia was designed in 1947 and lived up to the transfer of sovereignty in 1950. It consists of an orange triangle, black outline, two yellow bombs, blue lightnings and red number 18 with black shade. (via Gerben Tornij)

Most later models of the B-25J were equipped with solid strafer noses with eight .50 machine guns. Often the top turret located directly behind the cockpit was removed and most airplanes were then natural aluminium finished. The new serial with letter M was in black. The letter and number were painted on the vertical tail surfaces. The sequence number only on the nose. From July 1948, the full M-registration was painted in black on the fuselage rear part and the pre-war Dutch roundel was reintroduced. They were in six positions and the airplanes got a red/white/ blue fin-flash on both vertical tail surfaces. At left, the airplanes M-434, M-439 and M-433. Airplane M-434 in front is still partly camouflaged, hence the white registration number. (Royal Netherlands Air Force)

Left: *The numbers M-448 and M-450. The armament has been removed and there are still remnants of the Olive Drab camouflage. (Royal Netherlands Air Force)*

*A mighty strafer of No. 18 Sqn. at the aviation exhibition at Tjililitan in September 1948. The airplane is showing her "machine room".
Strafers of the RNEIAAF had no top turrets. (Collection Gerben Tornij)*

NETHERLANDS EAST INDIES TRANSPORT SQUADRON (NEITS)

There were no formal Dutch Transport Squadrons until September 1944. There were initially two transport sections: NEI-Transport Section, Brisbane (NEI-TSB) based at Archerfield and NEI-Transport Section, Melbourne (NEI-TSM). Both were equipped with a number of Lockheed Lodestars and B-25s that had been stripped of armament and converted for transport. Both these Transport Sections were used to ferry men and material to No. 120 (NEI) Squadron in Merauke (later Biak) and No. 18 (NEI) Squadron at Batchelor. In September 1944, TSM, was transferred to RAAF station Archerfield. At the time, it had an official squadron status and was referred to No. 1 NEI Transport Squadron. It is worth mentioning that on 1 September, 1944, No. 2 NEI Transport Squadron was formed in Brisbane with five B-25s. In practical terms, however, a separation between the two transport squadrons was a problem. Therefore, No. 2 Squadron had already disbanded in November 1944 and was assigned to No. 1 Squadron. The aircraft pool was expanded with C-47s and Lockheed 12A light transports.

Again N5-128 with "Donald Duck". The armament has now been removed and she has been stripped of paint, however, the "Donald Duck" artwork was maintained. The airplane served with the NEI Transport Squadron in 1944 and 1945 at Brisbane. (Collection Wim Nijenhuis)

At the end of December 1944, No. 1 Squadron counted five cargo B-25s. These were referred to as TB-25. On 15 August, 1945, the unofficial transports used by the Netherlands East Indies KLM (KNILM) were renamed No. 19 (NEI) Transport Squadron and officially taken on the strength of the RAAF. On the same date, No. 1 NEITS merged into No. 19 Transport Squadron. The squadron consisted largely of old crews of the pre-war KNILM, the support and technical personnel were a mix of both Dutch as Australians. In

N5-143 was a B-25D with s/n 41-29722. The Olive Drab/Neutral Grey ship was assigned to No. 18 Sqn. in 1942 but was converted into a transport plane and assigned to NEI-TSM in 1944. The transport aircraft were provided with Australian call signs on the vertical tail surfaces. For radio contact with transport airplanes, the RAAF made use of radio call signs. These consisted of a unique combination of three letters for each individual airplane, preceded by the VH-prefix of Australia. On the tail of N5-143 the call sign VH-RDF was applied. Late 1944, it went to No. 1 NEI Transport Squadron at Archerfield. (via Max Schep)

addition to the military supply flights, the daily task of No. 19 squadron was taking care of food flights, the transport of medicines, evacuation flights of ex-prisoners of war and ex-internees from the Japanese POW camps and the transport of many VIPS and civil servants. In May 1947, the squadron moved to Kemajoran, Batavia.

On 1 november, 1946, No. 20 Squadron was formed at Tjililitan as transport and ambulance service squadron and equipped with the TB-25 and Dakota C-47 aircraft. After 1 August 1947, the tasks of No. 19 squadron gradually phased out and were split into a civilian branch under the competence of the KLM, while the military flights were accommodated by No. 20 Sqn. On 1 april, 1948, No. 19 Sqn. was disbanded and No. 20 Sqn. was the only remaining Dutch military transport squadron. In 1948, the B-25s were replaced with Dakotas and on 20 June, 1950, the squadron was deactivated.

Centre: After service with No. 18 Sqn., N5-164 was converted to transport airplane. In 1947, she was renumbered M-364 and assigned to No. 20 Sqn. at Tjililitan. The airplane was then very weathered and partly stripped of her camouflage paint as can be seen in this picture. (NIMH)

N5-208, later renumbered M-408, was one of the few B-25s that flew for a short time with No. 19 Squadron. This is a B-25D-35, s/n 43-3833. The aircraft belonged to the last D-block produced in the Kansas City plant of North American. Like other cargo B-25s, she was a clean overall natural aluminium finished airplane with black airplane number, the national marking in six positions and with the red, white and blue fin flash.

(Royal Netherlands Air Force)

PVA

During the war, the B-25s of No. 18 Squadron made many photos. They were equipped with cameras above a hatch in the fuselage. They also had two folding windshield for making overboard pictures. A lot of experience was gathered this way and a photo service could be set up in Batavia. On 10 November, 1945, after these positive experiences, the Office Photo Service was founded. On 1 June, 1946, the name changed into Office Photo-Movie Service. At the same time the Photo Section Tjililitan and the Photo School at Andir were founded. In the beginning there was a great shortage of good film material, cameras, decent housing and staff. Gradually, the situation became better and this new unit of the ML-KNIL had two converted FB-25s and a large hangar at Tjililitan. On 1 January, 1947, the PVA (Photo Verkennings Afdeling - Photo Reconnaissance Department) was officially founded on Tjililitan. The task of the PVA was initially reconnaissance for military purposes. The outdated map material from the pre-war time had to be replaced with photo cards and drawn staff cards. The PVA worked intensively together with the Topographic Service of the Netherlands East Indies Army. A year after its foundation, the PVA had five FB-25s.

In addition to the military missions, the PVA also flew missions for civilian purposes of large businesses, the municipality of Batavia and press and information services. For the vertical aerial shots they used B-25s which were equipped with electrically-operated Fairchild K-17 cameras for vertical photography and Fairchild K-20 hand cameras.

Three times the same ship in different units, respectively No. 18 Sqn., NEI-PEP and the Photo Verkennings Afdeling (PVA). This former N5-148, a B-25C-10, s/n 42-32338, was assigned to No. 18 Sqn. In 1945, she was converted into transporter of the NEI-PEP and later assigned to the PVA.
Bottom: *She is seen with two other ships of the PVA with the squadron insignia. Crew members stand together and show the various cameras they use. (Collection Wim Nijenhuis)*

Before the start of the police actions, the PVA mapped roads, bridges and airports. During both police actions of 1947 and 1948, frequent use was made of the services of the PVA. Results of bombing and artillery firing could be analysed, as well as destruction of the TNI. During the actions, the PVA flew over 100 missions. The first three months of 1949, the PVA still flew many operational missions. During 1949, it became quieter and there were hardly any operational flights from the beginning of 1950. When the unit was disbanded on 1 March, 1950, No. 18 Squadron got its own photo section.

This was a former airplane of No. 18 Sqn. nicknamed "De Striet-ser". N5-154 was stripped of paint and assigned to the Netherlands East Indies Personnel and Equipment Pool. In 1947, she was re-numbered M-354 and in 1948 she was assigned to the PVA. Here she got a PVA squadron insignia on her nose.
(via Max Schep)

The early PVA squadron insignia was a blue circle with yellow outline, a mosquito with camera with above it the letters PVA in yellow. The mosquito had golden wings and the tail was alternating light green and gold yellow. On 1 January, 1947, the PVA was officially founded, to disbanded more than three years later on 1 March, 1950. (Collection Gerben Tornij)

Another natural aluminium finished unarmed ship of the PVA. The PVA had modified B-25s for photo missions which were termed as FB-25. It has a new unit insignia designed in 1948 painted on her nose. This was a blue circle with yellow red outline, a yellow camera with wings and feet and red letters PVA. (Collection Wim Nijenhuis)

The B-25 N-209 is being fuelled. Here the airplane is still Olive Drab/Neutral Grey, perhaps during her service with the NEI-PEP or No. 18 Sqn. Later, the paint was removed and the B-25D-35, s/n 43-3835, regularly flew for the PVA to make mapping flights. Large areas on Java were photographed and mapped. At right, the crew is getting ready for a new mapping flight. In May 1947, the airplane was renumbered M-409. On May 14, 1949, the airplane crashed at Kroya, Java, in which all crew members were killed. *(via Bert van Willigenburg, Collection Wim Nijenhuis)*

NEI-PEP

The NEI-APP Squadron (Netherlands East Indies Aircraft and Personnel Pool) was established on 1 September, 1943 for training and for transport of personnel and supplies. It was stationed at Canberra. The main task was keeping the staff skilled and maintaining the stock of spares for No. 18 Squadron and No. 120 Squadron. In the beginning, the NEI-APP had nine B-25s. In the second half of March 1944, some more B-25s were assigned to the NEI-APP. Also, B-25s came here after their operational tour with No. 18 Squadron.

On 1 April, 1944, the name was changed to NEI-PEP (Netherlands East Indies Personnel and Equipment Pool). In 1945, the NEI-PEP became a complete organisation for technical support for two operational squadrons and management of the stocks of spares. In addition, it arranged the flight training and exercises for bombers and fighters. Further expansion at Canberra was no longer possible. In June, 1945, due to the shift of the combat front further towards Japan, it was decided to move to the RAAF airbase Bundaberg. Mid September 1945, the move to Bundaberg was a fact. Bundaberg was a training base 260 km north of Brisbane and was sufficiently provide with buildings and

February 1944, ship number 426 at Jackson, Mississippi, is ready for the ferry flight to Australia. This is a B-25D-30 with s/n 43-3426. It carried nose art designed by the Disney studios and the name "Palembang I". The crew members also wear a badge on their jacket with the same image. The airplane got the registration N5-192 and was assigned to the NEI-PEP at Canberra and then went to No. 2 Squadron of the RAAF.

(Collection Gerben Tornij)

Again airplane N5-154. The armament had been removed and she was stripped of paint and assigned to the Netherlands East Indies Personnel and Equipment Pool. She is seen here in 1946 as a clean machine with only the national markings in four positions and the airplane number on her nose and tail. (Nationaal Archief)

facilities. Later around May 1946, the NEI-PEP was transferred to Biak. The squadron was disbanded in 1946.

N5-254, a B-25J-25, s/n 44-30900. In April 1945, she was delivered to the NEI-PEP at Canberra. Afterwards, she was assigned to No. 18 Sqn. On 21 November, 1945, she ditched at sea between Truscott and Broome, Australia. The Olive Drab is still fairly dark, which indicates that the airplane was still relatively new when this picture was taken. (Collection Wim Nijenhuis)

This plane was a B-25J-20, s/n 44-29260. She was part of the NEI-PEP at Canberra and was assigned to No. 18 Sqn. It is Olive Drab/Neutral Grey with the red white and blue flags on fuselage and wings.

Right: The fully armed N5-242 is testing her engines. Remarkable in this picture, in addition to the regular aircraft number on the nose, she also has this number in small figures below the cockpit.
(Collection Wim Nijenhuis)

RAPWI

In February 1945, at the headquarters of Admiral Lord Louis Mountbatten, the service Recovery of Allied Prisoners of War and Internees (RAPWI) was established. The organisation was responsible for the care of prisoners of war and internees in the areas under the control of South East Asia Command (SEAC). On 15 August, 1945, the command area was extended with the Dutch East Indies, the southern part of Thailand and Indo-China. It became clear that in dozens of former Japanese detention camps many tens of thousands of people were present. Not only Dutch, but also many other nationalities. They lived in miserable conditions in unsafe areas which, therefore, had to be improved.

In the Netherlands East Indies, the organisation consisted for the major part of Dutch employees who were recruited from former internees. The NEI RAPWI operated under British command. The central leadership

One of the few B-25s used by the RAPWI in 1945 was airplane N5-158. This is one of the modified B-25s used for transport. It was a B-25D-20 with s/n 41-30589. The airplane was stripped of the camouflage and armament. She has only a black airplane number on her nose and the Dutch flag in four positions. In July 1946 and January 1947, the airplane made a trip to Valkenburg airfield in the Netherlands. Here the ship is at Valkenburg airfield in 1947. (Collection Wim Nijenhuis)

was performed by the RAPWI Coordination Committee with a Dutch Adviser added. The RAPWI was responsible for the planning and implementation of reception, care and repatriation of all prisoners of war and internees in the command area of SEAC. Repatriation, however, was only for British, Canadian, Australian, New Zealand, Indian and American prisoners of war and civilians from the archipelago. Dutch prisoners of war and internees would be repatriated only if this was necessary on medical grounds. Thanks to the effort of this organisation, the situation in a number of camps on West Java and Sumatra were improved. Besides the C-47 Dakotas, the RAPWI was also equipped with eight B-25s. On 26 January, 1946, the RAPWI on Java was officially disbanded.

The N5-158 during a crowded Military Aviation Day at Kemajoran airfield on 9 March, 1947. (Nationaal Archief)

OTHER UNITS

No. 119 Squadron was a joint Dutch and Australian squadron. It was founded at Canberra on 1 September, 1943. As a Dutch-Australian squadron, the Netherlands supplied the aircraft and flight crews. The ground staff was predominantly Australian. The squadron operated under the command of the RAAF. The squadron was initially equipped with two B-25s, N5-134 and N5-142, and a Lockheed Lodestar. It was the intention that the new squadron, equipped with eighteen B-25s flown over from the U.S., could further work up to operational status in close co-operation with No. 18 Squadron. However, it proved to be impossible to maintain an extra bomber squadron for a longer period of time. As a result and owing to a shortage of manpower, the new squadron was disbanded already on 15 November, 1943. The Dutch and Australian personnel were transferred to the newly formed No. 120 Squadron.

Finally, there were still a few other training units that used the B-25. From mid 1946 to August 1948, the OOS (Overgangs Opleidings School) at Biak, which handled the conversion to the B-25, had more than twenty B-25s. Later, this became the Transition Training School. By the end of the Dutch presence in the Dutch East Indies, there was the GOS (Gespecialiseerde Opleidings School - Specialized Training School) at Tjililitan with a number of B-25s.

The airplane was renumbered in May 1947 as M-358. Here she is photographed upon arrival at the airfield of Palembang on 30 September, 1947, with on board Lieutenant-Governor-General Van Mook and Army Commander General Spoor.

Left: *On 3 May, 1949, the Army Commander Spoor arrived at the Talang Betoetoe airport at Palembang. On the nose is the "Zuiderkruis" (Southern Cross) emblem of the Cabinet of the Army Commander. This was the same emblem as mentioned earlier and carried on the N5-160 (M-360). (Nationaal Archief)*

N5-142, was one of the two B-25s initially assigned to No. 119 Sqn. It was the intention to equip the new squadron with eighteen B-25s flown over from the U.S. In 1943, the airplane was converted for transport and assigned to No. 119 Sqn. In 1944, she went to NEI-TSM and the Australian call sign VH-RDD was applied on her vertical tail surfaces. In the picture at left, the aluminium natural finished ship still with the emblem of No. 18 Sqn. on her nose. *(Collection Wim Nijenhuis)*

Skyline

The same airplane published in "Skyline". This was the major publication for all employees of North American Aviation at the plants at Inglewood, Dallas and Kansas City. This is the first page of an article about the Dutch B-25s of the Netherlands East Indies Air Force in the "Skyline" edition of November–December 1943. Notice the difference of the position of the name in both pictures. Probably a piece of old-fashioned "photo shopping" by the factory photographer.

(Collection Wim Nijenhuis)

A well-known picture of "Pulk", the B-25C N5-131, s/n 41-12916, of No. 18 Squadron. It shows personnel and aircrew in front of their bomber after returning from a raid against the Japanese. In 1947, this airplane was for a short time part of the OOS at Biak. The name "Pulk" was painted in yellow letters. *(Collection Wim Nijenhuis)*

YOU CAN'T BEAT

The Dutch

These Dutchmen, robbed of their homes and country by the Axis invaders, go all out for revenge and a final and lasting peace. Hitler and Tojo please take note.

Allied Headquarters in the Southwest Pacific, Aug. 6 (Aneta)—A flight of Netherlands-manned Mitchells bombed the enemy-held town of Lautem on Timor the night of August 5, it was disclosed today, starting one "very large" blaze and several small fires and causing several explosions from hits on ammunition dumps.

London, Aug. 20 (Aneta)—The Netherlands Navy Bomber Squadron in England, revamped for pre-invasion operations and newly equipped with medium Mitchells, has gone into action for the first time with attacks on enemy targets

yesterday and today, it was learned tonight.

The squadron today attacked an enemy aircraft factory at Flushing in Holland—believed to be the Schelde plant—after an attack yesterday on an enemy airfield at Poix, France.

The British Air Ministry communique on the Flushing attack said one plane was missing, but its crew was safe. Aneta learned that the missing aircraft was one of the Dutch B-25's, and that its crew had been returned to England safely. The Mitchells were escorted by Spitfires in the raid.

NORTH AMERICAN SKYLINE

N5-163 in the background was converted into a transporter in 1945 and after service with No. 18 Sqn. she went to the OOS at Biak in 1947. She is seen here at Biak in April 1947. Note the modified tail cone of the B-25 in the foreground. *(Nationaal Archief)*

ROYAL NETHERLANDS MILITARY FLYING SCHOOL

In addition to the aforementioned squadrons and units in the Netherlands East Indies, B-25s also have flown with the Royal Netherlands Military Flying School (RNMFS) at Jackson Army Air Base, Mississippi, U.S.A. This base was a military airfield that was opened in May 1941 and belonged to the U.S. Army and accommodated bomber and reconnaissance groups.

In February 1942, pilot training in the Netherlands East Indies was terminated. Continuation was no longer possible because of the Japanese advance. Pilot training was transferred to Australia. But soon it became apparent that Australia was not suitable for flight training because the airfields were fully in use for combat purposes. So, the training was moved to Jackson in the U.S. On this air base accommodation was reserved for two Dutch squadrons. Jackson became the home base of the Dutch training. Along

with the training at Sherman Field near Fort Leavenworth in Kansas, this flight school took care of the training of flight crews in the period from April 1942 to 15 February 1944. In addition, they used the reserve airfields Hinds Airbase, Tallulah Airbase and Forest Field. These were airfields not far from Jackson. The first group comprising the majority of the students and instructors

arrived at Jackson early in 1942 and shortly thereafter at Fort Leavenworth.

The entire training programme comprised from the primary training (PT), basic training (BT), the advanced training on single- and twin-engined aircraft (AT) and finally the operational training (OT). The PT-training was at Sherman Field. The BT-, AT-, and

Dutch wings over Jackson. Aircraft number 407 with s/n 42-53407 in flight. This airplane, a B-25C-5, made an emergency landing at West Palm Beach in 1943 without damage. Note the removed de-icers on the vertical tails and the traces of the exhaust gases on the engine nacelle.
(Mississippi Department of Archives and History)

Number 499 in flight. This is 41-30499, a B-25D-15, and one of the five D models operated by the RNMFS. (Collection Gerben Tornij)

OT-training took place at Jackson. The PT-training was the first phase of the training. This training took about 80 flight hours per student, about four months. The BT training was the follow-up training on a single-engine aircraft. This started in June, 1942 with student-pilots of the RNEIAAF and the Marine Luchtvaart Dienst (MLD), the Netherlands Naval Air Service. They used Vultee BT-13A training aircraft. The programme took 120 flight hours per student over four months. The AT-training was the third phase of the pilot training. There were two possibilities. Training in single-engine aircraft or training on twin-engine aircraft. AT Single Engine (SE) was for training of fighter pilots. AT Twin Engine (TE) the training for bomber pilots. The latter was intended for pilot training on the B-25 or the Catalina flying boat. Both programmes took 100 flight hours per student for four months. For the AT-TE the Beechcraft AT-11 and Lockheed L2-12 were used. Finally, there was the OT-training aimed at preparing the air crews for their operational tasks. The OT for bombers was established at Jackson on 8 February, 1943. At the end of November 1942, ten B-25Cs were delivered to the RNMFS for OT-training. By pure coincidence, these were B-25s from the original order of the 162 airplanes for the ML-KNIL which were taken over by the USAAF. In April and May 1943, another five Ds and five Cs were delivered. To be able to finish the training programme on time, a further ten airplanes were loaned. These were B-25s from the G-type and were owned by the USAAF. In October 1943, the number was thus extended to thirty. So, the

Dutch B–25s at Jackson Army Air Base. The airplane in front is a B–25C–25, s/n 42–64781. Second in row is a D–15, s/n 41–30491 and third is 42–64783, another C–25 model. All planes are Olive Drab/Neutral Grey with yellow USAAF serial, Dutch national markings in four positions and a three–digit white number on their noses. All three airplanes were delivered in the spring of 1943. (Collection Wim Nijenhuis)

ROYAL NETHERLANDS
MILITARY FLYING SCHOOL

JACKSON, MISSISSIPPI
1942

RNMFS in Jackson had fifteen B-25s type C, five D-types and ten G-types. These B-25Gs were the only B-25s of this type that were used by the Dutch. After gaining the necessary qualifications or certification, the crews went to both the ML-KNIL in the Netherlands East Indies as well as the Naval Air Service in England.

During OT, all pilots got the opportunity to make a long distance flight. Interest in long distance flights increased after the decision was made to ferry new B-25s from the United States to Australia with NEI crews at the controls. The first ferry flight comprising a Lockheed C-60 and eight B-25s, took place

The nose and tail of airplane number 782, a B-25C–25 with s/n 42–64782. This airplane was also one of the ten B-25Cs and Ds delivered in 1943. (Collection Wim Nijenhuis)

B-25C-25 with aircraft number 784, s/n 42-64784, is taxiing for a next training flight.
(Mississippi Department of Archives and History)

in August 1943. The various ferry flights included also B-25s which were not destined for the RNEIAAF. On 5 February, 1944, was the last ferry flight flown by RNMFS aircrew who had just received their wings. At the closing of the school, the remaining airplanes were returned to the USAAF as reverse Lend-Lease aircraft. On 15 February, 1944, the RNMFS was officially closed and disbanded.

The RNMFS B-25s were painted in the standard USAAF-camouflage of Dark Olive Drab and Neutral Grey. The national marking was the red/white/blue flag, however, without white border. Most of the B-25Gs retained their USAAF markings. The USAAF-serial number was yellow on both vertical tail surfaces and the last three digits of this numbering were repeated in white on the fuselage nose.

Two rare pictures of a B-25G with the Dutch flag. This is a B-25G-10, s/n 42-65102. This was the first airplane produced of the G-10 block series. The Olive Drab/Neutral Grey coloured plane of the RNMFS is seen here during an escort flight in November 1943. The then Dutch Princess Juliana, later Queen, visited Suriname and travelled in a Lockheed L14 accompanied by two B-25s. One USAAF ship with the name "Ponciforte" and the Dutch B-25 number 102. Note that the Dutch B-25 has no national markings on the upper wing surfaces. (Nationaal Archief)

November 1943, Princess Juliana in Suriname amidst the crew in front of the accompanying American B-25 "Ponciforte".
(Nationaal Archief)

Centre: *Two other pictures of Princess Juliana in front of USAAF B-25s. At left number 1645 and at right, number 1694 with the name "Betty Ann" painted on the nose. During the war, Princess Juliana lived with her small children in Ottawa, Canada. Her husband Prince Bernhard and her mother Queen Wilhelmina stayed in London. The Netherlands and the Netherlands East Indies were occupied, but the Netherlands Antilles and Suriname were free. In Canada, the Princess visited the U.S. more than once and she had several meetings with President Roosevelt. At the end of 1943, she went to Suriname and a few months later she made a visit to the Netherlands Antilles. On the trips, she was accompanied with these American B-25s.* (Nationaal Archief, John Fernhout)

MARINE LUCHTVAARTDIENST

The Marine Luchtvaartdienst (MLD) - Naval Air Service - was another military unit that has used the B-25. During the war period, many Dutch crews flew in B-25s with No. 320 Squadron of the RAF. After the war, a number of B-25s flew under the Dutch flag with the MLD.

The MLD was constituted on 18 August, 1917, and was part of the Royal Netherlands Navy. It was an independent organisation and has operated worldwide. In June 1940, the aircraft squadrons No. 320 and No. 321 were established with Fokker T-VIIIw and Avro Anson airplanes and were assigned to the British Coastal Command. These aircraft were found unsuited for war situations and were replaced with Lockheed Hudsons. These airplanes had to escort and protect convoys, but also had to attack enemy transports on the shipping route Narvik-Rotterdam. A big improvement came when No. 320 Squadron received the B-25 in 1943 and was assigned to the 2nd Tactical Air Force RAF. New aircrew were trained at the Royal Netherlands Military Flying School at Jackson in the U.S.
After the war, the MLD was restructured. There was new equipment and in October 1947, the Navy took over the airfield of Valkenburg from the Dutch Air Force. Following this transfer, the airfield got the name "Marine Vliegkamp Valkenburg" (Naval Air Base Valkenburg). The Navy then stationed the squadrons 320 and 321 at Valkenburg. In the 1950s, the MLD reached massive proportions with four airfields, eleven squadrons, more than two thousand men and an MLD contingent on the aircraft carrier HNLMS *Karel Doorman*. But in the following decades, the tasks changed and the size decreased dramatically. The MLD was down, Valkenburg was closed and the squadrons 320 and 321 were disbanded. The airbase is closed since July 2006. On 4 July, 2008, the MLD underwent a metamorphosis. The only flying material, the helicopters, were integrated with the helicopters of the Royal Netherlands Air Force into the new Defence Helicopter Command (DHC) under the command of the Royal Netherlands Air Force. With this, more than ninety years of MLD came to an end.

One of the B-25s that was obtained from the Dutch war inventory in England. She is seen here at the Gilze-Rijen air base in 1947, where she was temporarily stationed. The airplane still has the RAF serial FR-173 and is very weathered. After repainting she received the MLD serial number 1-15.
Below: Not a masterpiece colourful postcard, but nevertheless, a rare postcard from 1947 of the Gilze-Rijen air base. *(Collection Gerben Tornij)*

No. 320 Squadron

No. 320 (Dutch) Squadron RAF was a unit of the Royal Air Force during World War II, made up of the personnel of the Royal Netherlands Naval Air Service. The war period of the RAF is described in the chapter United Kingdom.

In the summer of 1945, No. 320 Sqn. operated from the German airfield of Achmer but came rarely in action. The aircraft were part of the Lend-Lease contract and, therefore, had to be returned to the USAAF. The aircraft were flown back to England and transferred to the RAF airbase Fersfield. Shortly thereafter, the B-25s were preserved at the RAF base Kirkbride. The squadron was passed to the control of the Dutch MLD on 2 August, 1945, retaining the same squadron number No. 320 Squadron. The squadron was decommissioned on 1 May, 1946, for the time being. At the post-war reconstruction of the Netherlands, the Navy considered shore-based aircraft necessary.

In 1947, for the restructuring of the MLD, 28 B-25s were obtained from the Dutch war inventory in England. Seven aircraft were directly scrapped for spare parts and a further three on arrival in the Netherlands. Two airplanes were used for ground instruction. All these airplanes were of the types B-25C and D. The 16 remaining airplanes were reserialled 1-11 to 1-23 and 18-1 to 18-3. These latter three were of the OSRD (Opsporings-en Reddingsdienst) (SAR, search and rescue service).

During the first post-war period, the airplanes were overall Sea Grey. On 22 March, 1949, the squadron was reactivated at Valkenburg with the original RAF number 320 and the original B-25 Mitchells for maritime tasks. The most important task was providing training and search and rescue service. For this last service, the OSRD, they had three B-25s of which one was continuously stand by. Already in September 1949, seven B-25s had been written off. In 1951, a complete overhaul took place of the remaining nine B-25s at the Avio-Diepen company at Ypenburg. During the overhaul, corrosion was removed as well as the belly

Two other B-25s at Gilze-Rijen in 1947. They still are in the RAF colours. (Collection Gerben Tornij)

gun turret. Armament was changed and the airplanes were painted in a new Extra Dark Sea Grey colour scheme. In 1951, because of the arrival of new aircraft types, No. 320 Sqn. moved to the U.S. for retraining and transferred her task and aircraft to new aircraft squadron VSQ. 5. After the departure of the Mitchells, Grumman Trackers flew with the squadron and in 1962 the Lockheed Neptune P2V-7B made its appearance. No 320 Sqn. was disbanded eventually on 14 January, 2005, after selling her Lockheed Orions.

The MLD used in its registration system a code letter for the assignment of aircraft. To distinguish Naval aircraft from their Air Force counterparts, the character in the registration was replaced with a figure representing the position of the character in the alphabet. So the A was number 1, the letter B was number 2, and so on. This number was followed by the aircraft number. The registration of the B-25s was 1-11 to 1-23 and 18-1 to 18-3, corresponding with A-11 to A-23 and R-1 to R-3. The numbers were painted in white on both sides of the fuselage behind the wings. The Dutch roundel was on six positions. On both sides of the fuselage and on top and bottom of both wings. Below the stabiliser was painted with small white letters the words "Kon. Marine". A red white blue flag was applied only on the outside of the two vertical tail surfaces. From 15 May, 1950, nine survivors were re-serialled 13-1 to 13-9, corresponding with M-1 to M-9, and they had the Dutch roundels in six positions and the white text "Kon. Marine" below the stabiliser. With the revision in 1951, the registrations were once

One of the Mitchells at Valkenburg during swearing-in of officers on 26 May, 1948. The serial number seems to be AC41-30794 and is painted in small white figures below the navigator's window. In that case this is airplane number 1-18, a B-25D-15.
(Nationaal Archief)

The overall Sea Grey no. 1-18 photographed in 1948. The registration number is painted in white on both sides of the fuselage behind the wings. Note the difference in size of the figures. The Dutch roundel is in six positions, on both sides of the fuselage and on top and bottom of both wings. Below the stabiliser, the text "Kon. Marine" is painted in small white letters. This plane has no fin flash on the vertical tails. The OSRD had an airplane with number 18-1 and should not be confused with this 1-18. (Nationaal Archief, Collection Wim Nijenhuis)

again changed to 2-1 to 2-9, also in white. The airplanes were now Extra Dark Sea Grey on top and Sky on the lower surfaces. They also had the rosettes in six positions and the text "Kon. Marine" in black below the stabiliser.

Number 1-21 was the ex RAF FR196. On 21 July, 1948, this airplane crashed in foggy weather conditions against the coastal rocks of Scotland, killing six crew members. (Collection Gerben Tornij)

This is airplane number 18-2 during an official Command transfer at Valkenburg on 14 October. 1947. Her USAAF serial is 42-87405. She is overall Sea Grey and is one of the three B-25s used by the OSRD (Opsporings- en Reddingsdienst) and has a registration number starting with number 18. (Nationaal Archief)

The registration starting with number 13 existed only for a short time. This is the overall Sea Grey 13-1 of No. 320 Sqn. formerly 18-1 and later renumbered 2-1, photographed in 1950. (Collection Gerben Tornij)

VSQ 5

VSQ 5 (Vliegtuigsquadron 5) was constituted on 7 May, 1951 at Valkenburg with the B-25s from No. 320 Sqn. The unit specialised in patrol and SAR duties. The unit also flew Sea Otters, Austers and Oxfords. Its tasks included performing exercises and retraining of pilots and SAR services. In 1952, the B-25s were transferred to VSQ 8, and the unit had standardised on the Fairey Firefly and the newly arrived Beech TC-45J Navigators.

1949, five overall Sea Grey Mitchells of No. 320 Sqn. at RAF Station St. Eval, Cornwall. In the centre is airplane 18-3 used by the OSRD. (Collection Wim Nijenhuis)

In 1951, a complete overhaul took place of the remaining MLD B-25s at the Avio-Diepen company at Ypenburg airfield. During the overhaul, the belly gun turret and corrosion were removed. Armament was changed and the airplanes were repainted. This is one of the airplanes with a new fresh Extra Dark Sea Grey and Sky colour scheme.

(Collection Wim Nijenhuis)

Left: *Two former ships of No. 320 Sqn. ship. After overhaul at Avio-Diepen and renumbering, they were transferred to VSQ 5 and later transferred to VSQ 8. No. 2-1 is a B-25C-15, s/n 42-32513 and 2-2 is a B-25D-25, s/n 42-87405. Both airplanes are Extra Dark Sea Grey on top and Sky on the lower surfaces.*

(via Klaas Folkersma)

Valkenburg in the early 1950s. One of the MLD's new painted Mitchells. On the background one of the squadron's Fairey Fireflies. (via Robert Jan Leerink)

VSQ 8

VSQ 8 was constituted on 1 February, 1950 at Morokrembangan, Netherlands East Indies. Already on 15 December, 1950, it was disbanded, and the squadron's Dakota aircraft were transferred to the Indonesian TNI-AU. The squadron was reactivated on 10 March, 1952 at Valkenburg, with the Mitchells and Sea Otters from VSQ 5 and took over that unit's duties including the SAR tasks. In 1953, the squadron became the first MLD helicopter squadron with the Sikorsky S-51. In February 1953, the B-25s were used after the big flood disaster in Zeeland in the night of 31 January/1 February. The B-25s remained in action until 16 February for dropping medicines, food and other relief goods. VSQ 8 had a total of four B-25s available for this purpose. Especially during the first three days of action, the B-25s were used almost exclusively for dropping rubber boats. So, the B-25s ended their flying career with the MLD in a very spectacular way. In the course of 1953, the first three planes were phased out and the last B-25s were written off in the spring of 1954 and replaced with Lockheed PV-2 Harpoons.

15 October, 1953, demonstration Safe Power for airplanes at Valkenburg. This is airplane no. 2-2, now of VSQ 8. The figures 2-2 are in white and the text "Kon. Marine" is in black below the stabiliser. It had the Dutch roundels in six positions. (Nationaal Archief)

Two other pictures of number 2-2. They show clearly the colours and markings of the Royal Netherlands Naval Air Service in the early 1950s. (Collection Gerben Tornij)

Five Mitchells of the MLD in flight over sea. They all have the new registration starting with a 2 and are Extra Dark Sey Grey with Sky. The roundels are on both upper wings.
(Collection Wim Nijenhuis)

Humanitarian aid

During the big flood of 1953, food droppings were carried out by B-25s. In the night of 31 January/1 February a devastating north-westerly storm reached the south-western coast of the Netherlands and carried the water to unprecedented heights. Dikes broke through and thunderous tidal waves of up to two meters high were flooding the polders. The disaster took more than 1,800 lives and that of thousands of animals. (Collection Gerben Tornij, ANP Archief)

Airplane number 2-6 in her last days after service. This is the former RAF airplane of No. 320 Sqn. with serial FR-193 and coded NO-L. This picture was probably taken in the mid-fifties at Deelen Air Force Base, in anticipation of the transport to its final destination in the Dutch National War and Resistance Museum at Overloon.

Bottom: *The airplane in 2007 in the museum with the newly painted RAF colours of No. 320 Sqn. during wartime.*

(Maritieme Historie, Collection Wim Nijenhuis)

FRANCE

The Free French flew B-25s under RAF control during the war with No. 342 (Lorraine) Squadron. This is described in the chapter United Kingdom.

After the war in November 1945, the Lorraine squadron moved to Dijon in France. The squadron was disbanded on 2 December, 1945, and transferred from RAF control to the French Air Force (Armée de l'Air) and renamed GB I/20 Lorraine. Most of the B-25s returned to England and were scrapped. At least one remained in French service and was stripped of armament and flew with the Groupe de Liaisons Aériennes Ministérielles (GLAM). This was a unit of the Armée de l'air française, constituted at the French air force base of Villacoublay in March 1945. The group successively got the names of GLAM 86, Groupe de Liaisons Aériennes I/40, Groupe de Transport et de Liaisons Aériennes I/60 and finally GLAM I/60. Another B-25 was taken from U.S. service in February 1945, and offered to the Armée de l'air française. The two Mitchells were converted to VIP transports. One airplane was number 330, and mainly used by General Leclerc for his inspection tours in North Africa. This was a B-25D-10 with s/n 41-30330. The airplane crashed in November 1947. The other airplane was a B-25J-20 with s/n 44-29678 and RAF serial KJ692. She crashed in July 1951 and was later sold to the U.S.A. Both airplanes were initially camouflaged Olive Drab with Neutral Grey undersides.

French roundel on camouflaged B-25s

French roundel on natural aluminium finished B-25s

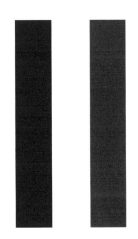

French flag on rudders

They were provided with French roundels on the fuselage and on both upper and lower wings. The ex-RAF ship had the Cross of Lorraine roundel on the fuselage. The blue, white and red French flag was painted over the entire outer surfaces of the rudders with the blue directly adjacent to the vertical stabiliser. Later, the camouflage paint was removed and the B-25s were both overall natural aluminium finished. The airplanes now had the French flag painted over the entire outer and inner surfaces of the rudders.

Two pictures of one of the converted VIP transports. The airplane was a B-25D-10 manufactured in Kansas City with s/n 41-30330 and delivered to the 12th Air Force in Oran, Algeria, in May 1943, and called "Bouncing Betsy". She was taken from U.S. service on 24 February, 1945, and offered to the Armée de l'air française which assigned her to the GT 1/60 GLAM, registered F-RAFC. She is seen here in North Africa, shortly after delivery. The Olive Drab/Neutral Grey airplane has the last three digits of its s/n 41-30330 on the rudder as well as a large letter C, the last letter of its call sign FRAFC. (Collection Wim Nijenhuis)

The emblem of the 2nd Free French Armoured Division commanded by Leclerc is on the nose of FRAFC with the name "Tailly" painted above it. (Collection Wim Nijenhuis)

Other pictures of F-RAFC in Morocco, 1947. The airplane is now natural aluminium finished. It has the French flag painted over the entire outer and inner surfaces of the rudders as well as the number 41-30330 on the outer surfaces of the rudders and vertical stabilisers. The airplane was used by General Philippe Leclerc de Hauteclocque (1902-1947). The airplane was christened "Tailly II". The first "Tailly" was an armoured car used by Leclerc during the liberation of Paris. On 28 November, 1947, this aircraft "Tailly II", carrying Leclerc and

his staff, crashed near Colomb-Béchar in French Algeria, killing the entire crew and all passengers. The causes of the crash of the Mitchell are still not known with certainty. Leclerc was a French general and war hero who achieved fame as the liberator of Paris. He was made Marshal of France, posthumously, on 23 August, 1952. (Robert Biancotti, Collection Wim Nijenhuis)

General Leclerc

General Leclerc in front of the Mitchell and a first day cover of 28 November, 1956, in memory of the accident. (Collection Wim Nijenhuis)

18 June, 1945, General Leclerc opened the victory parade on the Champs-Élysées aboard his command tank. On the tank "Tailly" is painted in white capital letters. General Leclerc lived in the castle of Tailly. He gave the name of "Tailly" to his armoured car as the head of the 2nd Armored Division during the liberation of Paris in August 1944, and later to his B-25 transport airplane. (Immersive)

Right: *A postcard of the castle of Tailly, dating from the 18th century. The castle is located in the department of the Somme in the region Nord-Pas-de-Calais-Picardie. It is the home of the family Leclerc de Hauteclocque. Nowadays in the outbuildings there is an exhibition showing the epic of General Leclerc and the liberation of France in 1944. This exhibition was set up by the son of the general.*

(Collection Wim Nijenhuis)

This is the former RAF Mitchell KJ692. It is a B-25J-20, s/n 44-29678 of the Groupe de Transport et de Liaisons Aériennes I/60 GLAM. It was registered F-RAFE. The airplane crashed on 28 July, 1951 at Luxeuil, France, and was summarily repaired and returned to the USA. The airplane has no camouflage paint but still has the Lorraine roundel on the fuselage with a blue Lorraine Cross. *(ECP Armées)*

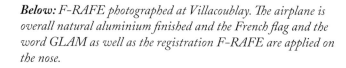

Below: F-RAFE photographed at Villacoublay. The airplane is overall natural aluminium finished and the French flag and the word GLAM as well as the registration F-RAFE are applied on the nose.

Left: Detail of the modified tail of the ship with the GLAM insignia painted on the vertical stabilisers. The French colours are painted on both sides of the rudders. *(Collection Wim Nijenhuis)*

A possible third ship of the GLAM was this Mitchell registered F-SCCZ. However, literature and sources make no mention of a third B-25 within the GLAM. So, most likely this is the same airplane as F-RAFE but with a different registration. It has the same colours, but the painted flag on the nose is different in shape. *(Musée de 'l Air, Collection Wim Nijenhuis)*

SPAIN

The Ejército del Aire de España or Fuerza Aérea Española (Spanish Air Force) did not flew with B-25s. However, during World War II, Spain interned several airplanes, both Allied and Axis. A B-25D-35 was interned in Spain with the serial number 43-3650. This airplane belonged to the 488th BS, 340th BG of the USAAF. The B-25 landed at Palma de Mallorca on 14 September, 1944. It is unknown what happened to this airplane, but was most likely scrapped.

Another interned B-25 served in Spain for a few years. This was Spain's only B-25 and was a B-25D-10 with s/n 41-30338 and was a VIP transport aircraft operating for the

Roundel on six positions

St. Andrew's cross on white rudder

RAF. On 4 August, 1944, this B-25 was flown by a British crew and made an emergency landing at the aerodrome of Tauima, Nador-Melilla in Morocco. The aircraft suffered a malfunction in the flight controls, coused by the breakage of two of the three hinges of a rudder. By mistake the pilot, who had flown

from Gibraltar en route to Tunis, thought he was in French Morocco. The crew was repatriated and the airplane remained in the workshops of the Maestranza de Nador. After the war, the Allied Control Commission had no interest in recovering the airplane so it remained at Nador until 1948. The then

Not very well known, but the Spanish Air Force had one B-25. It was a B-25D-10 with s/n 41-30338 and received the Spanish registration 74-17. Here is the B-25 in Morocco in 1950, with full colours and markings including the St. Andrew's cross.

(Collection Juan M. Gonzalez)

Captain Tordesillas managed to recover the airplane with the help of Iberia workshops there, and put it in flight condition. On 3 June, 1950, the airplane was flown to the Flight High School at the Air Base Matacán, Salamanca. The call sign *74-17* was assigned and she served here as a training aircraft and transport until 1953. But in practice it became the personal aircraft of Eduardo Gonzalez Gallarza. He was an early aviator who was Air Minister in the Franco regime from 1944 to 1955. In 1953, due to the lack of spare parts, the B-25 was retired from service and finally auctioned for scrap in 1956.

The Spanish B-25 was apparently camouflaged in Dark Olive Green and a Light Tan colour on the upper and side surfaces. The lower surfaces seemed to be Light Blue or Light Grey. The Spanish roundel used the colours of the national flag. On the upper and lower wings and fuselage were roundels of red yellow and red. On the rudder was painted a black St. Andrew's cross on a white ground. The registration number was painted black.

Right: In these pictures, the airplane appears very deteriorated so they must have been taken between 1953 to 1956. The black crosses on the white rudders have disappeared. (Paco Andreu)

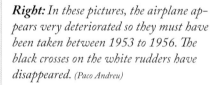

Left: Detail of the glazed nose and engine. (Paco Andreu)

~ 116 ~

CANADA

One of the many signs of the BCATP seen in Canada during the war. (RCAF)

A lot of Mitchells flew in the Canadian area during the war years. Most of these were new machines produced in North American's Inglewood and Kansas City plants. They were supplied by the United States, who used the common ferry routes via Canada to the United Kingdom and North Africa. During the war, the RCAF had no operational bombing squadrons with Mitchells. The greater part of RCAF personnel operating overseas in Mitchells did so as members of RAF squadrons in the United Kingdom. However, many Mitchells served the RCAF in Canada. The RCAF used the Mitchell for training during the war, although most of the RCAF use of the Mitchell was post-war into the 1960s. The first B-25s for the RCAF had originally been diverted to Canada from Royal Air Force orders. The RAF designated the B-25B model as Mitchell Mk.I, the

B-25C and D models as Mk.II and the B-25J was designated as Mk.III. This designation was also used by Canada. On 10 July, 1942, 7 Mk.Is were taken on strength. They were intended for use by No. 2 Operational Training Unit at Pennfield Ridge, New Brunswick, on the Canadian east coast. This unit was to train twin-engine and four-engine crews. It was the only unit within the RCAF that would be flying with the early B model. However, the unit was already disbanded on 20 August, 1942 and the Mitchells were assigned to the RAF at No. 111 Operational Training Unit in the Bahamas.

In February 1944, 70 Mk.IIs were taken on strength and 4 F-10 Mitchells a month later. The Mk.IIs of the RCAF were all B-25D models and the F-10 was a conversion of the D model specifically built for photo map-

ping. In 1945, the RCAF received 2 Mk.IIIs and in June 1951, it received an additional 75 Mk.IIIs from USAF stocks to make good attrition and to equip various second-line units. 37 of these 75 airplanes were fitted with Airborne Interception (AI) radar noses. They were designated by the USAF as TB-25K and TB-25M. Finally, the RCAF received 6 TB-25Ms in August 1954. These were borrowed from the USAF and served with No. 3 All-Weather (Fighter) Operational Training Unit. In total 164 B-25s were operated by the RCAF between 1942 and 1967.

Most of the Canadian Mitchells were taken on strength by Training Command, Western Air Command and No. 6 Repair Depot. Training Command, established at Trenton in October 1949, was responsible for the training of all personnel in the RCAF. In addition, under a mutual aid programme, they assumed the responsibility for training aircrews for Belgium, Denmark, France, Italy, Netherlands, Norway, Portugal and the United Kingdom. In September 1958, Training Command moved to Winnipeg.

Western Air Command (WAC) was part of the RCAF Home War Establishment. The wartime RCAF consisted of three main parts, two of which were in Canada and the third with its headquarters in London, was the Overseas War Establishment. The two in Canada were the British Commonwealth Air

Training Plan and the Home War Establishment. The latter was to deploy squadrons for coastal defence, protection of shipping, air defence and other duties in the western hemisphere. At the beginning of the war, the Home War Establishment had two operational commands, Eastern and Western Air Command. The biggest threat to Canada and the allies at the time were the German U-boats in the North Atlantic, so top priority was given to expanding the facilities and capabilities of the Eastern Air Command. In December 1941, when the Japanese attacked Pearl Harbor and later occupied the Aleutian Islands off Alaska, the priorities were reversed with the focus now on Western Air Command.

No. 6 Repair Depot (RD) was an aircraft modification and repair unit of the RCAF Air Materiel Command located at Trenton, Ontario. No. 6 RD cared for, among other things, the maintenance and modifications in Trenton and at other locations. Personnel of No. 6 RD ferried many aircraft types to and from Trenton, and flew aircraft to storage facilities after the Second World War.

During the war, Canada accomodated British training Mitchells. At the start of the Second World War, the British Government looked to the Dominions for air training help because the United Kingdom did not have the space to accommodate training and operational facilities, and because airfields in the United Kingdom were vulnerable to enemy attack. Canada's big open spaces and good climate for flying made it an ideal choice for large-scale flying training. In addition, it was beyond the reach of enemy forces. In December 1939, therefore, an agreement was made between Canada, the United Kingdom, Australia, and New Zealand, calling for Canada to train these countries' aircrews. This was done under the British Commonwealth Air Training Plan (BCATP). Nearly half of the pilots, navigators, bomb aimers, air gunners, wireless operators and flight engineers serving in all the Commonwealth air forces during the war were trained under the BCATP. The RAF moved a number of its training schools to Canada. It was a major Canadian contribution to Allied air superiority in World War II, and lasted until 31 March, 1945. At its peak, the BCATP maintained 231 training sites and required more than 10,000 aircraft and 100,000 military personnel to administer. RCAF control of the BCATP was performed by four regional commands. No. 1 Training Command at Trenton, No. 2 Training Command at Winnipeg, No. 3 Training Command at Montreal and No. 4 Training Command at Regina. These commands were created in early 1940 to replace the existing Air Training Command. By the end of the Second World War, the BCATP had graduated more than 131,000 personnel for the air forces of Canada, Australia, the United Kingdom and New Zealand.

After the war, 60 of the Mitchells supplied were held in storage. Most went to the bomber squadrons and a number went to the Air Armament School (AAS) at Trenton and were used as target tugs and gunnery trainers. Many of the new RCAF Mitchells supplied post-war incorporated a new exhaust system whith the top S-shaped stacks being replaced with a semi-collector rings. The Canadian post-war Mitchells were mostly used for aerial mapping, transport, and training. The RCAF retained the Mitchell until July 1964, when five Mitchells flew in a final salute at Winnipeg because of the termination of the training career of the Mitchell in RCAF service. Only two Mitchells remained in service with the RCAF's Central Experimental and Proving Establishment.

Roundel of the Royal Canadian Air Force from 1946 to 1965.

The Canadian Red Ensign flag was the de facto Canadian national flag from 1868 until 1965 when it was replaced by the maple leaf design. From 1958, it was used as fin flash on many of the Canadian post-war Mitchells replacing the RAF fin-flash.

CAMOUFLAGE AND MARKINGS

The RCAF schools operated RCAF owned aircraft with RCAF serials and RAF serials, and even a handful with USAAF serials. The RAF also funded and operated schools in Canada, using RAF owned aircraft with RAF serials. Until 1946, the RCAF used British roundels and other markings as described in the chapter United Kingdom.

During the war, the Mitchells of No. 5 OTU were all Olive Drab and Neutral Grey. The aircraft codes and numbers were just as in the RAF and were Medium Sea Grey. However, they had no squadron code on the rear fuselage. The RAF serial numbers were black. The serials of the D models comprised of 29 from the batch HD310 to HD345, 12 from the batch FW220 to FW280 and all 29 from the batch KL133 to 161. The four F-10's were serialled 891 to 894.

The roundels on the fuselage and on the wing upper surfaces were also the same as those of the RAF. The RCAF Mitchells used the British fin flash, which consisted of red and blue vertical bar separated by a white bar. Following the war, the RCAF Mitchells retained their RAF style markings. The Mk.III Mitchells supplied after the war were natural aluminium finished and had a four digit serial number from 5200 to 5283. From 1946, the maple leaf roundel, a distinctive Canadian character, began to be used on Canadian Mitchells. Tail markings generally consisted of the full serial number centred above the tri-coloured RAF fin-flash, with the red portion always leading in the direction of flight.

From June 1947, the RCAF introduced a five-letter registration with VC code as the first two letters. The third and fourth letters combined were to designate a unit, followed by the fifth letter that was used as an individual airplane code. The fuselage markings were to consist of the last three letters of the VC code, with a roundel separating the last letters on both sides of the fuselage. The full VC code was applied on the wing under surface with VC under the right wing and the remaining three letters under the left wing. The last three letters were also carried on the upper wing surfaces, inboard of the roundels, with the two letter unit identifier on the upper left wing and the last letter on the upper right wing. However, it is not fully clear whether Mitchells have flown with this registration.

In November 1951, the RCAF issued a new two-letter unit code. The fuselage marking included the retention of a two-letter unit code, the roundel and the last-three digits of the airplane serial number. The two-letter unit code, roundel and last three digits of the airplane serial, were applied to the under surface of each wing. Tail markings continued with the airplane serial number centred above the fin-flash. From February 1952, all RCAF aircraft had to have roundels on the upper and lower surfaces of the wings. In June 1954, on larger aircraft a standard full shadow title of red with black shadow was introduced spelling "ROYAL CANADIAN AIR FORCE" on a white fuselage top. In July 1958, new standard letter and number sets were released with roundel and last three of the serial number on the

fuselage. Also in 1958, the Canadian Red Ensign was introduced on airplanes based in Canada in place of the RAF fin-flash. The serial was moved to below the ensign, though several airplanes exist with the serial maintained above the ensign during the conversion period. Beginning in 1965, the new Canadian flag was used.

The TB-25Ks featured a fibreglass radome fitted to the front of the greenhouse nose. This radome was orange/red coloured. The TB-25Ms had a larger black radome fitted to the greenhouse nose.

Like in the USAAF and the RAF, the practice of painting distinctive art on airplanes reached a peak in the RCAF during the Second World War. Often starting out as a chalk outline and painted free-hand, nose art was as varied as the artists who created it and the crews who flew the airplanes. Since most of the Canadian aircrew flew operational missions over enemy-occupied Europe, most nose art was applied there. The crews adorned their planes with the names of their wives or sweethearts, names of the men themselves, at or near the positions the crewmen occupied in the airplanes and, of course, with pin-ups or cartoons. Above all, the large bombers such as the Halifax, Lancaster and Wellington had beautiful

forms of nose art. The opposite was the case with the Mitchells in Canada. Special paintings or nose art was hardly applied. Few aircraft had a modest form of nose art or texts affixed to the fuselage. The squadrons No. 406 and 418 were provided with the name of the town that adopted the squadrons. Especially the new post-war Mitchells were clean and shining machines.

During the war, the RAF Mitchells flew with No. 5 Operational Training Unit. The Mitchell entered Canadian service with No. 13 (P) Squadron in January 1943. After the war, this unit was renumbered as No. 413 (P) Squadron. Other squadrons that used the Mitchell after the war were No. 406 Sqn., No. 412 Sqn. and No. 418 Sqn. The Mitchells also served with many auxiliary units like OTU's, flying schools, observers and navigation schools. The major units that have used Mitchells are described below. In the units described, the numbers of Mitchells which have served in that unit are mentioned. Please note that an airplane may have flown with different units. Many Mitchells were, after their first assignment, transferred to other units, whether or not after a modification.

Embroidered badge of No. 5 OTU Boundary Bay, British Columbia.
(Collection Wim Nijenhuis)

This masterpiece on paper symbolizes very nicely the use of nose art in the RCAF. This is the cover of the magazine "Star Weekly" of July 1941. A Canadian Hurricane pilot is painting art under the cockpit of his fighter in England. The Canadians were applying nose art mostly in England and barely at the squadrons in Canada. The Star Weekly magazine was a Canadian periodical. It began publication in April 1910 in Toronto and it ceased publication in 1973. (Collection Pierre Lagacé)

No. 5 Operational Training Unit

Great shot of a busy Boundary Bay. Six Liberators and seven Mitchells are photographed in their Olive Drab/Neutral Grey camouflage scheme. They all have the RAF markings and some Mitchells have one aircraft letter painted on the nose and some have two letters. All the Mitchells are late D models with waist gun and tail gun positions. (RCAF)

By 1944, the RAF had decided to increase bombing operations in Southeast Asia and the Pacific and the bomber of choice was the B-24 Liberator. Boundary Bay, British Columbia, was chosen because of its close proximity to the mountains and ocean which, it was believed, helped to create similar flying conditions that would be found in the future theatre of operations. In addition to the Liberator, the Mitchell was used as a stepping stone to the four engined Liberators. No. 5 Operational Training Unit (OTU) was created for the purpose of training Commonwealth crews to fly the American built B-24 Liberator. No. 5 OTU was formed at Boundary Bay on 1 April, 1944 with 27 Mitchells and 17 Liberators. Training began on 24 April, 1944. The twin-engined Mitchell bombers were used as trainers allowing the pilots to step up to the big four-engined Liberators in stages and these were also supplemented with a flight of P-40 Kittyhawk fighters, used for fighter affiliation exercises. No. 5 OTU operated the Mitchell Mk.II in the training role, together with B-24 Liberators for Heavy Conversion as part of the BCATP. The course was to have approximately 35 hours of Mitchell flying and 70 hours on Liberators. Aircrews for No. 5 OTU came from both the RCAF and the RAF, second tour RAF aircrew direct from the UK, instructors from the Empire Air Training Scheme and newly trained aircrews from the flying training schools. By May 1944, the unit had already 37 Mitchells and 21 Libera-

Three ships in the winter of 1944-1945. At left, airplane L is HD320 (s/n 43-3788), centre N is HD323 (s/n 43-3794) and at right, AE is HD344 (s/n 43-3857). All airplanes are D-35 models. (Collection DesMazes)

tors. By August 1944, 41 Mitchells and 36 Liberators had been delivered to Boundary Bay and it had become apparent that a single aerodrome was not large enough to take this amount of day and night flying, so a satellite airfield was opened. On 15 July, 1944, No. 5 OTU Abbotsford Detachment was created and the Liberators moved to Abbotsford. This was a satellite field a few miles east inland. Boundary Bay was now responsible for the initial training and the Liberator crews would graduate from Abbotsford. The training ceased on 31 August, 1945 and the unit was disbanded on 31 October, 1945. No.5 OTU left the airfield of Boundary Bay and the RCAF decommissioned the station in 1946. RCAF Boundary Bay's last official function of the war was to act as a demobilisation centre for the Royal Canadian Air Force.

A total of 70 Mitchell Mk.IIs have flown with No. 5 OTU. The Mitchells of No. 5 OTU generally were painted in the RAF camouflage scheme. They were Olive Drab and Neutral Grey, with the airplane code letters in Medium Sea Grey on the fuselage noses. Some Mitchells had one letter painted on the nose and some had two letters. They had no letters on the rear fuselage. Gradually, the camouflage paint was removed to cut down fuel costs. This was done when

1944, another B-25D with the Olive Drab/Neutral Grey camouflage scheme and the aircraft letter U painted on the nose. (RCAF)

A weathered airplane KA at Boundary Bay. The letters are applied on a partially freshly painted surface. (Collection DesMazes)

each aircraft came in for its 30 hour maintenance. On the natural aluminium finished airplanes, the code letters were black. No. 5 OTU was first and foremost a training unit. Therefore, some airplanes of the unit had a lesser known paint scheme. On some airplanes wing tips and bands around the fuselage were painted in BCATP yellow. But very soon it was decided to simply strip them down to bare aluminium.

This unknown ship made an unfortunate landing. The picture shows clearly the standard RAF camouflage with the Type C.1 roundel on the fuselage, the Type B roundel on the wings and fin flash Type C. However, it has no letters next to the fuselage roundel. Note the roughly overpainted USAAF roundel and the waist gun and tail gun modifications. These modifications were made in later D models and became standard on the J model. (Collection DesMazes)

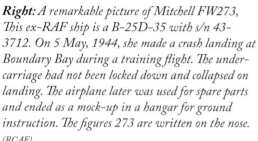

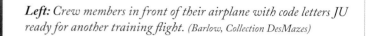

Left: Crew members in front of their airplane with code letters JU ready for another training flight. (Barlow, Collection DesMazes)

Right: *A remarkable picture of Mitchell FW273, This ex-RAF ship is a B-25D-35 with s/n 43-3712. On 5 May, 1944, she made a crash landing at Boundary Bay during a training flight. The under-carriage had not been locked down and collapsed on landing. The airplane later was used for spare parts and ended as a mock-up in a hangar for ground instruction. The figures 273 are written on the nose. (RCAF)*

Airplane AQ in flight in a lesser known paint scheme. Around late 1944, on some airplanes the wing tips and bands around the fuselage were painted BCATP yellow. But very soon it was decided to simply strip the aircraft down to bare aluminium. In time, the Mitchells were all stripped of their camouflage paint. (Collection Des-Mazes)

FW280 in flight with the code letters AT. The airplane was a B-25D-35 with U.S. serial 43-3753. In the post-war period, it would go on to fly with No. 418 Squadron City of Edmonton.
(Collection DesMazes)

Right: *Mitchells Mk.II of No. 5 OTU at the flight line at Boundary Bay. The airplanes are overall natural aluminium finished with RAF markings and black aircraft letters. Note the large RAF roundel Type B on the wings.* (Collection DesMazes)

Left: *Two overall natural aluminium finished Mitchells of No. 5 OTU. In front is KL147 with aircraft code letters BH. This B-25D-30 with U.S. serial 42-87501, was taken on strength by No. 5 OTU in January 1945. The other airplane is KL146 with code letters BG, an ex USAAF B-25D-35 with serial number 43-3629.*
(Collection DesMazes)

A Mitchell in the skies over the Vancouver area. The airplane is overall natural aluminium finished with black letters BA.
(Barlow, Collection DesMazes)

Left: It lookes like polished metal. The very shiny clean ship in this picture is KL136, a B–25D–15 with U.S. s/n 41–30757. She was taken on strength in November 1944, and went to Western Air Command for use by No. 5 Operational Training Unit at Boundary Bay. She was struck off charge in September 1960. (Collection Wim Nijenhuis)

No. 406 Squadron (Lynx) City of Saskatoon

No. 406 Squadron was formed at Acklington, England, on 10 May, 1941, as the RCAF's fifth (first Night Fighter) squadron formed overseas, flying Blenheims, Beaufighters and Mosquito's in the night air defence of England. During the war, the squadron moved several times to other bases in England. In November 1944, No. 406 Sqn. was redesignated an Intruder squadron and converted to offensive operations over Europe. No. 406 Sqn. was listed as the top-scoring RAF/RCAF intruder unit at the end of the Second World War and flew 1,835 sorties. The squadron was disbanded at Predannack, Cornwall, on 1 September, 1945. No. 406 Sqn. was reactivated at Saskatoon, Saskatchewan, on 1 April, 1947, as an Auxiliary Tactical Bomber unit. The squadron was equipped with B-25s previously used by No. 5 OTU. It flew the Mitchell in a light bomber role, as well as Harvard and T-33 Silver Star aircraft in an army co-operation role. It adopted the title "City of Saskatoon" on 3 September, 1952.

During the 1950s, Saskatoon became one of the major military centres in Western Canada. As a result of the RCAF's post-war expansion, RCAF Station Saskatoon reopened as an air training facility in October 1950. In March 1958, No. 406 Squadron was reassigned to a light transport and emergency rescue role and re-equipped with the Beech Expeditor and the De Havilland Otter. A reduction in the RCAF's Auxiliary Force resulted in No. 406 Sqn. being disbanded on 1 April, 1964. It reformed for a second time at Shearwater, Nova Scotia, on 12 July, 1972, as a maritime operational training unit flying the Grumman Tracker and Sea King. Today No. 406 Maritime Operational Training Squadron is the Helicopter Operational Training squadron for the Sikorsky CH-124 Sea King.

Car license plate from the 1950s.
(RCAF Saskatoon, Saskatchewan)

No. 406 Sqn. received the Mitchells in 1947 which were previously used by No. 5 OTU. They were stripped of their camouflage paint and their turret armament was removed. Only the machine guns in the right side of the glass nose were retained. The aluminium framework of the cockpit and nose enclosures was painted black. Most airplanes had the name of the squadron in beautifully stylized letters painted on the nose. No. 406 has flown with at least 11 Mitchells Mk.II and 5 Mk.III.

One of the few nose arts on Canadian Mitchells. This is "Saskatoon Sassy" of No. 406 Sqn. The cartoon "Sassy" was created by Margaret Theresa Fraser (1923-2015) and published in The StarPhoenix newspaper. Sassy was a mischievous cat that would do outdoor activities to portray the day's weather. Sassy was so popular she was painted on the nose of this Mitchell in the RCAF squadron based at Saskatoon. Fraser contributed other artwork to The StarPhoenix, the University of Saskatchewan Newspaper Sheaf and other publications. She was very active in the Saskatoon theatre scene, directing and acting in several plays. (Collection Wim Nijenhuis)

Women's Division RCAF

Two members of the Women's Division, RCAF, admiring one of the Mitchells at the Saskatoon airport. The "City of Saskatoon" sign on the aircraft represents the nickname of No. 406 Lynx Squadron. During the war, women played a significant role with the RCAF. The Women's Division was a non-combatant element which was active during the Second World War. The Women's Division's original role was to replace male air force personnel so that they would be available for combat-related duties. Women took on many different responsibilities. About 17,000 women wore its uniform before the service was terminated on 11 December, 1946. In 1951, five years after having discharged the last wartime Women's Division, the RCAF began recruiting again and the Women's Division was reborn in peacetime. In 1980, women were accepted as military pilots and in 1988 Canada became the first western country to license women as fighter pilots. At right, a WWII Women's Division recruiting poster. (RCAF)

Winter 1952. Airplane HD320, a B-25D-35 with s/n 43-3788, deployed in "Exercise Sun Dog III", is bombed up at Goose Bay, Labrador. "Sun Dog III" was a joint training exercise carried out by the RCAF and the Canadian Army in the Labrador–Ungava area from 4 to 14 February, 1952. The natural aluminium finished airplane has black glass framing. (RCAF)

Center: *After service with No. 5 OTU, this B-25D-30, s/n 43-3304, was used post-war by No. 406 Sqn. This old clean ship with serial KL154 and code DD-N, was struck off charge in September 1960.* (Collection Wim Nijenhuis)

This is AH-S with serial HD331, a B-25D-35 with USAAF s/n 43-3844. It is a clean ship of No. 406 Sqn. and at the moment of this picture without the Saskatoon text on her nose. Like the B-25J it has the large side windows and the tail turret. These were features of the late D models. The ship was assigned to the squadron in 1953 until it crashed in August 1954. (Collection Wim Nijenhuis)

A masterful winter landscape in 1952. Mitchells of No. 406 Sqn. are bombed up at a snowy and cold Goose Bay. (RCAF)

"The Moose" is an ex USAF B-25J-25 s/n 44-30601. This airplane was taken on strength in February 1953 and went to Tactical Air Command on 22 September, 1953, for use by No. 406 Sqn. at Saskatoon. It had the aircraft code XK259 and number 5259. On the nose a silhouette of a Moose with antlers and the text "The Moose" is painted. The moose has been an iconic figure for Canada's wilderness for centuries. The Moose is the greatest living deer species and lives among others in the Canadian coniferous forests.

Left: *Moose country. A postcard from the 1930s by Photogelatine Engraving Co. Ltd., Ottawa, showing a moose somewhere in Nova Scotia.*

(RCAF, Collection Wim Nijenhuis)

A flying masterpiece this B-25D-35 built for the USAAF with s/n 43-3848. This was one of the Mitchells loaned to the RAF under Lend-Lease in WW II and transferred to the RCAF with the serial number HD335. After assignment to No. 5 OTU, it went to No. 406 Sqn. Note the post-war engine modification. (RCAF)

Gabriel Dumont

Ex USAF B-25J-25 with s/n 44-30625 is nicknamed "Gabriel Dumont". The airplane with number 5267 and code XK267 went to No. 406 Sqn. at Saskatoon, on 27 January, 1955, and served the squadron till 1958. It has a large astrodome behind the cockpit at the place of the former gun turret. It is one of the few Canadian Mitchells still with side gun packages. Gabriel Dumont (1837-1906) was a Métis hunter, merchant, ferryman, and political and military leader. Dumont raised to political prominence in an age of declining buffalo herds and was concerned about the ongoing economic prosperity and political independence of his people. He was a prominent hunt chief and warrior, but is best known for his role in the 1885 North-West Resistance as a key Métis military commander.

(Collection Wim Nijenhuis)

Dumont was a Métis buffalo hunter. The North-West Rebellion (or North-West Resistance) was an insurrection of five months against the Canadian Government, fought mainly by the Métis and their First Nations allies. Dumont was an ally of Louis Riel, the Canadian politician and founder of the province of Manitoba, and political leader of the Métis people of the Canadian prairies.

(Library and Archives Canada)

Winter and summer in Canada. The engine is protected from the cold and technicians maintain the left engine at Saskatoon. On both airplanes the engines are still in their original condition. In the 1950s, the engines of most of the Canadian Mitchells were modified. Note the addition of the word RESERVE on the nose in the summer picture. *(RCAF)*

Left: *A very fine picture of a black engined ship with aircraft code XK-266. This ex USAF B-25J-25, s/n 44-30599, with aircraft number 5266 flew with No. 406 Sqn. from August 1954 to March 1958.*

(Collection Wim Nijenhuis)

No 412 Squadron

July 1959, Mitchell No. 5220 at the ramp at Goose Bay. The airplane is on its way to an air show in Europe. The natural aluminium finished airplane has a white roof and red lightning bolt on the fuselage as well as a red front edge of the engine. The tail is extended and behind the windows are curtains. The greenhouse glass nose is painted. This was an ex USAF B-25J-30/32 with s/n 44-86729. The ship crashed on 19 April, 1960 at Milwaukee, killing the entire crew. (Don Hodgson)

No. 412 Squadron of Air Transport Command flew with two Mitchells along with other types from September 1956 to November 1960. The squadron was constituted at Digby, Lincolnshire, England, in June 1941 with Spitfires. It moved several times to other fields and joined No. 126 Wing of the 2nd TAF at Biggin Hill in October 1943. After D-day, it moved to France, the Netherlands and Germany. After the war it was re-organised at Rockcliffe, Ontario, as No. 412 (Transport) Squadron on 1 April, 1947. In 1955, it was transferred to Uplands, Ottawa, Ontario. Upon unification No. 412 Sqn. was the VIP squadron for the Canadian Forces. Today the squadron performs the VIP and general transport duties from Ottawa International Airport with the Bombardier CC-144 Challenger.

The Mitchells used by No. 412 Sqn. had the serials 5220 and 5248. Both were Mk.III models. They served until 1960. The airplanes were highly polished and had luxury accommodation. They were equipped with the latest in avionics, and the rear was quite nicely appointed as a VIP passenger compartment. They both had a fuselage tank installed in the top portion of the bomb bay giving a total of 8.5 hours of fuel. Below the bomb bay tank was a large cage for cargo or luggage. This could be lowered and hoisted to and from the ground for loading and unloading. Ship 5220 was destroyed on 19 April, 1960, during a crash landing at Milwaukee, USA, when an engine failed. All six crew members on board were killed. The aircraft was not replaced and the squadron carried on its role with the Mitch-

ell 5248 for only about another six months. This airplane with serial number 44-86698, was taken on strength in January 1952. Her last operational flight in the RCAF was an Air Member mission. Number 5248 was then retired from the squadron and soon after from the RCAF. She was sold to the civil market in 1961 and is nowadays still flying and owned by Fagen Fighters WWII Museum, Granite Falls, Minnesota, and is flown as "Paper Doll" after an extensive restoration.

Below: *A picture of number 894. Note the RAF roundels and fin flash on the airplane. As mentioned earlier in the text, during the war, the Canadian Mitchells carried the RAF roundels and fin flash.*

(Library and Archives Canada)

No. 413 Squadron (Tusker)

No. 413 Squadron was preceded by No. 13 (Photographic) Squadron. This squadron was formed as No.13 (Operational Training) Squadron on 13 July, 1940 from the Seaplane and Bomber Reconnaissance School authorised on 1 May, 1940. In 1942, land-plane training was discontinued, and the squadron concentrated on the training of flying boat crews. It was disbanded at Pa-

tricia Bay, British Columbia, on 9 November, 1942. The unit reformed as Photographic Flight on 14 January, 1943, stationed at Rockcliffe in Ottawa. On 15 May, 1944, the flight was unofficially recognised as No. 13 (Photographic) Squadron, yet it was not until 15 November, 1946 that it was officially a squadron. On 1 April, 1947, it was redesignated No. 413 (Photographic) Squadron

One of the four F-10s of No. 13 Sqn. Note the revised oblique camera port on the nose of shiny natural aluminium finished number 892. This is ex. USAAF s/n 41-29924. The four F-10s were numbered 891 to 894. The F-10 was originally a B-25D with modifications for the camera system which resulted in the so-called "bug eye" nose.
(*Library and Archives Canada*)

and the unit flew Mitchells and Avro Lancasters on aerial photography. On 1 April, 1949, it was redesignated Survey Transport Squadron and flew transport aircraft in logistical support and for the transport of survey parties in the far north. The squadron was disbanded on 1 November, 1950. In later years, it was several times reformed and redesignated.

No. 413 Sqn. used four F-10 Mitchells. For photo mapping the RCAF needed a fast and high-flying platform and ordered three F-10s from USAAF stocks in January 1944. A year later, a fourth aircraft was available. The F-10 was a conversion of the D model specifically built for photo mapping. All the armour, armament and bombing equipment were removed. Three synchronised cameras, forming a so-called trimetrogon mapping system, were installed in the greenhouse nose. This resulted in a "bug eyed" chin fairing on the nose. The centre camera photographed directly downward. The two side cameras photographed at an oblique angle left and right. After arrival, they were again modified to specific Canadian requirements. The photo Mitchells were mostly used for development of topographical and hydrological surveys. The Mitchells had the airplane numbers 891 to 894. After disbanding of the squadron, the remaining numbers 891 and 892 served with auxiliary squadrons.

Station Rockcliffe, Ottawa, July 1944. Personnel in front of their F-10 number 894 of No.13 (P) Squadron. On the nose the emblem of the squadron is painted. (*Library and Archives Canada*)

Two of the four F-10s of No.13 Sqn. at Norman Wells, Northwest Territories, 1944. (Collection Wim Nijenhuis)

No. 418 (Eskimo) Squadron City of Edmonton

No. 418 Squadron was the RCAF's only Intruder squadron, and was formed in 1941 when Canada was called for help in the defence of England after the "Battle of Britain". It flew with the Douglas Boston and converted in 1943 to the De Havilland Mosquito. They were the only Canadian unit given free rein to "intrude" into the enemy's lair from the fjords of Norway, through the Mediterranean, to the steppes of Eastern Europe. They performed a multitude of tasks, ranging from dropping money and supplies for clandestine operations, to lightning quick strikes at grass-top level against railway yards and airfields. During this period, No. 418 Sqn. was adopted by the City of Edmonton, Alberta, and became known as the No. 418 "City of Edmonton" Squadron. After the war, the squadron was called back to service now flying the Mitchell in the tactical bomber role from the Edmonton Municipal Airport. No. 418 Sqn. was restructured on 15 April, 1946, as a fighter-bomber unit. On 26 December, 1946, the squadron was reorganised as a light bomber squadron and equipped with Mitchells previously used by No. 5 OTU. At the time the majority of Canada's air defence was made up of reservists and No. 418 Sqn. was no exception. By 1958, defence cuts reduced the squadron's activities to a transport role flying the De Havilland Single Otter and Beechcraft C-45 Expeditor from RCAF station Namao.

Home of the City of Edmonton Squadron. Personnel of No. 418 Squadron with a Mitchell Mk.II in front of hangar No. 14. The ex-RAF airplane is a B-25D-35, s/n 43-3752, with Canadian serial FW279. The hangar is a tall rectangular, one-storey, wooden flat-roofed aircraft hangar built in 1942. It is the last remaining example of a "double-double" hangar. These hangars, built for the BCATP across Canada, were made of pre-cut wooden timbers of British Columbia fir. They could be built as single units, double units, and the "double-double" which is 4 units. Hangar No. 14 has heritage value as a significant surviving example of the hangars built in Canada under the British Commonwealth Air Training Plan during World War Two. The hangar is currently the location of the Alberta Aviation Museum.

(418 squadron archives)

Another ship of the "City of Edmonton" squadron was KL149 with the code HO149. She is an ex USAAF B-25D-35 s/n 43-3647, and was taken on strength at No. 5 OTU. After the war, she served with the squadron at RCAF Station Namao, Alberta, in the mid 1950s. She has black painted engine nacelles. (RCAF)

Left: *Mitchell Mk.II FW251 showing her Canadian colours. The fuselage marking is HO251. The figures are the last-three digits of the airplane serial number FW251. This is a B-25D-35 with the U.S. s/n 43-3686. The two-letter unit code, roundel and last three digits of the airplane serial were applied to the lower surface of each wing. The Canadian serial number is centred above the fin-flash. The airplane from No. 418 Sqn. has full search markings applied, consisting of a black anti-glare panel and engines. It has red wing tips on upper and lower surfaces as well as red horizontal stabiliser on both upper and lower surfaces. (RCAF)*

Bottom: *On 16 May, 1957, a hydraulic line failure resulted in no brakes when the pilots attempted to park HO251 but crashed into a hangar wall at Edmonton. Although both pilots were injured and hospitalised for a few days, they miraculously escaped being killed when their seats were thrown backwards. The Mitchell was scrapped. The airplane had a nose art from Al Capp's "Li'l Abner" comic strip. The attractive and ever faithful Daisy Mae was painted on the nose of the airplane.*

(Collection Wim Nijenhuis)

Its duties ranged from aid to the civil power to aerial re-supply. Upon unification of the armed forces, the squadron converted to the De Havilland Twin Otter. With the advent of the Twin Otter, the squadron's role was redefined as search and rescue and light tactical transport. No. 418 City of Edmonton Squadron is currently inactive.

No. 418 Sqn. received its Mitchells in 1947. They were stripped of their camouflage paint and their turret armament was removed. Only the machine guns in the right side of the glass nose were retained. The squadron operated nearly 20 Mitchells until March 1958 with a mix of mostly Mk.IIs and a few Mk.IIIs.

All Capp

Al Capp and his characters Li'l Abner and Daisey Mae on the cover of Time Magazine of 6 November, 1950. The illustration was made by the Russian artist Boris Chaliapin. A noted portraitist and illustrator for "Time Magazine", Chaliapin (1904-1979) did about 400 of these cover illustrations between 1939 and 1970. The strip "Li'l Abner" became famous and No. 418 Sqn. obtained permission from its creator Al Capp to put his characters on airplanes of the squadron.
(Collection Wim Nijenhuis)

During the Second World War, No. 418 Sqn. obtained permission from Al Capp, creator of "Li'l Abner", to put his characters on Mosquito fighter-bombers flown by the squadron. Post-war, when the squadron flew Mitchell bombers, this tradition continued.

Al Capp (1909-1979), was an American cartoonist. "Li'l Abner", was a satirical American comic strip that appeared in many newspapers in the United States, Canada and Europe, featuring a fictional clan of hillbillies in the impoverished mountain village of Dogpatch, Arkansas. The strip starred Li'l Abner Yokum, the simple and muscular, poor but lazy, uneducated but good-natured hero of Dogpatch. Abner lived with Mammy and Pappy Yokum and devoted much of his energy into avoiding matrimony with the beautiful and industrious Daisy Mae, his devoted and ever-faithful girlfriend. The strip ran for 43 years, from 1934 through 1977. Many of Capp's creations decorated the airplanes of No. 418 Sqn.

A nice detail of the insignia as applied to Mitchells of No. 418 Sqn. (RCAF)

A picture of HO891, the former F-10 photo-ship 891 of No. 413 Squadron. It shows the red colours on the outer wings and horizontal stabiliser as well as the insignia of No. 418 Sqn. on her nose. Next to the insignia the text "City of Edmonton" and underneath "418 SQUADRON" in black letters. It has the greenhouse nose closed and painted. (Collection Gerben Tornij)

Another unfortunate accident. HD312 made a wheels up landing in July 1957 at the RCAF Station Whitehorse, Yukon. This
B-25D-35, s/n 43-3780, was an ex RAF Mitchell Mk.II.
The ship was scrapped after the landing accident. Featuring on
the left side of the bomber is the Grey Cup nose art that paid
tribute to the championship victories of the Edmonton Eskimos
in the Canadian Football League during the 1950s. The Grey
Cup is both the name of the championship of the Canadian
Football League (CFL) and the name of the trophy awarded to
the victorious team. The trophy is named after Albert Grey, the
Governor General of Canada from 1904 until 1911. Grey donated the trophy to the Canadian Rugby Union in 1909 to recognise the top
amateur rugby football team in Canada. It was first awarded in 1909. *(Collection Gerry Hagan)*

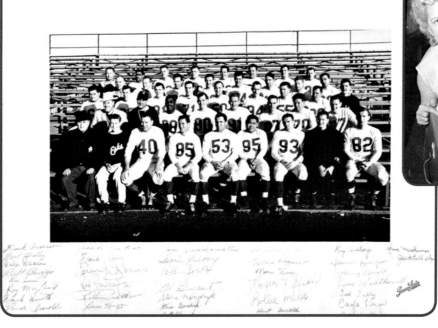

Grey Cup

A woman with the Grey Cup in
November 1955. At right, a picture
of the 1954 champion Edmonton
Eskimos team signed by 37 members
of the great Canadian football squad.
*(Vancouver Public Library Historical Photographs,
Collection Wim Nijenhuis)*

No. 1 Advance Flying School

No. 1 Advance Flying School (AFS) was based at Saskatoon. RCAF Station Saskatoon was a World War II BCATP base operated by the RCAF. It was located at Saskatoon, Saskatchewan. It was re-opened as an air training facility in October 1950. Students at the school trained on Mitchell bombers and Beech Expeditor aircraft trainers. The RCAF's No. 1 Advanced Flying School opened at Saskatoon with B-25 Mitchells on 1 January, 1952, due to a decision made by the Department of National Defence to provide more schools to train regular pilots in advanced flying on multi-engine aircraft. It was one of the many Flying Training Schools opened across Canada to train RAF, RCAF and NATO aircrews. A total of 16 Mitchell Mk.IIIs have flown with No. 1 AFS at Saskatoon. Solid nosed Mitchells were used for multi-engine crew training. On 8 December, 1958, the Mitchell trainers retired from Saskatoon's No. 1 AFS.

Rest In Piece. The cover of Twinaire, the newspaper of the Air Force base in Saskatoon. It shows the last Mitchell to apparently be flown from Saskatoon in 1958. The Mitchell is number 5230, a B-25J-30/32 with s/n 44-86727. It served the Training Command at RCAF Station Saskatoon and went to No. 1 AFS in 1958. (CBC)

Airplane number 5239 in flight. This ship went to Training Command in August 1954 for use by No. 1 Advanced Flying School. In January 1959, she was transferred to No. 2 Air Observer School at Winnipeg. This solid nose ship is a B-25J-30/32 with s/n 44-86697. It has the black number 5239 below the fin-flash and the black number 239 on her nose. (RCAF)

This clean natural aluminium finished airplane is number 5243, photographed at Saskatoon. She is an ex USAF B-25J-30/32 with s/n 44-86725, and was delivered to Training Command in January 1952. After modification it served No. 1 Advanced Flying School at Saskatoon. In 1959, it served No. 2 Air Observer School at Winnipeg. She has the serial number above the fin-flash.
(Collection Wim Nijenhuis)

No. 1 Flying Instructor's School

The RCAF began the Second World War with a small number of trained flying instructors. Instructional flight was first formed at Camp Borden in April 1939 and moved to Trenton, Ontario, in January 1940, with No. 1 Flying Instructor's School (FIS). Having regard to the increasing need for instructors in the schools of the BCATP, an agreement was signed in June 1942, which made provision for three separate flying instructor schools in Canada. No. 1 at Trenton, Ontario, for twin-engined aircraft, No. 2 at Vulcan, Alberta, for Harvard instructors and No. 3 at Arnprior, Ontario, for instructors at elementary flying schools. Trenton was the largest training centre of the BCATP during the Second World War. As the home of the Central Flying School, Trenton was known as "The Hub" and was responsible for training more than 5,000 flying instructors who were in turn responsible for training 131,000 aircrew. The station's training role continued after the war with the establishment of Training Command Headquarters at Trenton. No. 1 Flying Instructor's School was first formed at Trenton on 3 August, 1942. When the demand eased with the reduction of the BCTAP at the end of the war, the No. 1 FIS amalgamated with the Central Flying School and was disbanded on 31 January, 1945. But in the post-war years, again more RCAF flying training schools and advanced flying units were opened. To supply the instructors needed for the greatly increased training programme, it became necessary to reform No. 1 FIS at Trenton. So, it was reformed on 1 April, 1951, at Trenton and flew with a few Mitchells.

This Mitchell served Training Command after the war and was used by No. 1 Flying Instructor's School and the Central Flying School at Trenton. It is ex USAF B-25J-30/32 s/n 44-86724, with the Canadian serial number 5203. It was struck off charge in April 1962 and is photographed here at the Air Force Heritage Museum and Air Park at Winnipeg. This museum is located inside the headquarters of Canada's Air Force in Winnipeg, Manitoba. The airplane is natural aluminium finished with a white roof and the well-known Canadian red lightning bolt. (Collection Wim Nijenhuis)

Action shot of 5203 with four Canadair Sabres in the early 1950s. The airplane is overall aluminium finished and still carrying the RAF fin flash. During her entire career, the airplane was assigned to RCAF Training Command. (RCAF)

No. 2 Air Navigation School

Royal Canadian Air Force specialty navigator training started in March 1942 as part of the BCATP. The two former Air Navigation Schools, No. 1 ANS and No. 2 ANS, amalgamated on 11 May, 1942, to form the Central Navigation School (CNS). After the Second World War ended, all observer and navigator schools were disbanded, as there was no longer a need for new navigator trainees. The specialist wing of CNS was moved to

Summerside, Prince Edward Island, to form the basis of a new Air Navigation School (No. 1 ANS). The Korean War and Canada's increased commitment to NATO created a demand for more navigators and a second Air Navigation School (No. 2 ANS) opened in Winnipeg in 1951. The majority of the students at the time were from the RCAF and RAF. However, students from France, Belgium, Netherlands, Denmark, Portugal,

Norway, Italy and Turkey also trained in Winnipeg. In 1953, No. 1 ANS closed and incorporated into No. 2 ANS at Winnipeg. The Central Navigation School moved to Winnipeg in 1954. It operated three different Mitchell models. The solid nose was a pilot trainer and was used to convert pilots from the Beech Expeditor. There were two types of the glass nose. One had a black glass fibre nosecone and had interception radar installed for training CF100 Navigators. The other had a red glass fibre nosecone and had radar installed to train navigators for the transport role. No.2 ANS operated over 20 Mitchells Mk.III.

A post-war masterpiece, a Mitchell in full colours of the RCAF. This is airplane number 5258 of No. 2 ANS. Natural aluminium finished, black engine nacelles and red wing tips and a red horizontal stabiliser and nose cone. This is a B-25J-25 with s/n 44-30642. The airplane was transferred to Training Command on 5 March, 1954, for use at No. 2 Air Navigation School at Winnipeg, were it served until 1958. The two-letter unit code, roundel and last three digits of the airplane serial, are applied to the lower surface of each wing. The serial number is centred above the fin-flash. (RCAF)

Another ship of No. 2 ANS in 1953. Number 5274 in front is a B-25J-20 with s/n 44-29726. It has a black coloured fibreglass radome fitted to the front of the glass nose. The last three digits of the number are also applied to the cockpit access door at the bottom of the fuselage. The airplane was taken on strength by Training Command on 18 September, 1953.

(Collection Wim Nijenhuis)

training activities which graduated over 5,000 aircrew members from foreign countries. No.2 AOS has operated with at least 6 Mitchells Mk.II and nearly 30 Mk.IIIs. The school was redesignated as the Air Navigation School in April, 1961.

NO. 2 AIR OBSERVER SCHOOL

During the war, No. 2 Air Observer School (AOS) operated from 5 August, 1940 until 14 July, 1944 at Edmonton, Alberta. No. 2 AOS served as a specialty training facility with three distinctive courses offered, each lasting twelve weeks. Navigation was the primary duty of an air observer, with bomb aiming and air gunnery as secondary duties. Also included was the wireless operator, a category in which recruits could enrol directly. All air observers who graduated would continue their training at a Bombing and Gunnery School or a Wireless Operators School. Following the war, RCAF Station Winnipeg, continued to provide training for pilots and navigators from many allied countries, as well as base active RCAF squadrons. The formation of No.2 Air Observer School and Central Navigation School was created from the increased

Ex USAF B-25J-25/27, s/n 44-30478, at Winnipeg. It has the Canadian number 5219 with aircraft code SV219. After some earlier assignments it went to Training Command on 17 December 1957, for use by No. 2 AOS at Winnipeg. It has a radome fitted to the front of the former glass nose. The solid nose ship in the background is aircraft number 5247, also assigned to No.2 AOS in 1957. (RCAF)

"Bristol"

Ship number 5213 is photographed at Bristol Aerospace at Winnipeg in 1958. After her modification here, she went to No. 2 Air Observer School at Winnipeg. This is a B-25J-25/27 with s/n 44-30479. It is natural aluminium finished with a red lightning bolt shaped stripe and the Red Ensign flag on the vertical stabilisers. The top of the fuselage is white with the words "ROYAL CANADIAN AIR FORCE" in red with black shadow. The brothers MacDonald formed MacDonald Brothers Aircraft Company in 1930. They developed it into a full-fledged aircraft factory by 1940. During the Second World War the factory built training aircraft. At the end of the war, MacDonald Brothers became an important repair and overhaul centre for the Royal Canadian Air Force. In 1954, MacDonald Brothers Aircraft was purchased by the British Bristol Aeroplane Company, becoming their Canadian division. Bristol did work on many Canadian Mitchells in the late 1950s consisting of modifications and installation of Stromberg carburettors. In 1967, the company was renamed Bristol Aerospace.

(Collection Wim Nijenhuis)

This airplane is a B-25J-25 with USAAF s/n 44-30475. In the early fifties she was transferred to the RCAF. The airplane went to Training Command on 17 December, 1957 for use by No. 2 Air Observers School at Winnipeg. She has a large astrodome behind the cockpit. The Canadian Red Ensign flag is on her vertical stabiliser with the number 5231 below the flag. The maple leaf roundels are on the fuselage and wings. A former aircraft code on the fuselage has been overpainted. (RCAF)

Right: An ex USAF B-25J-30/32, s/n 44-86726. In February 1952, it was received from the USAF at Mobile, Alabama, and assigned to Training Command at Saskatoon. In March 1959, it went to No. 2 Air Observer School at Winnipeg. Struck off charge in October 1960. The airplane had a solid nose and modified engine and was registered No. 5237 with letters QP237. In February 1962 it was struck off strength and went to the civilian market.

(Collection Wim Nijenhuis)

No. 3 All-Weather (Fighter) Operational Training Unit

No. 3 All-Weather (Fighter) Operational Training Unit was formed at North Bay, Ontario, on 1 November, 1951. This station had been founded a month earlier and was part of the expansion of Canada's air defences in face of the rising threat of nuclear air attack from the Soviet Union. No. 3 (AW) OTU was a school teaching military flying, interception and fighter combat in all weather conditions, day or night. The OTU was the world's leading all-weather interceptor school during its service at North Bay in the early 1950s. In June 1955, No. 3 All Weather (Fighter) Operations Training Unit moved from North Bay to Cold Lake, Alberta, to train crews up to operational standard with the Avro Canada CF-100 Canuck all-weather interceptor. Cold Lake became a major Cold War facility after 1954, eventually housing an establishment of more than 2,000 service personnel. When the CF-100 was

Number 5217 is shown in the markings of No. 3 (AW) OTU which operated some Mitchells. The airplane went to Hughes Aircraft for modification to TB-25M configuration, including APG40 radar, in September 1954. In June 1955, she was assigned to No. 3 (AW) Operational Training Unit at RCAF Station Cold Lake, Alberta. Note the large astrodome behind the cockpit and the nose and engine modifications. (Collection Ron Dupas)

phased out in 1961, the military created operational training units to convert pilots to Lockheed Starfighter and later successors. The RCAF received 6 B-25Js in August 1954. These were borrowed from the USAF and served with No. 3 All-Weather (Fighter) Operational Training Unit at North Bay for a short time until June 1955. Furthermore, No. 3 (AW) OTU at Cold Lake has flown with about 10 Mitchells supplied by other RCAF units. In 1953, the unit adopted the nickname "Night Witches", suggested by the wife of the unit's Engineering Officer, and the unofficial orange and black logo seen on the nose of its airplanes, denoting its all-weather day-or-night operations. It is not known whether this also was applied on the Mitchells.

A squadron shoulder patch used by RCAF aircrew with No. 3 AW(F)OTU in the late 1950s. (Crest Craft Ltd.)

AIR ARMAMENT SCHOOL

The Air Armament School was established at RCAF Station Trenton. This station, located on the shores of Lake Ontario, was the largest training centre of the BCATP during the Second World War. Schools included the RCAF Central Flying School, No. 1 Air Navigation School, No. 1 Flying Instructor School, and No. 1 Composite Training School. In 1951, the Air Armament School (AAS) was opened at Trenton. In 1953, the school moved to Camp Borden. After the war, a number of Mitchells were used as target tugs at the AAS at Trenton. The target tug Mitchells of the AAS were very colourful with a yellow and black striped paint scheme. The gunnery trainers were natural aluminium finished. The Air Armament School has flown with at least 7 Mitchells Mk.II.

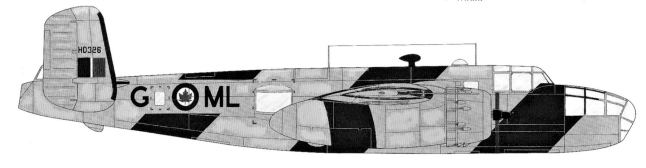

A colourful Mitchell was this airplane of the Air Armament School at Trenton and used as a target tug. It was overall painted yellow with black diagonal stripes on the fuselage and wings. The ship is coded G-ML, had the former RAF serial HD326 and is a B-25D-35 with s/n 43-3797. In February 1944, the plane was taken on strength by Western Air Command as a new aircraft. After service during the war, it went to Avro Canada at Malton, Ontario, for conversion to a target tug, from 10 October, 1948, to 28 July, 1949. Then it was transferred to Training Command for use at Air Armament School. After November 1952, it was used by Central Experimental & Proving Establishment at Cold Lake, Alberta. It was struck off strength in September 1960. (Collection Wim Nijenhuis)

CENTRAL EXPERIMENTAL AND PROVING ESTABLISHMENT

Rockcliffe 1960. This is number 5243 again. After use by No. 1 Advanced Flying School and No. 2 Air Observers School, she went to the Central Experimental & Proving Establishment at RCAF Station Uplands on 14 May, 1959. She served here until 1962. The airplane with serial 5243, is natural aluminium finished with a white top of the fuselage and the red Canadian Red Ensign flag on the vertical stabilisers. Note the difference in colours and markings compared with the picture shown at No. 1 AFS. Today, the Mitchell is still an airworthy warbird of The Oklahoma Museum of Flying, Oklahoma City, with the name "Super Rabbit". (RCAF)

In the early days of the Canadian Air Force, test and development work was carried out at Ottawa Air Station (at Rockcliffe and Shirley's Bay). For this purpose a special Test Flight was formed. In 1940, the RCAF Test and Development Establishment was formed to replace the Test Flight. In 1946, its name was changed to Experimental and Proving Establishment. On 1 September, 1951, the Central Experimental and Proving Establishment was formed by the amalgamation of the Experimental and Proving Establishment at Rockcliffe, the Winter Experimental Establishment at Edmonton, and the RCAF (National Research Council) Unit at Arnprior. Headquarters of Central Experimental and Proving Establishment (CEPE) were at Rockcliffe, with detachments at several sites across Canada. In 1957, CEPE was moved to RCAF Station Uplands, Ottawa, Ontario. This move was necessary because of the longer runways required for testing new jet aircraft. At the end of the 1950s, CEPE had flown with at least 7 Mitchell Mk.IIs and 5 Mk.IIIs

July 1952, an unidentified Mitchell of the RCAF at Rockcliffe.
(Library and Archives Canada)

The restored B-25 of the Alberta Aviation Museum has a nose art from Al Capp's "Li'l Abner" comic strip. The attractive and ever faithful Daisy Mae was painted on the nose of one of the RCAF ships.
(Collection Wim Nijenhuis)

AUSTRALIA

*Aircraft camou-
flage? Mitchell
men, a masterful
pose at Hughes
Field of members
of No. 2 Squad-
ron for a group
portrait with their
Mitchell.*
(Mile Pegs NT)

The first B-25 Mitchells arrived in Australia almost immediately after the Japanese attack of Pearl Harbor. However, these planes were originally intended for the ML-KNIL, the military aviation component of the Royal Netherlands East Indies Army, the RNEIAAF. But these airplanes were quickly taken over by the 3rd Bomb Group of the USAAF. The NEIAAF did not get their first permanent B-25s until late in 1942. These served with No. 18 Squadron, which was formally a part of the Royal Australian Air Force (RAAF). These Mitchells carried the Dutch flag insignia of the NEIAAF and were flown largely by Dutch crews. This is further described in the Netherlands chapter.

It was not until the spring of 1944 that the Australians were to get B-25s that were flown in RAAF insignia and which carried RAAF serials. The RAAF took 50 aircraft on charge, most of which came from Dutch orders. The first batch of 20 B-25Ds was transferred from the Dutch contracts to the RAAF in late April 1944. Between May and September, they were followed by 10 more B-25Ds and 9 B-25Js. Many of the later B-25Ds carried field modifications which included a tail gun, waist gun positions below the mid-upper turret, and "cheek" gun packs mounted on the side of the fuselage. The final 11 Mitchells that were delivered to the RAAF were B-25Js. They were handed over

between April and August 1945. These aircraft came directly from the USAAF stocks. Nearly all the B-25s of the RAAF served with No. 2 Squadron. Only a few were assigned for some time to second line units. The Central Flying School (CFS) at Point Cook had four B-25Js and No.1 Aircraft Performance Unit (APU) had temporarily two B-25Js. The Mitchell was not selected for the postwar inventory of the RAAF and they were withdrawn from service and put into storage awaiting disposal. All the surviving airplanes were struck off charge on 1 October, 1946. They remained in storage until March 1950, when they were sold for scrap.

CAMOUFLAGE AND MARKINGS

RAAF colour schemes were officially promulgated by "Aircraft General Instructions", issued to units as a guide and were accompanied by appropriate drawings. Camouflage patterns and colours were determined by Headquarters in Melbourne, as were squadron codes, their colour and application. Individual squadron commanding officers had the authority to allocate individual aircraft code letters and other squadron markings. From December 1943, the camouflage scheme for operational aircraft was Green for the upper surfaces and Grey for the undersurfaces. These standard colours were not directly prescribed for aircraft which were delivered from abroad such as the B-25 Mitchells. From the end of May 1944, it was directed that all bombers were to be delivered and employed operationally uncamouflaged. Camouflage was no longer considered necessary. However, not all operational aircraft were immediately stripped back to bare metal or delivered uncamouflaged. By mid 1945, the first effects of this directive were visible. But at the same time some airplanes were also painted overall Foliage Green. This colour was pretty much similar to the U.S. Army Air Forces colour Medium Green No. 42. The 39 B-25s were transferred in different batches from the RNEIAAF contracts to the RAAF. These airplanes had the standard USAAF camouflage scheme of Olive Drab upper surfaces and Neutral Grey undersurfaces. The B-25s from USAAF stocks were also in this camouflage scheme and some were aluminium finished. Some ships had the lower surfaces painted black. This was a modification by the RAAF of the Neutral Grey scheme.

During the Second World War, RAAF flying squadrons were identified by an alphabetic code.

In early 1943, the coding system consisting of a group of three letters was adopted for use on RAAF aircraft in Australia and the South West Pacific. Two letters to identify the squadron and one to identify an individual aircraft. On the camouflaged Mitchells these letters were Medium Sea Grey. Although it is quite likely that White may sometimes have been used for the painting of codes. After the war, the squadron codes were abandoned.

Roundel Type A

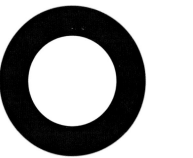

Roundel Type B

Fin flash

The RAAF allocated the airframe number A-47 to their Mitchells. This prefix was a part of their RAAF serial number. The serials assigned were A47-1 to A47-39. The final 11 B-25Js had the Australian serial numbers A47-40 to A47-50. The colour for the marking of airframe numbers on camouflaged B-25s was Medium Sea Grey or sometimes White. They were Black on natural aluminium finished airplanes.

Originally, the RAAF used the existing red, white and blue roundel of the British RAF. However, during the Second World War the inner red circle, which was visually similar to the Japanese Hinomaru, was removed. The B-25s had the Australian roundel Type A in six positions, two on the rear fuselage and two on both upper and lower wingsurfaces. Some B-25s only had roundels on the upper wingsurfaces. At the end of the war, the B-25s had roundels Type B with a smaller white centre. The fin flash was painted on the outside and inside of both vertical stabilisers. Although there have been B-25s with the fin flash only on the outside.

NO. 2 SQUADRON

A total of 50 Mitchells were operated by No. 2 Squadron. They were type B-25D and B-25J models. Originally, No. 2 Squadron of the Australian Flying Corps was formed as 68 (Australian) Squadron, Royal Flying Corps (RFC), at Kantara in Egypt on 20 September, 1916. The squadron was redesignated No. 2 Squadron, Australian Flying Corps, on 4 January, 1918, and disbanded in 1919. It was reformed at Laverton, Victoria on 10 January, 1937. During the pre-war period the squadron underwent training, took part in air shows and co-operated with the Royal Australian Navy. At the outbreak of the Second World War, the unit searched for enemy vessels in Australian waters using Avro Anson airplanes. In June 1940, the squadron began a convert to the Lockheed Hudson. For the remainder of 1940 the squadron carried out a limited number of maritime patrols. The level of activity increased dramatically at the start of 1941, with more patrols being carried out, but no enemies were sighted.

The squadron moved to Darwin in April 1941 to perform anti-submarine activities and general reconnaissance. In December 1941, a detachment was sent to Koepang in Dutch Timor to provide cover for Australian troops moving within the islands and to attack Japanese shipping. By 10 December, the whole squadron was based at Koepang. Numerous raids were made on Menado, where a considerable amount of Japanese shipping was located and damaged. The greater part of the squadron withdrew to Darwin in mid February 1942. On 20 February, the squadron moved to Daly Waters and

Most of the B-25s of No. 2 Squadron were camouflaged Olive Drab upper surfaces and Neutral Grey under surfaces. Nose art on the aircraft was generally modest or not present, such as on this ship. (Australian War Memorial)

No. 2 Squadron was the first and only Mitchell squadron in the RAAF. The ground crew did the preparatory work and made sure that the B-25s were operational. So, the flying crew members were able to smoke their cigarette and talk after a successful mission. Such teamwork is extremely important in the world of aviation. The picture show very well the Type B roundel on this natural aluminium finished Mitchell. (State Library of Victoria)

in May to Rapid Creek. In August it moved again and now to a new base at Batchelor. Between May and October 1942, the squadron attacked Japanese positions and shipping at Ambon, Timor, Koepang, and other islands in the Banda Sea. Reconnaissance, search missions and limited attacks continued for the remainder of 1942 and into 1943. On 12 April, 1943, the squadron moved to Hughes Field, an airbase half-way between Batchelor and Darwin. The year also saw a continuation of attacks on Timor and nearby targets as well as air-sea rescue and anti-submarine warfare flights. In January 1944, the squadron was re-equipped with the Bristol Beaufort and started 1944 with attacks on enemy shipping and villages in Timor.

Ground staff is busy around the Olive Drab/Neutral Grey KO-S. This aircraft is a B-25D-30, s/n 43-3607, and joined No. 2 Sqn. on 26 April, 1944. She had the Australian serial A47-7. (Collection Wim Nijenhuis)

Hughes Field 1944. Number A47–16, KO-L, was one of the few Australian B-25s with some form of nose art. On the nose of this Olive Drab/Neutral Grey ship is written "Ell for Leather". It was an ex-Dutch aircraft renumbered from N5–203. The remnants of the previous Dutch name "Kalidjati" (a former Dutch airfield near Bandoeng on Java) are still visible forward of the RAAF name.

(Australian War Memorial, Collection Wim Nijenhuis)

In July, 1945, the squadron began to move to Balikpapan, Borneo, operating from nearby Sepinggan. The squadron had only just arrived in its new quarters when the Japanese surrendered, ending the war. The squadron remained on Borneo for the remainder of the war, flying reconnaissance missions to locate prisoner-of-war camps and dropping supplies to camps in the Celebes. The last operational flight was carried out on 25 September, a supply mission to Makassar. Soon after, ground crew removed all weapons from the B-25s and converted them into transports. On 14 November, 1945, the squadron ceased flying operations, and preparations for its disbandment and the move of the aircraft were begun. The squadron moved to Laverton in December 1945. By the end of December, the squadron had no aircraft. It was reduced to a cadre basis and eventually disbanded on 15 May, 1946. The aircraft were phased out of service and were placed in storage until March 1950 when they were sold for scrap.

Most of the B-25s of No. 2 Sqn. were camouflaged Olive Drab/Neutral Grey and some with black undersurfaces. A few airplanes were overall Foliage Green and late in the war, a few were natural aluminium finished.

In April 1944, No. 2 Sqn. replaced its Bristol Beauforts with B-25s. By May 1944, the squadron had 27 of these bomers. The arrival of the B-25s meant that No. 2 Sqn. was the first and only Mitchell squadron in the RAAF. On 1 May, pilot training on the B-25 began, with instructors from the RNEIAAF. Between May and June 1944, the squadron was withdrawn from operations and then concentrated on converting to the B-25. The first operation with two B-25s was already on 11 June, 1944. In July anti-shipping operations were added to the list. The squadron operated over the islands south of New Guinea and Timor, flying a mix of search missions, reconnaissance, strike missions and anti-shipping strikes. Between February and August 1944, a part of the squadron was temporarely based at Jacquinoy Bay and Morotai. The end of 1944 was spent targeting enemy barges and freighters. This was continued in early 1945, but then in conjunction with No. 18 Sqn. of the RNEIAAF. The B-25s of No. 2 Sqn. and No. 18 Sqn. formed No. 79 Wing of the RAAF, and these aircraft carried out many successful strikes against enemy targets.

KO-G serial number A47–19, s/n 43–3790, is a B-25D-35. Many of the later B-25Ds carried field modifications which included a tail gun, waist gun positions below the mid-upper turret, and "cheek" gun packs mounted on the side of the fuselage.
Above: *The code KO-G is remarkably thinly outlined in black.*
Left: *She is stripped of camouflage. The code letters are painted black and the roundels on the wings are now of the Type B.*

(ADF-Serials via Mike Mirkovic)

No. 2 Squadron used the squadron letters KO. Some of the B-25s of the squadron had a name or a cartoon painted on the fuselage nose.

This ex Dutch aircraft is a B-25D-35, s/n 43-3789. It is coded KO-L with serial A47-21. It is one of the Mitchells with a large nose art on the left side of the fuselage nose. The ship is Olive Drab with Black undersurfaces. The aircraft code letters seem to be White. (Collection Gerben Tornij)

This is the nose art of A47-27. This B-25J-1, s/n 43-27691, was received from the NEIAAF in June 1944 and was coded KO-A. She was assigned to No. 2 Sqn. The nose art is a wolf head with aviator goggles and a bomb in his mouth. Wolf figures, wolf heads or wolf names were a much chosen object in aircraft nose art during the Second World War. (Collection Wim Nijenhuis)

Big Bad Wolf

One of the most famous wolves is the fictional "Big Bad Wolf" appearing in several cautionary tales and animated films. "Little Red Riding Hood" is a European fairy tale about a young girl and a big bad wolf and she is a character that stars in "Silly Symphonies" titled "The Big Bad Wolf". "Silly Symphonies" was a series of animated short films produced by Walt Disney Productions from 1929 to 1939. This is the cover of the 1934 book "The Big Bad Wolf and Little Red Riding Hood".

(Collection Wim Nijenhuis)

Australians too, knew teeth motifs on their planes. Here a rare picture of a B-25J-5, s/n 43-27928, at Balikpapan, Borneo, 1945. This B-25 is Olive Drab/Neutral Grey with serial number A47-29 and aircraft code KO-D. It is the only known Australian B-25 to have carried sharp teeth as nose art. (Australian War Memorial)

B-25 Mitchells of No. 2 Sqn. lined up at Hughes Field, 1945. The first in row is A47-35, a B-25D-25, s/n 42-87416. The airplane is coded KO-R. The Olive Drab/ Neutral Grey ship was forced landed on 27 August, 1945, at Sepenggang airstrip Borneo when her nose wheel failed to lock down due to hydraulic failure from dust accumulation from the unsealed airstrip.

Below: A detail of the cockpit with the U.S. serial number in small letters painted below the window in contrast to the American method of information stencil-ling behind the cockpit of B-25s.

(State Library of Victoria, Australian War Memorial)

"My Favourite" is a B-25D-30 with s/n 42-87608. The ex RNEIAAF was received in November 1944 and coded KO-E with serial A47-34. The airplane is painted in the later overall Foliage Green paint scheme and has the Type B roundels.

(State Library of South Australia PRG 1614/2/69)

A picture of KO-P. The crew of this airplane is unloading their gear after returning from a mission. The airplane is Olive Drab/Neutral Grey with the serial A47-31. This is a B-25J-10, s/n 43-28183 and another ex-RNEIAAF ship.

(Australian War Memorial via Gerben Tornij)

A clean machine was this natural aluminium finished B-25J with the serial A47-44 in flight over Brisbane. This is a B-25J-25 with USAAF s/n 44-30896. In April 1945, she was received directly from the USA. The Type B roundel is in six positions and the fin flash on both sides of the vertical stabilisers.

(Collection Wim Nijenhuis, RAAF)

A47-36 is stripped of her camouflage paint. The bare metal ship is coded KO-Z with black letters and is a B-25D-25 with U.S. s/n 42-87255. *(ADF-Serials via Mike Mirkovic)*

An atmospheric image. Two B-25s of No. 2 Sqn. are hidden among the trees. The airplane left in the picture, is largely stripped of her camouflage colours and the airplane on the right is still completely camouflaged. *(RAAF)*

1940. After movements to Camden, Tamworth and Parkes, New South Wales, it returned to Point Cook in September 1944. It continued to operate after the end of the war. By the end of World War II, the school had produced more than 3,600 instructors. CFS relocated to East Sale in Victoria, in November and December 1947.

Two B-25Js were delivered to CFS in October 1944. These were the airplanes A47-38 and A47-39. The first mentioned remained until April 1946 and A47-39 served only one month at CFS. In October 1945, airplane A47-30 joined CFS for about six months and in January 1946, number A47-50 was assigned to the school until May of that year.

CENTRAL FLYING SCHOOL

The Central Flying School (CFS) at Point Cook had four B-25Js for some time. The purpose of the school was flying training and administrative duties for selected officers and airmen of the RAAF so that they could be employed as flying instructors at RAAF Service Flying Training Schools throughout the country.

The Central Flying School was established at Point Cook, Victoria, in March 1913, and became the training and assembly point for Australian Flying Corps units proceeding overseas. After the First World War, the CFS was disbanded on 31 December, 1919. It was reopened at Point Cook on 29 April,

February 1945, Point Cook, Victoria. A general view of RAAF aircraft assembled on the airfield for a static display during the visit of the Duke and Duchess of Gloucester to Point Cook. Shown are several aircraft types of the CFS with at the top right Mitchell A47-38, one of the four Mitchells that have served at CFS.
(Australian War Memorial).

This B-25J-30 s/n 44-86855, was the last Australian B-25 directly received from the USAAF in August 1945. She went to the Central Flying School at Point Cook in January 1946 until May 1946, and had serial A47-50. She is unarmed and the fuselage gun turret behind the cockpit has been removed. The ship is overall natural aluminium finished with the Type B roundels. (ADF-Serials via Mike Mirkovic)

No.1 Air Performance Unit

In the Second World War, a link was required between the developing aircraft industry in Australia and the operational elements of the Australian Air Force. No.1 Air Performance Unit (APU), originally Special Duties and Performance Flight, was established in December 1941 at Laverton, Victoria and attached to No. 1 Aircraft Depot, a maintenance unit of the RAAF. The unit was reformed as No. 1 Air Performance Unit in December 1943. No. 1 APU was responsible for the testing of aircraft types from local production and overseas introduced into RAAF service during the conflict. It carried out flight trials of new aircraft as well as aircraft modifications. After the war, the unit moved from Laverton to Point Cook before being renamed Aircraft Research and Development Unit (ARDU) in August 1947. Returning to Laverton the following year, ARDU's role in aircraft test and evaluation expanded to include two detachments, operating out of Mallala in South Australia and Richmond in New South Wales. The unit conducts development, testing and evaluation tasks on aircraft, aircraft weapons and associated systems, and provides electronic warfare operational support for the Royal Australian Air Force and other designated organisations.

No.1 APU had temporarily two B-25Js, one of which made a crash landing after just five days.

A47-30 was received in August 1944 and remained with an interruption until October 1945. A47-40 was received on 7 October, 1945. But on 12 October, the airplane crash landed shortly after take-off at Laverton and was converted to components.

A47–40 after her crash landing at Laverton on 12 October, 1945. As a result, she was only five days in service of No. 1 APU and was thereafter reduced to a supplier of components. The natural aluminium finished airplane was a B-25J-25 with s/n 44–30888. (RAAF)

Right: *This is A47-30, a B-25J-10 s/n 43-28185, at Laverton. She is an ex NEIAAF aircraft renumbered from N5-229 and was assigned to No. 1 APU in August 1944. In October 1945, the airplane joined the Central Flying School at Point Cook for about six months. She is camouflaged Olive Drab/Neutral Grey and has full armament. (ADF-Serials via Mike Mirkovic)*

INDONESIA

With the surrender of Japan on 15 August, 1945, the war ended in the Pacific. Directly afterwards, the popular Indonesian nationalist leader Sukarno formed a large militia ready to fight the Dutch upon their return to the Netherlands East Indies. On 17 August, 1945, he proclaimed the Indonesian independence. On 9 April, 1946, the fledgling state, at war with the Dutch, formed its own Air Force, named Angkatan Udara Republik Indonesia (AURI). The AURI, was the forerunner of the contemporary Indonesian Air Force Tentara Nasional Indonesia-Angkatan Udara (TNI-AU). The aircraft used from 1945 until 1950 were mainly of Japanese Army and Navy origin and reclaimed from large dumps all over Java. As described in the Netherlands chapter, the RNEIAAF was still active in the Indonesian area searching for prisoners of war and concentration of civilians and dropping food, medicines and other basic necessities. In addition, there were the guerrilla attacks from the militia and the country became insecure. Finally, after two Dutch police actions in 1947 and 1948, the military actions were terminated and resulted in the independence of Indonesia in December 1949. On 17 August 1950, exactly five years after the proclamation of independence, Sukarno proclaimed a single unitary Republic of Indonesia. The RNEIAAF was disbanded on 26 July, 1950. Following the transfer of sovereignty, the aircraft of the RNEIAAF were transferred to the Indo-

The impressive nose of an Indonesian strafer photographed in 1958. (Collection Wim Nijenhuis)

nesian Air Force. The transfer of the B-25s took place in May and June 1950 and comprised 42 aircraft. The B-25s of the AURI saw action against several regional rebellions in Indonesia in the 1950s and 1960s. The rise of the communist party in Indonesia drew Indonesia closer to the Eastern Block. Several Soviet-built aircraft began to arrive in the early 1960s. In 1961, Indonesia became the second country to receive and operate Soviet bombers and fighters. These aircraft served along with the remaining western aircraft such as the B-25 and A-26 Invader. In July 1977, the B-25 and A-26 were removed from the inventory of the AURI.

As said, the AURI received a total of 42 B-25s. This number consisted of 7 B-25Cs, 11 B-25Ds and 24 B-25Js. A number of these J models were the heavily armed strafers. The Js had no top turrets. These were previously removed by the Dutch. Because the "old" strafers were widely used, also former photo ships and bombers were converted to strafers. The AURI used the B-25s as tactical bombers until the 1970s. They served with No. 1 squadron (Skadron Udara 1) at Tjililitan near Batavia (now Halim Perdanakusuma Airport, Jakarta). The squadron was formed on 1 July, 1950, and became non-active on 29 July, 1977. The first historic event in the history of No. 1 Sqn. was on 30 April 1950, when the B-25 M-456, successfully carried out the first flight with an Indonesian crew. After an hour's flight it proceeded with a low pass flight around Tjililitan. In 1958, No. 1 Sqn. was transferred to the air base Abdul Rachman Saleh, East Java. The AURI made use of the B-25 for more than twenty years and the airplanes were deployed in various conflicts such as rebellions against the Central Government in Jakarta in 1950-1955. The B-25s played an important role in supporting the crackdown operation in the country during the Pemerintah Revolusioner Republik Indonesia (PRRI)/Permesta rebellion. The Permesta rebels were actually a separate movement in Sulawesi, East Indonesia, which had pledged allegiance with the PRRI. Furthermore, the B-25 was also used as air support during operations in Dutch-New Guinea in 1962-1963 and against the Malaysia Federation in 1964-1965. Even during the major military operation Seroja in 1975, a B-25 was still supporting the operations of ground forces.

CAMOUFLAGE AND MARKINGS

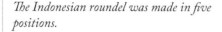

The Indonesian roundel was made in five positions.

The Indonesian flag was painted on the vertical stabilisers.

Most of the B-25s were already stripped of camouflage paint by the Dutch and were natural aluminium finished. However, the AURI also flew some camouflaged B-25s. These were Olive Drab and Neutral Grey. Some airplanes were painted over after overhaul or modification and had Dark Green upper surfaces and Light Grey undersurfaces. The rudders were painted white.

The black Dutch registration numbers starting with the letter M remained unchanged. On camouflaged airplanes the black numbers had a white border.

The Indonesian national marking was applied in five positions. Two on the rear fuselage and two on the upper wings and one on the right lower wing. On the left lower wing was painted the word AURI in black capital letters. Some airplanes had the emblem of No. 1 Sqn. on the left side of the nose and outside of both vertical stabilisers. The Indonesian flag was added on the outside of the vertical stabilisers. The Indonesian B-25s were not very colourful and had no special markings. Only the national markings and the squadron emblem gave some colour to the airplanes.

M-378 of Skadron Udara 1 of the Angkatan Udara Republik Indonesia (AURI). The ex-Dutch natural aluminium finished airplane is a B-25D-25, s/n 42-87312. It has only black registration numbers and the Indonesian flag on the outside of the vertical stabilisers. It has no national markings on the fuselage.

(Collection Wim Nijenhuis, Collection Coert Munk)

1952, again M-378 with M-464, a B-25J-30 s/n 44-31258, in flight. Both natural aluminium finished airplanes were ex RNEIAAF planes turned over to the Indonesian Air Force. In 1971, M-464 was donated by the Indonesian Air Force to the Military Aviation Museum at Soesterberg in the Netherlands, where it is still exhibited. (Indonesian Defence Ministry)

B-25J-1, s/n 43-27688, with registration number M-421. This airplane has modified engines and was converted to a strafer configuration. She is painted over after modification and has Dark Green upper surfaces and Light Grey undersurfaces with white rudders and prop spinners. (Collection Coert Munk)

Centre: M-464 after engine modification and after applying the new Indonesian camouflage scheme. At right, on 23 October, 1971, the M-464 was officially transferred to the Dutch museum at Soesterberg by Prince Bernhard of the Netherlands. The natural aluminium finished aircraft is now provided with the former Dutch markings of No. 18 Squadron of the RNEIAAF but still with her number M-464. (Collection Coert Munk, Nationaal Archief)

M-408 was USAAF s/n 43-3833, a B-25D-35. The Indonesian national marking is applied in five positions. The emblem of No. 1 Sqn. and the Indonesian flag are on the outside of both vertical stabilisers. The emblem is also painted on the left side of the fuselage nose. The Green/Grey camouflaged ship has black registration numbers with a white border. The rudders and prop spinners are white. (Collection Coert Munk)

Another strafer was number M-434, serial 44-29023. The black number has a white border. The camouflaged ship is unarmed and has the Indonesian roundels on five positions. (Collection Wim Nijenhuis)

This is M-444, a natural aluminium finished B-25J-20, s/n 44-29262. The ship is unarmed and has the red/white Indonesian flag and the squadron emblem on her vertical stabiliser. The emblem was mirrored on both tail surfaces. Note the modified tail cone

(Collection Wim Nijenhuis)

Two other natural aluminium finished B-25s of No. 1 squadron. M-449 is a B-25J-20, s/n 44-29517, and M-372 is a B-25D-25 with s/n 42-87256. Note the unarmed waist gun position on M-372. Both airplanes are ex-RNEIAAF ships.

(Collection Wim Nijenhuis)

M-458 is a B-25J-25 with USAAF s/n 44-30399. She has survived her military life and is since 1976 exhibited in the Museum Satria Mandala, Jakarta. (Collection Wim Nijenhuis)

Below: *Not the best but nevertheless interesting picture of two camouflaged B-25J models. In the background stands M-459 and in front is M-423 with white painted rudders and prop spinners. The Indonesian B-25s had no top gun turrets.*

(Collection Wim Nijenhuis)

Left: *A B-25J of No. 1 Sqn. with the squadron insignia painted on the nose.*

(Collection Wim Nijenhuis)

Two B-25s ready to take off. The natural aluminium finished airplane in front has black window frames.
(Collection Wim Nijenhuis)

Two B-25J gunships. Both natural aluminium finished ships have the post-war engine modification and the fuselages at the location of the machine gun barrels under the cockpit are painted black. Due to the nature of operations, the AURI in particular used the heavily armed strafer gunships. The Indonesians used the B-25 among others in Operation Mandela in 1962. This was a joint army-navy-air force command and formed the military side of the campaign to win Western New Guinea, from the Dutch who were preparing it for its own independence, separate from Indonesia. (Collection Wim Nijenhuis)

Above and left:
Two other fully armed ships have the Olive Drab/ Neutral Grey or Dark Green/Light Grey scheme.
(Collection Wim Nijenhuis)

CHINA

The B-25 played a significant role in China. The main part of it took place during the Second World War. The B-25s were at the time in service with the Chinese-American Composite Wing (CACW). This is described in the book *"Mitchell Masterpieces Vol. 1"*.

CHINESE NATIONALIST AIR FORCE

The CACW was initially formed on 31 July, 1943 as the 1st Bomb Group (Provisional) and the 3rd Fighter Group (Provisional) Chinese Air Force. The CACW was a joint United States Army Air Forces and Republic of China Air Force organisation. The operational units were jointly commanded by both American and Chinese Air Force officers and the unit's aircraft were jointly manned by American and Chinese pilots and aircrew. The backbone of the CACW consisted mainly of Chinese fliers. It was administratively assigned to the 14th Air Force in China. The bomb group was formed after American pilots arrived at Malir, India. One hundred Chinese cadets returned from training in the United States at Luke Air Advanced School to fly for the CACW. Training began at Malir using B-25s that had been used in China. The Chinese and American officers had segregated facilities, and each maintained separate quarters and mess from enlisted personnel. Organised as two fighter groups of P-40s and one bomber group of B-25s, CACW units began their first combat operations in October 1943. The four squadrons of the 1st Bomb Group (1st, 2nd, 3rd, and 4th) were formed during the war. They formerly operated Russian-built Tupolev SB bombers, then transferred to the B-25. Following the end of the war in the Pacific, these four bombardment squadrons were established to fight against the Communist insurgency that was rapidly spreading throughout the country. During the Chinese Civil War, Chinese B-25s fought alongside de Havilland Mosquitos. The B-25s of the squadrons included the B-25C and D, with the B-25H and B-25J following over a period of time. More than 100 B-25Cs and Ds were supplied to the Nationalist Chinese during the Second World War and about 30 B-25H and Js. When the Chinese Communists won the civil war in 1948, the Nationalist fled to Taiwan, leaving behind a few Mitchells that were operated by the Communists for a time.

The CACW was a joint United States Army Air Forces and Republic of China Air Force organisation. USAAF ground personnel explaining the B-25 ground handling task using a B-25 model and American and Chinese men standing next to each other under the blue white Kuomintang star. (Collection Wim Nijenhuis)

B-25J crew members together in front of their Kuomintang starred airplane numbered 603. The engine cowling is coloured and has a remarkable painted checkerboard motive. (Collection Wim Nijenhuis)

Center: *American and Chinese colours in the skies over China. Four American P-51 Mustangs, one American B-25J and two Chinese B-25Hs. The nearest airplane is called "Marie" and carries the insignia of the 4th Bombardment Squadron on her nose. (Life)*

of C-46 and C-47 transports. In 1950, the Kuomintang Air Force had about 330 aircraft. The B-25Js remained active until 1958. The most intensive bombardments the Nationalists carried out against industrial objects, electrical power stations, railroad junctions, and airfields.

After the end of World War II, the Chinese Civil War resumed between the Chinese Nationalists (Kuomintang) and the Communist Party of China. The United States were concerned about the widespread communist influence, and decided to continue the support of the Nationalists. By 1949, a series of Chinese Communist offensives led to the defeat of the Nationalist army, and the Communists founded the People's Republic of China (also named Communist China or Red China) on 1 October, 1949. The Nationalists Republic of China, originally based in mainland China, has since 1945 governed the island of Taiwan (former name Formosa). When the Nationalist fled to Taiwan, they were taking many of their B-25s with them. Some B-25s were left behind and went into service with the air force of the new People's Republic of China. By 1949, the Kuomintang Air Force was a well-developed and equipped service with, according to some reports, 28 B-25s. In addition to the B-25, it flew also P-47 Thunderbolts, P-51 Mustangs and even B-24 Liberator bombers, as well as a considerable number

G.A.C.W. INSIGNIA

SUBMITTED BY:
HARRY L. KEBRIC

Right: *The Chinese American Composite Wing was a force of Chinese and American airmen trained side by side, flying wing tip to tip, fighting shoulder to shoulder. The B-25 pilots of the CACW bombardment groups were famous among their Chinese and American comrades as fine formation fliers. The beautiful insignia of the CACW with the flying tiger and the dragon with a Japanese flag was designed by Capt. Harry Kebric, Combat Liaison Officer with the CACW. (USAF)*

CAMOUFLAGE AND MARKINGS

The B-25s of the CACW were both Olive Drab with Neutral Grey and natural aluminium finished. A part of the aircraft was flown by Americans and had the standard USAAF markings. Most B-25s dipslayed the Kuomintang twelve-pointed blue and white star on wings and fuselage in four positions in place of the USAAF star and bar insignia. Some airplanes had six horizontal blue and white stripes painted on the outside of both rudders. The airplanes had different tail numbers consisting of the U.S. serial number, a five-digit number preceded by a letter B or a three-digit CACW number. They were painted in black or white.

The post-war B-25s were newly painted Olive Drab with Light Grey or Medium Grey and some were natural aluminium finished. They had the Kuomintang stars in six positions, four on the wings and two on the fuselage. The airplanes had six horizontal blue and white stripes painted on the inside and outside of both rudders. The airplanes carried a five-digit black or white number preceded by a letter B, but also other combinations at the same time as in the war during the CACW service.

The B-25s of the Chinese Nationalist Air Force had the Kuomintang twelve-pointed blue and white star in four or six positions and horizontal white and blue stripes on the rudders.

This is how you make a Kuomintang star on an American airplane. First patient taping and then spraying paint. In this case, white paint for the circle and star on a blue background on a P-51 Mustang, another successful airplane from North American Aviation Inc. (Life)

The Kuomintang star disposed on the bottom of the right wing of a B-25. The picture clearly shows the remains of the American roundel. (USAF)

One of the many C and D models supplied to the Nationalist Chinese. Note the loop antenna on top of the fuselage. (Collection Wim Nijenhuis)

Above and right:
Two overall natural aluminium finished B-25Hs in the colours of the CACW and even with a shark mouth nose. (USAF)

Below:
Rare picture of eight Olive Drab/Neutral Grey camouflaged B-25s of the CACW. Crew members are walking to the four canon nosed ships and the four glass nosed ships.

(Collection Wim Nijenhuis)

Centre:
Chinese crew members in front of a sign indicating the insignia of the 1st Bombardment Squadron of the CACW. But remarkably, this insignia was later used by the 2nd BS. The legendary monkey god Sun Wukong is incorporated as the squadron's mascot. Sun Wukong is one of the major characters in the classic tale "Journey to the West".

(USAF)

A picture depicting a scene from the Chinese classic "Journey to the West". The painting shows the four heroes of the story, left to right: Sun Wukong, Xuanzang, Zhu Wuneng and Sha Wujing. The painting is a decoration on the Long Corridor in the Summer Palace in Beijing, China. "Journey to the West" is a great Chinese novel published in the 16th century during the Ming dynasty and attributed to Wu Cheng'en. The story follows the adventures of an immortal monkey demon–turned–Buddhist monk named Sun Wukong. Sun Wukong is also found in many later stories and adaptations. *(Rolf Müller)*

Great action shot of a B-25H of the 3rd BS of the CACW on a bombing and strafing mission to Burma in the summer of 1944. The Olive Drab/Neutral Grey airplane has the squadron insignia of a black and white skunk with a clothespin painted on her nose as well as a number 715. At right, a detail of the insignia on number 714. *(Solyn Jr., via Margaret Mills Kincannon, Collection Wim Nijenhuis)*

Two other pictures of the skunk insignia on the B-25Hs numbers 716 and 717. In front of the canon nosed airplanes are both American and Chinese crew members. (Collection Wim Nijenhuis)

American crew members in front of a natural aluminium finished B-25J of the 3rd BS.
Some men wear the squadron insignia on their flying jacket. *(via James H. Mills)*

Unfortunately two pictures
of poor quality, but the more
interesting. The canon nose
of a B-25H and the glass
nose of a B-25J of the 4th
BS. On both noses the squadron insignia of a nude that
lifts up her right leg.
(Collection Wim Nijenhuis)

Right:
*A crew member with the sign
of the 4th BS.*
(John Ching)

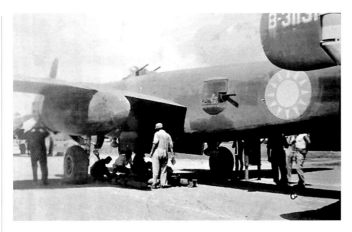

Crew members next to an Olive Drab/Neutral Grey and an overall natural aluminium finished B-25. The natural aluminium finished airplane is a B-25H-10. The U.S. serial number is still painted in black on the vertical stabiliser and rudder.

(USAF, pixnet)

Centre:
The Chinese also flew with the B-25J strafer. Here an Olive Drab/Light Grey or Medium Grey example with full armament and white number 371 on her nose. The top turret has been removed.

(Collection Wim Nijenhuis)

An unarmed B-25D of the 12th Reconnaissance Squadron shortly after the war. The number on the vertical tail seems to be F-10-002. The number 002 is just visible on the nose. The emblem on the nose is similar to that of the 35th Photo Reconnaissance Squadron of the USAAF. In 1944, this squadron arrived in China and used the F-5E Photo Lightning.

Right: The squadron emblem on the nose of an F-5E Photo Lightning of the 35th PRS at Yunnanyi Airfield in China.

(Collection Wim Nijenhuis, USAF)

After the war, two B-25Js are fraternally standing next to each other. The armament has been removed and the blue stripes on the rudders of the camouflaged B.31306 are largely gone.

(Collection Wim Nijenhuis)

A solid nose B-25 of the 12th RS with number 003 and the squadron emblem on her nose.

(Collection Wim Nijenhuis)

A late 1940s Chinese Nationalist Air Force B-25J with white serial number B31387. She has a modified tail and it looks like she has been freshly painted. The finish is Olive Drab on the upper surfaces and Medium Grey or Light Grey on the lower surfaces. The rudders have six blue and six white stripes. *(Collection Wim Nijenhuis)*

Again B31387 in the background. In front another B-25 with number B31388. Both airplanes are B-25J models and are unarmed.

(Collection Wim Nijenhuis)

Left: *A B-25C with serial number B31393 in San Francisco, November 1949. (William T. Larkins)*

Right and Centre:
Personnel of the Chinese Nationalist Air Force in front of two of their B-25s. Both are B-25J models. The first one is camouflaged with white serial number 398, the second is natural aluminium finished with black serial number 386. **Above:** *A good view of the camouflage pattern of number 398. Note the different numbers on the vertical stabiliser. The lower number is 8830, standing for the U.S. serial 45-8830. This is one of the last produced series of the B-25. (Collection Wim Nijenhuis)*

PEOPLE'S LIBERATION ARMY AIR FORCE

The Chinese People's Liberation Army (PLA) represents the armed forces of the People's Republic of China. In 1944, the Red Army of China Air Force, was still in development. It captured a number of Japanese Tachikawa Ki. 54 aircraft, and after the Japanese capitulation it was reformed and almost completely equipped with different types left behind by the Japanese Air Force and Navy. In 1946, the Communist Party formed the new armed force, the People's Liberation Army. They eventually won the Chinese Civil War, establishing the People's Republic of China in 1949. On 11 November, 1949, the Central Military Commission formed the People's Liberation Army Air Force (PLAAF) command. It was manned by Chinese pilots who had crossed over to the communists, while Soviet instructors and even Japanese prisoner of war "volunteers" helped with training. Equipment was sourced from wherever it could be found, most of it Japa-

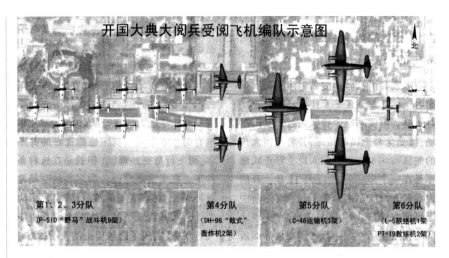

开国大典大阅兵受阅飞机编队示意图

| 第1、2、3分队 | 第4分队 | 第5分队 | 第6分队 |
| (P-51D "野马" 战斗机9架) | (DH-98 "蚊式" 轰炸机2架) | (C-46运输机3架) | (L-5联络机1架 PT-19教练机2架) |

开国大典大阅兵受阅飞机编队示意图

On 1 October, 1949 the new Chinese People's Liberation Army Air Force held a flypast over Tiananmen Square at Beijing. At that time, a total of 17 aircraft participated in the founding ceremony. Of the 17 aircraft, nine were P-51 fighters, two were Mosquito fighters, three were C-46 Commando's, one was an Stinson L-5, and the last two were Fairchild PT-19 Junior trainers. (Collection Wim Nijenhuis)

nese, left behind by the occupying forces, or captured from the Kuomintang. The PLA started with over 100 aircraft of various types, half of which had to be repaired before use. The aircraft were mostly fighters and trainers, but also included four American B-25J bombers. At its first air display, on 1 October, 1949 the young communist republic's air force was represented by American Mustang fighters and C-46 Commando transport aircraft, British Mosquitoes and a few American-made light trainers. Large-scale supplies of Soviet aircraft began only at the end of 1949. In 1952, the last two B-25s retired. In the 1960s, the Beijing Military Museum has exhibited a B-25J strafer but the machine was broken down in the Cultural Revolution.

Photos of communist Chinese B-25s are quite rare. This photo shows a part of the People's Liberation Army Air Force fleet at Beijing Nanyuan Airport in 1949. The young communist republic's air force was represented by a variety of aircraft. A lot of P-51 Mustangs in front of a couple of C-47 Skytrains and C-46 Commando's. In the upper left corner a natural aluminium finished B-25J without top turret. (
Collection Wim Nijenhuis)

A Chinese propaganda photo of B-25s with P-51 Mustangs, all showing their red and yellow PLAAF marking on the fuselages.
(Collection Wim Nijenhuis)

Below: *Two other shots of the same location showing two B-25s with the red and white striped rudders.*
(Collection Wim Nijenhuis)

CAMOUFLAGE AND MARKINGS

Little is known about the colours of the PLAAF B-25s. Most likely they were overall natural aluminium finished. The B-25s had the national marking in six positions, four on the wings and two on the fuselage. The airplanes had five horizontal red and four white stripes painted on the outside of both rudders. The serial number was also painted in red.

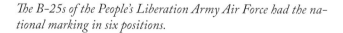

The B-25s of the People's Liberation Army Air Force had the national marking in six positions.

Fin flash

Crew members stand in line before their B-25s. The airplane behind them is number 5229 and has a red coloured engine cowling ring and red serial number. At right, a better detail of the same picture. *(Collection Wim Nijenhuis)*

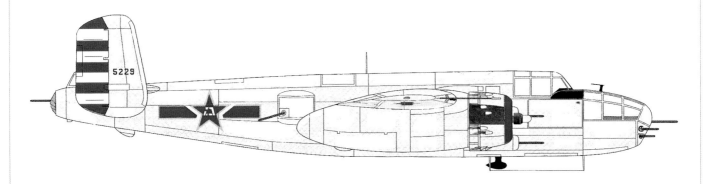

A B-25 bomber in front of a P-61 Black Widow night fighter at the Beijing Military Museum. She has number 5230 and was obviously a B-25J strafer. In the 1960s, she was the only intact B-25 and was sent to the Beijing Military Museum. But during the Cultural Revolution, she was shredded into aluminium. In 1966, China's Communist leader Mao Zedong launched what became known as the Cultural Revolution in order to reassert his authority over the Chinese government. The Cultural Revolution was a socio-political movement that took place in China until 1976. At right, a picture of the same B-25. *(Sina.com)*

A cover from a 1964 aviation magazine with the same picture at the time the Beijing Military Museum still retained the B-25J. Nowadays, there is only the left engine part.
(Sina.com)

Centre:
Another rare picture of the Chinese bomber of the Beijing Military Museum.
(Sina.com)

Below:
A close-up of one of the B-25s of the People's Liberation Army Air Force fleet at Beijing Nanyuan Airport in 1949.
(Collection Wim Nijenhuis)

Soviet Union

The Allied Powers in World War Two were led by Great Britain, the United States and the Soviet Union (Union of Soviet Socialist Republics - USSR). This war was often referred to the Soviets as the Great Patriotic War. The Soviet Union received aid from the U.S. under the Lend-Lease programme bringing together former enemies in the fight against the Nazi Germany and the Axis powers. From 1941 until 1945, the United States and the Soviet Union ferried about 14,000 warplanes from the U.S. to the Soviet Union. A total of 865 of these airplanes were B-25s and assigned to the Soviet Air Forces (Voyenno-Vozdushnye Sily - VVS).

In late August 1941, a delegation of the Soviet Air Forces arrived in the U.S.A. for study and selection of heavy bombers to

The Soviet Lend-Lease Б-25 Митчелл. A group of P-63 Kingcobra fighters with a leading B-25J over the Verkhoyansk Range in eastern Siberia during a ferry flight of the ALSIB-route. The entire route represented a path of about 14 thousand kilometres: about 5 thousand from the factory plants in the United States through Canada and Alaska to Fairbanks, 6.5 thousand kilometres from Fairbanks to Krasnoyarsk and approximately 2.5 thousand kilometres to the fronts. It was an arduous journey over some of the most remote and inhospitable terrain on the planet. The B-25 bombers were supplied to the Soviets via the Lend-Lease programme and they ultimately received 861 B-25s. (Wio.ru)

be delivered to the Soviet Union. Their first preference was the B-17 Flying Fortress, but that was refused by the Americans who proposed buying B-25s or B-26s instead. In September, the Soviets agreed to three B-26 Marauders and two B-25B Mitchells. But the Soviets finally settled for five B-25Bs because of its advantage in ease of handling over the B-26. Before delivery of the

B-25B, installation of additional de-icing equipment was requested. On 6 November, 1941, the first two B-25s were delivered in crates by a Soviet ship to Murmansk. In January 1942, the aircraft were put together but could not fly. Only on 5 March, the B-25s were flown from Murmansk to Moscow. None of the five B-25Bs has been used as a fighting machine and all of them were used

1943, one of the early B-25s while ferrying from Basra, Iraq, and Iran to Moscow.
(Collection Wim Nijenhuis)

der the Lend-Lease programme. Apart from B-25s, many other aircraft were supplied via the ALSIB-route to the USSR. The American part of the route began in Great Falls, Montana State and ended in Fairbanks, Alaska. The Soviet part of the route continued from Fairbanks to Krasnoyarsk. Total distance for aircraft to get from the American manufacturers to the Soviet battle fronts exceeded about 14 thousand kilometres. Thousands of pilots, navigators, radio operators, and engineers worked in the unbearable conditions of the Far North, flying over the most dangerous areas of the globe, including the permafrost zone. Using primitive and inaccurate maps, they often flew in poor visibility, not knowing what waited ahead.

for training purposes. After this, the delivery of B-25s on a large scale began via Brazil and Iraq to Iran. In March 1942, pilots of Pan Am ferried 72 B-25s via Iran. Over the same southern route, in all 102 B-25s were flown to the Soviet Union until the end of 1942 and another 16 in the beginning of 1943.

Only after the opening of the northern AL-SIB-route (Alaska-Siberia) in October 1942, the thrue mass-delivery of B-25s for the Soviets became a reality. ALSIB was an air route between Alaska and the former USSR. It was opened in 1942 and was operational until 1945. This air route was used to ferry American warplanes from the USA to the USSR un-

American crews delivered the B-25 bombers from the North American plants in the U.S.A. through Canada to Ladd Field, Fairbanks, Alaska, where they were accepted by representatives of the Soviet military mission. Selected experienced Soviet ferry pilots flew the B-25s onward via the Bering Strait in five regiments to the Krasnoyarsk airfield in Siberia. Each of the regiments, 1 PAP to 5 PAP (Ferry Air Regiment), flew a separate part of the route. Mid 1943, these regiments were grouped into 1 PAD GVF

American and Soviet crew members at Ladd Field around one of the first B-25s which were intended for the VVS. This is one of the early C models. In contrast to the standard U.S. colours, this airplane is painted in Soviet camouflage with red stars and the U.S. serial number has been painted over. (U.S. National Archives)

Above:

Rare pictures of a B-25J with P-63 fighters during a ferry flight in 1944. The B-25 is leading the flying formation. The B-25 is camouflaged with black lower surfaces but still has the yellow U.S. serial number on her vertical tail.

(Peregon.wmsite.ru)

Centre:

Late B-25DP models in Soviet colours in Alaska are ready for departure to Krasnoyarsk. The nose of the aircraft in the foreground features the written text "All armament OK" with date 2-5-44 and signed by Staff Sergeant Cook.

(USAF)

(Ferry Air Division of the Civil Air Fleet). Bomber aircraft and transport airplanes were ferried individually or in groups of two or three. The Krasnoyarsk Territory was an industrial centre and a large transportation node through which the latest overseas fighter and bomber aircraft were sent from the U.S.A. to the Soviets using the secret air route. Division pilots received the aircraft at Krasnoyarsk and flew them to the frontline units.

A total of 865 B-25s of different versions were delivered to the USSR until the end of the war, but actually 861 arrived. These B-25s were B, C, D and J models. It should be noted that the Soviets had designated the

Two other pictures of B-25s during an ALSIB ferry flight. The airplane with serial number 44-30039 is a B-25J-25. The pictures are probably taken at the military airfield of Yakutsk in North-Eastern Russia. Yakutsk was the administrative centre of ALSIB and was one of the stopovers on the ALSIB air route for the American airplanes flying to Krasnoyarsk. (Trinixy.ru)

B-25C as B-25S and the B-25D-30/35 models as B-25DP. The P stands for perehodnoy (intermediate) because the late type D retained the dorsal turret in the same position as on the C and D. But the major change was that the waist gun stations (like the B-25J) were added and a tail gun station was added as well, however, with a single machine gun. The ventral turret was removed. The Soviet Union received also at least six B-25Gs. After a few test flights and combat missions, it was clear that this variant was unsuitable for long range bomber units. All B-25Gs were delivered to naval aviation. The Gs were converted for transport duties after the war. The Soviets had no H models. Finally, there were some American B-25s interned during the war. These were aircraft that had made an emergency landing or had escaped to Soviet territory. They were used as trainers for crew training to fly American bombers as well as for various support purposes.

In the beginning, the B-25s caused many problems to the Soviets. The flight and maintenance instructions published by North American were written in the English language. In the Soviet Union there were no training facilities for the type and one had to develop these for the flight crew and supporting staff. Despite the number of the B-25's technical advances, the first in-cidences of freezing temperatures showed that the airplane was not equipped for utilisation in Russian winter conditions. Almost immediately, it turned out that the Soviet diesel destroyed the inner layers of rubber. They had many problems with the rubber fuel and oil cells, which were made from several layers of rubber with varying physical characteristics. Because of cold weather some B-25s were equipped with adjustable air intakes for the radial engine, which could be removed again in the warm season. And there were various other problems and failures of individual components such as electrical instruments, armaments, frozen and burst hydraulic brake lines, the controls for raising and lowering the landing gear, flaps and bomb bay doors. But with time, the Soviets developed all kinds of solutions and adjustments that were sufficient for their specific situation. Generally, the Soviet pilots were pleased with the B-25. The airplanes were easy to control and easy in take-off and landing, even in the snow.

The Soviet Mitchells were predominantly used in the Air Armies of the VVS. The Air Armies were integrated formations of the Fronts. From May until November 1942, seventeen Air Armies were created and in December 1944 a long-range aviation Air Army was created as the 18th Air Army. The Air Armies consisted of fighter, bomber, as-sault and mixed Aviation Divisions and separate Aviation Regiments. The Air Regiment was the standard tactical unit. It officially comprised 40 aircraft divided into three squadrons of 12 plus four spares. Squadrons were sub-divided into three flights of four aircraft. A Bomber Aviation Regiment (BAP) only had 30 aircraft, with 9 per squadron. Three or sometimes four regiments made up a Bomber Air Division (BAD), so on paper a bomber division had 90-120 aircraft but in practice they were usually under strength. Likewise, two to four divisions made up a Bomber Aviation Corps (BAK).

In April 1942, the first operational B-25Cs were handed over to 37 BAP of 222 BAD at Monino south of Moscow, and soon also the other two regiments, 16 BAP and 125 BAP of this division were equipped with B-25s. After rather heavy initial losses, the Soviets considered the B-25 more suited for night operations, and in September 1942, 222 BAD was transferred to ADD (long-range air division). In order to ensure the range required by ADD, additional fuel tanks were installed. In September 1942, the bombing of German targets was started. From August 1942 to April 1943, 222 BAD saw action on the Western, Kalinin, Stalingrad and Bryansk fronts. In April and May 1943, B-25s attacked major administrative centres in Germany and Poland. In the meantime, it was

A B-25 on a winter airfield. Because of the cold weather circumstances, some B-25s were equipped with adjustable air intakes for the radial engines, which could be removed again in the warm season. (via Carl Geust)

decided to embark on nocturnal long range attacks. The division's combat success with B-25s earned it the "Guards" title. In March, 1943, 222 BAD received the guards designation. It had been elevated to 4 GBAD (4 Guards Bomber Aviation Division) and into 4 GBAK (4 Guards Bomber Aviation Corps) in July 1943. The 125th regiment later became 15th Guards and even later became 15th Guards Red Banner, Sevastopol. The 37th regiment was re-designated 13th Guards and the 16th regiment was re-designated 14th Guards. 4 GBAK became the main Soviet operator of B-25s within the 18th Air Army, consisting of two divisions, 4 and 5 GBAD, renamed respectively 14 GBAD and 15 GBAD. 4 GBAK participated in almost all major operations of the Air Force in 1943 to1945. It played a significant role in the strategic bombing attacks against Helsinki in February 1944 and supported the Slovakian uprising by dropping supplies at the Tri Duby airfield in Central Slovakia in September 1944. During the war, 4 GBAK carried out a total of 13,407 bombing sorties, dropping 80,584 bombs with total of 17,035 tons. It also carried out a total of 2,336 supply flights to partisans, during which 1,447 tons of cargo and 864 men were dropped.

The other ADD aviation corpses used smaller numbers of B-25s. In early 1944, the B-25s amounted to approximately ten percent of all ADD aircraft. After the reorganisation of ADD as 18th Air Army on 6 December, 1944, the ADD Guards regiments and divisions were renumbered in order to "fit" into the VVS numbering scheme. On 1 May 1945, the inventory of VVS included 552 B-25s, including 398 at the front. Another 98 airplanes were stationed in the interior military districts, and 56 were in transit to their destination. Total B-25 losses in the USSR during the war amounted to 201 bombers.

Number 2 GBAP, 337 BAP, 362 BAP and other units flew the B-25, too. The B-25s performed also long-range reconnaissance tasks in various VVS and naval regiments. In particular the strategic recce regiments of the Soviet Supreme Command 48 GDRAP (Guards Long-Range Reconnaissance Aviation Regiment), 118 ODRAP (Independent Long-Range Reconaissance Aviation Regiment) and the 15 ORAP (Independent Reconaissance Aviation Regiment) of the Red Banner Baltic Fleet, used a number of

One B–25J-5 with the U.S. serial number 43–28112 was used in the post–war years for testing parachute systems.
(via Carl Geust)

Main B-25 units with renumbering 4 GBAK 18th Air Army VVS during World War Two.

Number BAP	Number GBAP ADD	Number GBAP 18th Air Army	Number GBAD
125	15	198	14
113	27	199	14
37	13	229	14
335	34	250	14
16	14	201	15
747	22	238	15
337	35	251	15

Also after the war, some B-25s were used for rocket and turbojet engine tests. Here is a B-25 as a test bed for the Type 93-1 rocket booster and a B-25J-20, s/n 44-29347, converted into a flying laboratory for testing the RD-10F turbojet engine on top of her fuselage. From October 1946 until May 1947, a total of 17 flights were made with this ship. (via Carl Geust)

specially equipped B-25s. In the two years after the war, considerable numbers of aircraft were destroyed under the supervision of American inspectors. However, several B-25s were retained for post-war use. 330 BAP used B-25s from 1946 until 1949, 132 BAP converted from Tu-2s to B-25Js in 1950, and a Kamchatka-based regiment operated B-25s still in 1953. In the early 1950s, the test-pilots school at Kratovo still had a number of B-25s in its inventory. 121 GODRAP (Guards Detached Long-Range Reconnaissance Aviation Regiment) used reconnais-

Great detail of the tail of another test bed. This was the B-25J-25, s/n 44-30041, for testing the D-5 ram jet engine.
(via Carl Geust)

sance B-25s until 1953. Also a number of B-25s were used as so-called departmental aircraft after the war. Among the owners of the B-25s were Polar aviation, the main Department of Hydro meteorological Service, the General Administration of Geodesy and Cartography, the Ministry of Aviation Industry, Geology and the Fishing industry and the Directorate of Camps, the Mining and Metallurgical Industry of the Ministry of Internal Affairs. B-25s that remained in Soviet Air Force service after the war were assigned the NATO reporting name "Bank".

In general, the B-25 was operated as a ground support and tactical daylight bomber. It was operated from Stalingrad in 1942, until the German surrender in May 1945. Most of the B-25s operated alongside the Douglas A-20 Havocs in the North-Western part of Russia against the Germans on the Kola Peninsula. Many airplanes went to the Guards units. The Guards units were elite units and formations in the armed forces of the former Soviet Union. In September 1943, B-25s were used for the bombing of port cities in Poland and Germany and they also bombed Leningrad. In February 1944, Helsinki in Finland was bombed. From 1943 to 1945, B-25s took part in operations in Belarus, Ukraine and Poland. B-25s were also used for aid to partisans in Poland and the Czech Republic. They flew in at altitudes of 400 to 500 m for which the B-25s received special adjustment. The Soviet B-25s were regularly used for night bombing and supply dropping purposes in 1944 and 1945. Among their most famous mission-series were the supply dropping missions over Yugoslavia for Tito partisans. In February 1944, B-25s were used for the first time in a transport role on a large scale during troop relocations in the Ukraine. At the end of 1944,

Despite the major problems in the beginning, the B-25 was a successful aircraft in the Soviet Union. A reason for the Soviet crew members to have fun.

(Collection Wim Nijenhuis)

B-25s were even used for dropping special secret agents in the Czech Republic, Poland and Austria. In April 1945, B-25s attacked Berlin and Prague. In the Far East, B-25s of the Pacific Fleet Air Arm were also used in attacks on Japan and Chŏngjin in Korea. On 9 May, 1945, B-25s participated in a large parade over Moscow.

Because of the good flying characteristics and strong structure permitting extensive modifications, the B-25 was a very popular test bed for various research and developments projects in the late 1940s. B-25s were used in tests in 1947 until 1949, like flight testing of early jet engines, development of air-to-air tanking methods, testing of rocket-assisted take-offs and catapult experiments. Two B-25Gs participated in the programme of using torpedoes. One plane carried a mock torpedo and the second a guidance system in the capacious fuselage. Several B-25s were also converted to VIP-transports. After the war, some demilitarised Mitchells were also entered into the civil register and were used e.g. as courier aircraft by 2 AD GVF (Civil Air Fleet).

COLOURS AND MARKINGS

The B-25B, C, D and G models given to the Soviets were painted Dark Olive Drab and Neutral Grey according to the American specifications. These airplanes were generally painted at the factory in accordance with the requirements of the U.S. Army Air Corps and later Army Air Forces. In 1940, the standard colour of bombers was matt Dark Olive Drab No. 41 and matt Neutral Grey No. 43. The great majority of B-25s of the 4 GBAK had these traditional American camouflage colours of Olive Drab above and Neutral Grey below. When the B-25 switched to a "nocturnal" role, the lower surfaces were repainted black with bottom markings on the wing. The colours sometimes matched the original, sometimes not. The colour scheme was basically simple, though it might change with time.

The later delivered J models were greatly similar to the 1943 NKAP scheme. This scheme was brought in after the U.S. discontinued painting their airplanes. By January 1944, most airplanes coming off the production line were left unpainted. At the time, the U.S.A. began to deliver the B-25J in natural aluminium finish, devoid of camouflage. But the Soviets wanted their airplanes camouflaged.

The NKAP was the Narodniy Kommisariat Aviatsionoy Promishlinosti (People's Commissariat for the Aviation Industry) and was during the war responsible for making recommendations and policies on the painting of military Soviet aircraft. The NKAP suggested schemes were actually more recommendations. They were not requirements in any sense of the word, neither was their use enforced by the Government at any time. The specific patterns suggested by

Fine colour picture of the B-25J-25 with s/n 44-30004 with the Soviet camouflage pattern. (Collection Wim Nijenhuis)

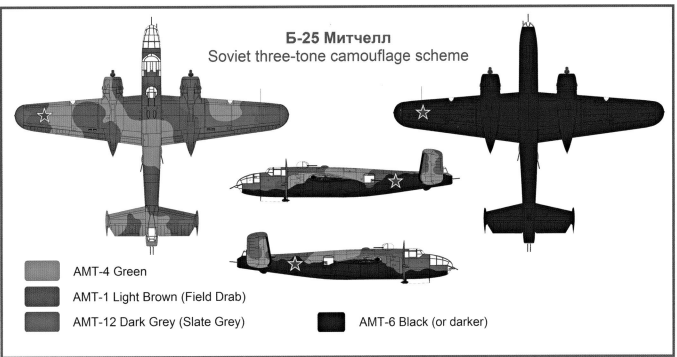

Б-25 Митчелл
Soviet three-tone camouflage scheme

AMT-4 Green

AMT-1 Light Brown (Field Drab)

AMT-12 Dark Grey (Slate Grey)

AMT-6 Black (or darker)

Factory picture of a B-25J-25, s/n 44-30052. The airplane is painted in the Soviet three-tone scheme Field Drab, Green and Slate Grey on the top and side surfaces. Underneath the entire plane is painted black. This was done by North American's Fairfax plant at Kansas City.
(North American Rockwell)

the NKAP were in the form of a three-view 'template' showing the desired application. They were known as the "NKAP Templates". For the medium bombers, these were made on the basis of the Standard 407. This introduced a three colour camouflage for the upper surfaces, consisting of AMT-1 Light Brown (Field Drab), AMT-4 Green and AMT-12 Dark Grey (Slate Grey). These colours were pretty much similar to the colours ANA 617 Dark Earth, ANA 613 Olive Drab and ANA 603 Neutral Gray. The undersides of the long range aviation airplanes were AMT-6 Black or even darker. The wavy demarcation lines for the black colour varied, ascending to the top and descending to the very bottom of the fuselage. However, several B-25s also had the undersides painted AMT-7 Blue. On most of the B-25Js, the camouflage colors were applied in the Soviet Union, but on a number of airplanes they were applied at the Kansas City factory.

Centre and below:
Two other colour pictures of a B-25J-30 with s/n 44-31162. They show very well the three-tone Soviet camouflage pattern and the black lower surfaces.
(Collection Wim Nijenhuis)

The later American B-25DP models as well as the B-25J models had additional machine guns beneath the pilot's cabin. But these were removed in the Soviet Union and the uncovered areas were painted over with a wide variety of paints from silver to black.

Sometimes, the B-25s were provided with a winter camouflage. Just prior to the war, the Soviet materials industry produced a white aviation paint that could be easily applied over existing camouflage, even under very low temperature conditions. The paint produced a very matte surface with a nice white colouration, and visually it was considered to be very suitable for seasonal camouflage. This winter camouflage of white paint, also called whitewash, was intended for quick and easy concealment of airplanes in snowy areas. The whole or parts of the plane were provided with white paint. This paint was often also fairly easy to remove so that if necessary, the underlying

A well-known publicity picture at the North American flight line at the Inglewood plant with the B-25C s/n 41-12525. The airplane is almost ready for delivery to the Soviet Union and has the Plain Red star painted on the Olive Drab fuselage. The other B-25Cs are intended for the U.S., the Netherlands East Indies and the United Kingdom.

(North American Rockwell)

Plain Red star on white disc

White Border star

Victory star

Other pictures taken at the Kansas plant with a B-25 intended for the Soviet Union. Number 43-28111 is a B-25J-5 model. It is painted Olive Drab over Black. The great colour picture was taken during an engine test run. (Collection Wim Nijenhuis)

A picture taken in the armament hangar at the Kansas City plant. The Soviet B-25J in the centre left is painted in the three-tone scheme and the Plain Red star is painted on a white disc in four positions. (Collection Dan Desko)

colour or camouflage emerged again. But, that also meant it weathered quickly and the underlying colour soon reappeared in many places.

Different markings. Soviet crews in front of their early B-25s with the White Border star and the Plain Red star on a white disc on the rear fuselage. The ship with the waist gun was designated B-25DP by the Soviets. (Collection Wim Nijenhuis)

A crew member holds a bomb for this B-25J-20. The airplane has the Soviet three-tone camouflage scheme with black lower surfaces and the White Border star. Soviet B-25s also had de-icers on the wings and vertical stabilisers. (Collection Wim Nijenhuis)

The national insignia of the VVS changed over the years. The Plain Red star was more or less standard at the outbreak of WWII. During 1941-1942, it was a bit of a fad at some Soviet factories to apply a thin black outline to the marking, but units in the field did likewise, and also used white paint in the same way. This practice gave way to a general convention during 1942-1943 that national markings should have a white outline. In practice, the White Border star with a medium-to-wide border became standard until 1945. Just after the war, the VVS Command issued a regulation that a new star would be the correct insignia, being a medium border White Border star with an additional thin red outline. This marking, the so-called Victory star, was actually again taken from the practise of field units, and examples like this can be seen as early as very late 1943. By 1944, many units thought that this was certainly the preferred marking, and during that year it became as common on service aircraft as the White Border type. Soviet national insignia were usually applied in four or six positions on the machine. The wing under surface application was standard, and one always sees them here. Stars were then applied either to the fuselage sides, or to the fin/rudder, or to both. The B-25C and D, however, arrived in the Soviet Union with U.S. markings. These were the white star on a blue disc, located on both sides of the rear fuselage and on the upper left wing and lower right wing. Large red stars were so painted as to fully cover the blue disc. On some airplanes the red star was applied over the U.S. insignia on the fuselage and upper wings, leaving the blue disc visible. However, there were also airplanes which received the Soviet marking of a white circle with the red star applied at the factory. Often, additional stars were applied on the bottom of the left wing and on top of the right wing. Standard 407 specified that the red star with border, without any background was to be painted at the factory in Kansas City. Therefore, the sizes of these various markings, their skill in execution and suitability of orientation were quite random.

Men are working on the tail of a ship of 22 GBAP. The most common colour for the Soviet aircraft numbers was white or red with a white border. They were often the last two digits of the aircraft's production number. On this aircraft of 5 GBAD, later renamed 15 GBAD, the white bordered red number has been placed on the rudders.

(Collection Wim Nijenhuis)

A B-25DP at Baranavichy airfield in the western Brest Region near Poland. This airplane with number 2 on her nose is a B-25D-35 with the U.S. serial number 43-3730 still on her vertical stabilisers and rudders. The tail is equipped with a gun turret position.

(Collection Wim Nijenhuis)

Soviet aircraft have always used a number to identify the airplane. During the war, these numbers were unique in design, font, placement, and execution. Usually, the numbers were applied by the receiving regiment in the field when any new aircraft arrived. The most common colour for the numbers was white or red with a white border. Early in the war, the numbers would appear virtually anywhere on the rear fuselage, the fin, and/or the rudder. Later, by 1942, it was common that such numbers mainly appeared on the rear fuselage sides. Airplane numbers were sometimes applied at the factory. They were often the last two digits of the aircraft's production number. Red and black paint were used to mark airplane numbers at times, particularly on winter schemes, and occasionally even yellow might have been used. In the 4 GBAD, the number was applied below the cockpit. The numeration was separate for each regiment, but

the script was the same. In the 5 GBAD, the numbers were applied on the rudders. The shapes of the numbers were different and their colour regularly changed according to orders or local initiative.

The guard's badges, honorary names, and other orders at first were barred from display on aircraft. From 1943, the Guards badges began to appear on the B-25s. The Guards insignia was applied on airplanes

The Guards' unit symbol

The Order of the Red Banner emblem.

Both emblems were awarded to elite units and units which had accomplished exceptional achievements in combat operation.

The Guards insignia was applied on airplanes belonging to units which had distinguished themselves in combat and been accorded Guards status. Here an example with the emblem on the right side of the nose. *(Collection Wim Nijenhuis)*

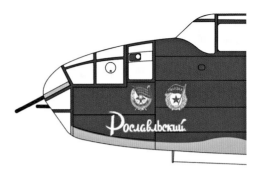

13 GBAP "Roslavl"

14 GBAP "Smolensk"

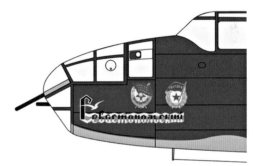

15 GBAP "Sevastopol"

The names of the guards units were applied to the noses of the B-25s.

belonging to units which had distinguished themselves in combat and been accorded Guards status. The Order of the Red Banner was awarded to units and crews who had accomplished exceptional achievements in an operation. Before the establishment of the Order of Lenin in 1930, the Order of the Red Banner functioned as the highest military order of the USSR. During World War II, it was presented both to individuals and to units for acts of extreme military heroism.

Another ship of 13 GBAP at Novodugino with almost complete winter camouflage.
Collection Wim Nijenhuis)

In some ways, the Order of the Red Banner was more prestigious, as it could only be awarded for bravery during combat operations whereas the Order of Lenin was sometimes awarded to non-military personnel and political leaders. B-25 units as 13 GBAP "Roslavl", 14 GBAP "Smolensk" and 15 GBAP "Sevastopol" received the Order of the Red Banner. In December, 1944, 13 GABP was renamed 229 GBAP, 14 GBAP was renamed 201 GBAP and 15 GBAP was renamed 198 GBAP. The names of the guards were painted below the emblems on the nose. Proving more effective and stable at distinguishing the regiments, the decision was taken to follow the practice. Various individual emblems and inscriptions began to spread quite widely.

Like most of the U.S. airplanes, B-25s had a yellow serial number on the vertical stabilisers and rudders. These were mostly painted over by the Soviets, but occasionally left in place. More rarely, the serial numbers were removed from the tail and placed on the rear fuselage. On the B-25C and D, the fuselage had a red propeller warning stripe.
Finally, many airplanes had nose art. One of the things they had in common were patriotic references to Stalin or the motherland, markings detailing who paid for the aircraft i.e. paid by the workers of the steel factory at some town, markings for death to the Germans and, of course, also personalised markings.

A poor but interesting picture of a B-25 of 13 GBAP with the words "Смерть Гитлеру!" (Death to Hitler!) painted on the rear fuselage. In December 1944, the unit was renamed 229 GBAP. (Collection Wim Nijenhuis)

B-25D-30, s/n 42-87594, of 13 GBAP
"Roslavl". The Guards' unit symbol and
the Order of the Red Banner emblem are
painted on the nose. The emblem of the
Order of the Red Banner is painted below
the escape hatch. The unit's name is applied
below the emblems. It still has the yellow
U.S. serial number on her vertical stabiliser
and rudder. The remnants of the American
roundel on the rear fuselage are still clearly
visible. The upper surfaces are Olive Drab
and the lower surfaces are Neutral Grey.

(Pavel Zakutin, via Ilya Grinberg)

Airmen of 13 GBAP in front of B-25J
number 37. The number is painted in
white. This regiment was awarded the
Order of the Red Banner for its part in the
liberation of the city of Roslavl in 1943.
During World War II, the town was occupied by the German Army from 3 August,
1941 to 25 September, 1943.

(Scalemodels.ru)

Left: The crew of airplane No. 19 in front of their B-25D of 13 GBAP "Roslavl". Above Again number 19. Note the different style of the inscription and the black lower surfaces. It is not certain whether this is the same but repainted aircraft, or another ship with the same number. (Pavel Zakutin, via Ilya Grinberg)

Airmen in front of a B-25D-25, s/n 42-87241, of 229 GBAP at Novodugino, 1944. On the nose of the airplane the word "Мститель" meaning "Avenger" is painted in white. The word was repeated on the right fuselage side behind the wing. The airplane is Olive Drab with a winter camouflage of white paint, also called whitewash. (Collection Wim Nijenhuis)

Pilots and mechanics of 13 GBAP in front of their airplane. The Olive Drab/Neutral Grey airplane still seems relatively new and without nose painting. (Collection Wim Nijenhuis)

B-25Ds of 14 GBAP "Smolensk". In December 1944, the regiment was renamed 201 GBAP. The airplane is Olive Drab with black lower surfaces. The Guards' unit symbol and the Order of the Red Banner emblem are on both sides of the fuselage nose as well as the name "Смоленскчч" (Smolensk).
(Collection Wim Nijenhuis, via Carl Geust)

Airplane number 10 of 14 GBAP "Smolensk" in winter camouflage. Note the Plain Red star on the vertical stabiliser and rudder and the white or yellow number 10 on the inner side of the right rudder.
(Scalemodels.ru)

Two B-25Ds of 15 GBAP "Sevastopol". Number 03 was photographed in Poland, 1945. Number 10 was photographed at Uman airfield, Ukraine, August 1944. All upper surfaces are Olive Drab and lower surfaces are Neutral Grey. The inscription "Sevastopol" is white, but on number 03 partially light blue. The numbers 03 and 10 and the seagull are also white. In December 1944, the unit was renamed 198 GBAP. (Collection Aleksandr Dudakov)

Another airplane of former 15 GBAP was No. 17. This B-25J-5 with U.S. serial number 43-28017, completed 286 combat missions. Curiously, it seems that the tail star has a darker colour than the fuselage star. The lower surfaces are black. The airplane photographed at Mielec airfield in Poland, 1945, is the airplane from Major I.M. Pavkin, commander of the 2nd Squadron 198 GBAP. *(Collection Wim Nijenhuis)*

Four crew members in front of their B-25Js of 112 BAP, 26 GBAP. The airplanes are painted in the three-tone Soviet camouflage pattern with black lower surfaces. *(Zaika70)*.

May 1945, Rzeszów, Poland, again B-25Js of 112 BAP, 26 GBAP. The airplane in front is a B-25J-20, s/n 44-29320, and was transmitted to the Soviet Air Force in October 1944. She still has her U.S. serial number painted on the vertical tail as well as the Soviet number 64. *(Zaika70)*.

Nose art of a polar bear on this B-25J of 251 GBAP, Uelkal, Chukhotka, July 1946. The nose art was applied on the airplane over a former unit emblem after transfer of the ship between the units.

(Collection Wim Nijenhuis)

Centre:

A great nose art was painted on this B-25D-35, s/n 43-3729, of 251 GBAP, 15 GBAD, Hungary, 1945. The U.S. insignia and serial numbers have been painted over in the appropriate places on the fuselage, upper left and lower right wings. The tactical number 85 on the rudder is red with a white border. All upper and side surfaces are Olive Drab and the undersides are Neutral Grey. The nose art is painted at the pilot's request on the port side only. It consisted of a tiger's head with yellow background and a white lightning. However, some sources mention a panther head. The inscriptions in red read "Za krov' Vityebska" meaning "For the blood of Vitebsk". Vitebsk (Витебск in Russian) was the home town of the pilot and a big city in Belarus. During World War II, the city was under Nazi Germany occupation from July 1941 until June 1944. Much of the old city was destroyed in the ensuing battles between the Germans and the Red Army soldiers.

(via Carl Geust)

Two other examples of Soviet nose art with a lightning. The inscription on the airplane at right says "Za Stalina!" meaning "For Stalin!".

(via Carl Geust)

Two B-25s with bird nose art. At right, Pudov's crew in front of their airplane. Fedor Pudov was commander of the B-25 of the 45 Gomel Long Range Aviation Division and did not return from a night mission in the night of 15-16 September, 1944.

(Scalemodels.ru, Sovietwarplanes.com)

A fine picture of another ship of the Gomel Long Range Aviation Division. The nose and side guns have been removed. The under surfaces are painted black.

(Collection Wim Nijenhuis)

Below: *This B-25J was flown by Vladimir V. Doveiko of 341 BAP. The airplane has a clown nose art and inscription " For the Soviet art". Doveiko (1922-2002) was an outstanding artist and acrobat, a legend of the Soviet and Russian circus. During the war, he left the arena to become a bomber pilot. He was the crew commander on the B-25 and flew 46 sorties. After graduating from Novosibirsk flight school and then high school for night pilots, Doveiko was appointed squadron commander on the long-range bomber. The first thing he did upon arriving at the airfield was painting the laughing clown on the fuselage nose and writing the text. He flew over enemy cities, bombing Breslau and Berlin. He was awarded several times. After the war, he returned to the circus. Doveiko travelled very successfully around the world in the circus circuit.*

(Karopka.ru)

A post-war poster of Circus Barlay Berlin with the announcement of the 5 Doveikos with Vladimir in the centre.

(SCDR.RU)

A B-25C of the NII VVS (Scientific Test Institute of the Air Force) in June 1942. Note the Plain Red star on both wings and the inner and outer sides of the vertical stabilisers. On the left upper wing the star is painted on a white disc.

(Collection Wim Nijenhuis)

Left: *Another B-25 of NII VVS was this B-25C-10, s/n 42-32244. The airplane was converted to a VIP passenger transport in 1945. The U.S. roundel has been painted over and the White Border stars have been applied on the vertical tails and on the wings. The yellow U.S. serial is still present.*

(via Carl Geust)

As with any air force, also at the VVS sometimes accidents happened. Number 21 made an unfortunate landing.

(Collection S.P. Shilov)

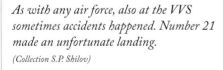

Ceremony with Major General of Aviation Lebedev. In the background a B-25D-35 with s/n 43-3831.

(Collection Wim Nijenhuis)

A clean machine. Working on the left engine of an unknown Soviet B-25. The airplane is Olive Drab with black undersides, she has no other markings except the star on her vertical tail.

(Collection Wim Nijenhuis)

Soviet B-25G

One of the very few pictures of a Soviet B-25G. Lieutenant S.M. Nakorâkov in front of his B-25 converted into a transport aircraft of 118 ORAP. Because all Soviet B-25s were operated by ADD units, the first two B-25G were delivered to these units too. After a few test flights and combat missions, it was clear that this variant was unsuitable for long range bomber units. All B-25Gs were delivered to Naval Aviation. In 1944, two went to the Northern Fleet, two to the Baltic Fleet and two to the Pacific Fleet.

(Collection Wim Nijenhuis)

Maintenance crews at work. At least six B-25Js of the Soviet fleet are in this picture. All the airplanes are painted in the three-tone Soviet camouflage pattern with black lower surfaces. *(Aviaforum.ru)*

An early B-25 is running up her engines. The bombardier in the greenhouse nose seems to be ready for the flight.

(aviaforum.ru)

BIAFRA

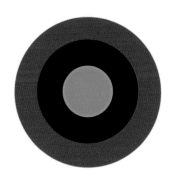

Biafran roundel on the lower surfaces of the B-25 wings?

The flag of Biafra was painted on the out-side of the rudders.

As far as known, two B-25Js were sent to Biafra. The Republic of Biafra was a secessionist state in South-Eastern Nigeria that existed from 1967 to 1970. In that period the Biafran War raged, a very gruesome civil war between the central authority in Nigeria and the rebellious region of Biafra. After two-and-a-half years of war, Biafran forces agreed to a ceasefire with the Nigerian Federal Military Government, and Biafra was reintegrated into Nigeria. The war cost the lives of millions of people, mainly as a result of a conscious starvation policy. Therefore during the war, Joint Church Aid airplanes brought lots of food to improve the human situation. The Biafrans managed to set up a small yet effective air force. Early inventory included two B-25 Mitchells, two B-26 Invaders, a converted DC-3 and one De Havilland Dove. The B-25s were sent in 1967 to fight against the Nigerians during the war. They served for a few months only.

The B-25s were equipped with new and modified fuel tank fittings. This was carried out in Miami in July 1967, possibly for the trans-atlantic ferry flight to São Tomé International Airport. In October 1967, the airplanes were flown from São Tomé to Biafra's main operating base at Port Harcourt. Here they underwent modifications before going into service. The two bombers were fitted with machine guns and locally made rockets and bombs. The B-25s made attacks on shipping and river gun boats and were used for sporadic bombing attacks during the period to December 1967. However, Biafra had big problems with the B-25s because of the maintenance of the old aircraft and the lack of spare parts. They were flown by European and American mercenaries with Biafran support crews.

This B-25J-25, s/n 44-29919, was registered as N9868C and flew in the U.S. as "Manana Express". It was later used by the rebel Biafran Air Force in Africa. She is photographed here in 1967 in Miami, before being ferried to Biafra, and still in her last civil colours.

(Collection Coert Munk, Collection Wim Nijenhuis)

The other B–25J–30, s/n 44–31491, was registered as N8013 and also used in Biafra. She is camouflaged in Biafran colours. This B-25 was continually plagued by engine trouble and for almost the whole of November 1967, she was permanently grounded.

(Collection Coert Munk)

One of the B-25s was s/n *44-29919*, a B-25J-25, and registered with the U.S. civil number N9868C. It was purchased at the end of 1964 by John Osterholt of Homestead, Florida. In June 1967, the airplane was sold to a company called Aerographic Inc. President of this company was also John Osterholt. The airplane was operated by Tripoint Associates, Miami, Florida. This was a manufacturers' representative dealing in reconditioned aero engines, aviation spares of all types and, during the Biafran conflict, in leasing and operating cargo carrying aircraft. Whether, in fact, Tripoints had any direct involvement in the B-25 deal is not known. The aircraft arrived in Biafra in August 1967. The ferry pilot of this B-25 was possibly of Cuban nationality and was accompanied by an American ex-TWA pilot and a U.S. engineer who stayed to install SNEB rockets on the aircraft. The SNEB rocket is an unguided air-to-ground rocket projectile manufactured by the French company TDA Armaments, designed for being launched by combat aircraft and helicopters. Following a bombing raid with this

B-25, one of Biafra's B-26 Invaders was damaged in a belly landing at Port Harcourt in the night of the 2/3 December, 1967. As a result, the B-25 was unable to land at Port Harcourt owing to the presence of the B-26 bomber which had made a wheels up landing and was blocking the runway. Running desperately short of fuel, the B-25 attempted a go-around but, while doing so, first the starboard and then the port engine cut out. The bomber ploughed through a stand of trees which ripped the engines from their mountings. The accident killed the bombardier/gunner and injured the other crew members. The aircraft was written-off.

The identity of the second B-25 was N8013, ex USAAF s/n *44-31491*, a B-25J-30. In 1964, this former RCAF ship with the Canadian number 5245 and with a solid nose, was sold to Intercontinental Trading Corporation, Miami, Florida. The airplane was operated by Intercontinental from 1964 until 1967. The airplane was delivered to Port Harcourt in October 1967 and was fitted with armament. The B-25 seems to have been abandoned when it became unserviceable sometime in December 1967. When Federal forces recaptured Port Harcourt airport on 20 May, 1968, they destroyed the B-25.

Little information has been found regarding the colours and markings carried by the Biafran B-25s. Most likely, they were painted in the same way as the B-26 Invaders which means the lower surfaces Light Blue Gray and the upper surfaces Dark Green with Dark Tan. Probably they had no roundels or only on the lower surfaces of the wings. The Biafran flag was painted on the outside of the rudders.

A plastic scale model giving an impression of a possible colour scheme of the Biafran B-25s.

(Collection Wim Nijenhuis)

BOLIVIA

There is much uncertainty about the B-25s in Bolivia. In all probability, a total of 13 B-25s have flown in this country. Seven went to the Bolivian Air Force and in addition to the military aircraft, at least six B-25s got civil registrations and were often used as a meat hauler.

The Bolivian Cuerpo de Aviación (Aviation Corps) was actually the first in the Latin Americas with air combat experience. The Cuerpo de Aviación was further re-organised in 1944 along USAAF lines to become the Fuerza Aérea Boliviana (FAB, Bolivian Air Force), with most of its aircraft of U.S. manufacture. The FAB was at first under partial Army control, but became totally independent in 1957. After Bolivia signed the Rio Pact in 1947, the FAB received small quantities of training and transport aircraft from the United States. However, Bolivia did not acquire B-25s until late 1973 as part of a package deal with Venezuela. It received 7 B-25Js and the first four were delivered on 7 November, 1973. They were assigned to

This is number 541 of the Fuerza Aérea Boliviana (FAB) after delivery in November 1973. The airplane just arrived from overhaul in Venezuela. This is s/n 44-86725, a B-25J-30. She was transferred from the Fuerza Aerea Venezuela to Bolivia as FAB-541. By 1979, she was stored as derelict at the La Paz Airport, but the aircraft was not removed from La Paz until 1985, when she was sold to Doan Helicopters of Daytona Beach, Florida. She has been with the Oklahoma Museum of Flying since 2003 undergoing a complete restoration. Nowadays she flies in the U.S. warbird circuit as "Super Rabbit".
(Collection Wim Nijenhuis)

the transport unit Transporte Aéreo Militar (TAM). This is a branch of the Bolivian Air Force, dedicated to transport passengers to the most remote areas of Bolivia, where other airlines could not come. The first three

Roundel and fin flash of the Fuerza Aérea Boliviana.

A B–25J survivor of the Fuerza Aérea Boliviana photographed in 2006 and 2008. The airplane is No. 542 and has been rebuilt and is now a static display at the Plaza Gral. Walter Arze Rojas, approximately 1,000 feet east of Cochabamba Airport.
(Robert Domandl, Flickr)

B-25s received the serial numbers 541, 542 and 543. Number 544 was destroyed during training in Venezuela in December 1973. Number 545 and 546 arrived on 14 December, 1973, at La Paz. About number 547 there is no clarity. In February 1979, only one B-25 was still in service and this airplane was eventually sold back to the U.S.A. in 1984.

The airplanes were natural aluminium finished with black engine nacelles. The registration number was also black and the B-25s had the abbreviation FAB painted on the bottom of the left wing and on the top of the right wing. The Bolivian roundel was applied in four positions and the Bolivian flag was painted on both sides of the rudders.

BRAZIL

Brazil was the first Latin American country that had the B-25 bomber in its armed forces. The Fuerza Aérea Brasileira (FAB) was the only Latin American air arm to receive B-25s under the terms of USAAF Lend-Lease during the war. The Lend-Lease deliveries were six B-25Bs, one B-25C, 11 B-25J-15s, and ten B-25J-20s. The six B-25Bs were delivered between August and December 1941. Their U.S. serials were *40-2245, 2255, 2263, 2306, 2309* and *2310*. They were assigned to the Agrupamento de Aviões de Adaptação (Aircraft Adaptation Group) based at Base Aérea de Fortaleza. One of them was used only as a ground instructional airframe.

The B-25 has the privilege of being the first Brazilian aircraft to enter in combat

Left: *The first attack on a German U–boat made by a Brazilian B-25 is nicely illustrated in this 1943 propaganda poster of the of the Departamento de Imprensa e Propaganda (DIP). It says "The FAB hits the enemy target".* (FAB)

The war-weary old B-25C, s/n 41-12872, served in combat in the 82nd Bomb Squadron of the 12th Bomb Group and was baptised with the name of "Desert Lil". She was converted into a transport by the removal of armament, and allocated to the 1° Grupo de Aviação de Caça (1st Fighter Aviation Group) at Pisa. The names "Earthquakers" and "Desert Lil" were retained, but the beautiful painting of the girl on the nose was covered by a coat of paint before delivery. The ship was never officially transferred to the FAB, although she served for several months in the 1st Fighter Aviation Group. She never received a load number, and never belonged to the aircraft of the Brazilian Air Force inventory. After the war, the airplane was recovered and taken back to the United States, where she served for some time. (Cultura Aeronáutica)

in the Second World War. The first attack on a German U-boat made by a Brazilian B-25B was made on 22 May, 1942. Around October 1944, a seventh B-25B was delivered to the Technical Training School. This airplane was s/n 40-2316 and received the Brazilian number 5144.

The B-25C, s/n 41-12558, was delivered in July 1942 to the Technical Training School for training ground crews. This airplane received the serial number 5075. The remaining 21 Lend-Lease aircraft were all B-25Js and delivered in September and October 1944. All were assigned FAB serials in the 5000 and 5100 range. The FAB received one B-25D model in 1944.

In addition, a war-weary B-25C with serial number 41-12872 was allocated to the 1º Grupo de Aviação de Caça, based at Pisa in Italy, 1944-1945, by the 12th U.S. Air Force. This airplane was to be used as the squadrons liaison aircraft, but it was not formally transferred to the FAB. At the end of the war in Europe, it was used to bring back to Italy the Brazilian fighter pilots which had been liberated from POW camps.

The B-25s were used initially for maritime patrol missions. The FAB B-25s participated in the war against the U-boats in the southern Atlantic. Later, with the end of the conflict, the B-25 continued its career in the FAB as bomber and reconnaissance aircraft and for aerial photography. Some were converted for transport, involving the replacement of the glass nose with a solid nose. Yet, some transport B-25s retained the glass nose.

Brazil received additional B-25s from the United States after the war. With the end of the war, thousands of airplanes of the United States became available for military assistance programmes. The USAAF developed the American Republics Projects (ARP). This was essentially a Lend-Lease follow-on programme that gave the USAAF, and later USAF, a legal way to transfer airplanes from its inventory to Latin and South American countries on behalf of the U.S. Department of State. Between July 1946 and October 1947, 64 additional B-25Js were delivered to Brazil under the ARP programme. These were low-time aircraft and most came from storage at Kelly field, Texas. Because of the complex introduction in both old and new units, this introduction proceeded fairly

A masterpiece, this formation of 15 B–25Js of 5º Grupo de Aviação at Natal, 1955. (FAB)

slowly. By January 1949, 43 of these B-25Js were assigned to operating units and the remaining airplanes were waiting at several depots. By April 1949, most of the B-25s had been assigned to the units. Around August 1949, a redistribution of B-25 units began, aiming at four operating units with a strength of about 17 airplanes per unit and an Air Tactical School with five B-25s. By the end of 1952, another unit was equipped with 15 B-25Js. By 1955, there were still a number of 62 B-25s in service with the FAB and mid 1958, the total number of B-25s in the FAB was still 57. But many of these airplanes were inoperative for lack of spares and some undergoing a number of modifications. These aircraft were used in different missions, including photographic reconnaissance by the 1º/10º Grupo de Aviação

and as transports, designated as CB-25. At least five B-25Js were converted to CB-25J and were used as VIP transporter. On some airplanes the greenhouse nose was all or partially faired over and painted. The guns and gun turrets were mostly removed. The B-25s were deployed at several bases and in the final years of their service, the B-25s were used in second-line PR and transport roles.

In Brazil, the B-25 was used in anti-submarine patrol missions during World War II, operating mainly from Fortaleza. Later, with the acquisition of the 64 B-25Js, there were medium bombardment groups at the bases of Recife, Salvador and Fortaleza. The Brazilian B-25 was finally declared surplus in 1974.

Few colours on number 5067 as seen at Natal Air Base. The airplane is a B–25J–20, s/n 44–29497, has the green/yellow rudders and the four–digit number added vertically on the vertical stabilisers. (FAB)

The main FAB units that employed the B-25 were:

Unit	Period	
1º Grupo de Bombardeio Médio	1943 - 1947	This group of the 6º Regimento De Aviação at Recife AFB, received three B-25Bs from Fortaleza in 1942 and the other three from Natal in 1943. It was deactivated in 1947.
3º Grupo de Bombardeio Médio	1944 - 1947	The unit was formed as Unidade Volante do Galeão at Base Aérea do Galeão, Rio de Janeiro in 1943. It flew with B-25Js and other airplanes and was renamed the 3º Grupo De Bombardeio Médio in 1944 and deactivated in 1947.
4º Grupo de Bombardeio Médio	1944 - 1947	The unit was formed as 4º Grupo de Bombardeio Médio at Base Aérea de Fortaleza, in October 1944 with Lockheed Hudsons, North American Texans and B-25Js in the light bomber role. It became the 1º/4º Grupo de Aviação in 1948 with B-25Js and flew them until 1956.
5º Grupo de Bombardeio Médio	1945 - 1947	The 1º Grupo Misto de Aviação received three B-25Bs from Fortaleza in 1942. In 1943, they exchanged them for eight new B-25Js. The unit became the 5º Grupo de Bombardeiro Médio in August 1945 and the 5º Grupo de Aviação in March 1947. It had two squadrons, 1º/5º GAV and 2º/5º GAV and was equipped with B-25s, B-26s and P-47 Thunderbolts. From 1958, the B-25s were replaced with the Douglas B-26 Invader. 5º Grupo was the major user of the B-25 in Brazil.
5º Grupo de Aviação	1947 - 1958	
7º Grupo de Aviação	1947 - 1951	The 2º Grupo de Bombardeio Médio was formed in August 1944, at Base Aérea de Salvador. It received some B-25Js. The group became 1º Esquadrão "Orungan"/7º Grupo de Aviação in November 1947 and flew the B-25s until 1951.
10º Grupo de Aviação	1955 - 1969	The 2º Grupo de Bombardeio Leve was based at Cumbica AFB, São Paulo city, and used a B-25J as a transitional trainer from 1945. It became the 1º/10º Grupo de Aviação in 1947 and operated 6 RB-25s adapted with cameras for photo-reconnaissance from 1955 to 1969.
Agrupamento de Aviões de Adaptação	1942	This was the first Brazilian unit that received the B-25. It was formed in February 1942 at Fortaleza AFB under the supervision of American military. Their mission was the transfer of knowledge to FAB crews to participate in actual combat missions. The group had six B-25Bs and several other airplanes. The unit was deactivated in the same year and the surviving B-25s were distributed to operational units at Natal and Recife Air Force Bases.
Escola Técnica de Aviação (ETAv)	-	This unit was stationed at São Paulo city, with several planes including one B-25C in 1942 and the B-25B from 1944. It was absorbed by the Escola de Especialistas da Aeronáutica (EEAR) at Guaratinguetá, São Paulo State in 1953 and conserved its two B-25s up to this date. The aircraft were based at Hipódromo da Mooca, next to the school.
Escola de Especilistas de Aeronáutica (EEAR)	-	The unit was formed in March 1941 at Base Aérea do Galeão, Rio de Janeiro and moved to Guaratinguetá, São Paulo in May 1950. The school merged with the Escola Técnica de Aviação (ETAv) in October 1953.
1º Grupo de Aviação Embarcada.	-	The group was formed in February, 1957 to operate the Grumman S-2A Tracker. The crews were trained in 1957 and 1958 utilizing a Lockheed Neptune, some SNJ-5C Texans and B-25Js borrowed from others units.
1º Esquadrão Misto de Instrução	1948 - 1951	Was formed in 1948 at Cumbica AFB, São Paulo and had six B-25Js. It was deactivated in 1951.

In addition to the units mentioned, several other operational squadrons, base flights and air depots operated some B-25s until their final retirement in 1974.

Colour and markings

The seven B-25Bs flew in the standard U.S. Air Forces colour scheme of the time. This was Olive Drab upper surfaces and Neutral Grey undersurfaces. Some of the undersurfaces were later painted black. At first they retained their yellow U.S. serial numbers, but later these were replaces with a two-digit white or yellow number on the nose and on the rudders. These were the last two digits of their Brazilian serial number. Later, some of the B-25Bs got the four digit FAB serial number. The Brazilian serial numbers were for the B-25B 5028 to 5033 and 5144. For the B-25C 5075 and the B-25D 5078. The B-25Js received the numbers 5052 to 5072, and the 64 B-25Js after the war received the Brazilian numbers 5077 and 5079 to 5143. The two-digit serial numbers on the natural aluminium finished airplanes were black and added on the nose. The full serial number and aircraft identification number were painted in small figures on the outside of the vertical stabilisers.

The B-25Js were natural aluminium finished. At the time, on old airplanes all camouflage was removed and the new B-25s were delivered uncamouflaged by the factory. After the war, the Brazilian B-25s had a variety of colour schemes. Some airplanes had the upper surfaces painted Dark Green and the lower surfaces Neutral Grey. Others had the upper surface of the fuselage painted white over the natural aluminium.

When the FAB was created, in 1941, the national marking was applied in six positions, four on the wings and two on the rear fuselage. There was also a variant of this marking which had a wider white ring. In early 1942, after the FAB received its first B-25s, the Brazilian stars were applied to these aircraft. There were at least two versions used on the B-25Bs; one with the FAB star painted over the U.S. Insignia Blue disc and one over a white disc. After the end of World War Two, FAB aircraft used the stars in four positions on the wings, two on the rear fuselage and the green/yellow fin flash was painted en-

FAB national marking

Variant with wider white circle

FAB star over the U.S. Insignia Blue disc

FAB star over a white disc

Fin flash entirely on the rudders

This B-25J-15, s/n 44-29007, is taxiing on the tarmac at Guaratinguetá in 1966. The airplane with number 5052 is from the Escola de Especialistas de Aeronáutica (EEAR). The airplane has black engine nacelles and Day-Glo bands around the rear fuselage and nose as well as Day-Glo wing tips. The name Força Aérea Brasileira is added in black on both sides of the fuselage above the wings. Note the double loop antenna on the fuselage. (FAB)

This nose art on "Super Maconha" is the cartoon character Amigo da Onça. This is perhaps the most important character in the history of Brazilian graphic humour in the 20th century.
(Plastimodelismo Santos)

Pericles de Andrade Maranhão

"O Amigo da Onça" (Friend of the Jaguar) was created by Pericles de Andrade Maranhão (1924-1961) and was published as a political cartoon for the first time in the magazine "O Cruzeiro" on 23 October, 1943. Satirical, ironic and critical, he appears on several occasions unmasking his interlocutors or placing them in the most embarrassing situations. This is the edition of October 1956. Maranhão, at left, committed suicide on New Year's Eve 1961.
(Collection Wim Nijenhuis)

tirely on the inside and outside of both rudders. However, B-25s also had the national marking in four positions on the wings and not on the fuselage.

As mentioned above, the Brazilian B-25s had a variety of colour schemes after the war. Some were very colourful like the trainers of the EEAR. These natural aluminium finished or sometimes grey trainers often had black engine nacelles and Day-Glo bands around the rear fuselage and nose as well as Day-Glo wing tips. In some cases, the B-25s were identified with colours for their air base by painting the engine cowling rings. Those of the Salvador Air Base were painted green, the Recife airplanes were red, and the Fortaleza airplanes blue and those from Natal were yellow. During the war, the FAB B-25s hardly knew nose art. After the war, some airplanes had a very modest form of nose art. Some had female or cartoon caricatures and others flew with female names or other names. Sometimes the airplanes carried a unit insignia on the nose.

This is one of the first B-25s of the FAB. It is a B-25B with U.S. serial number 40-2310. She was assigned to the Agrupamento de Aviões de Adaptação at Fortaleza and nicknamed "Lero-Lero". Her Brazilian number was 5033. On 22 May, 1942, this B-25 was the first Brazilian airplane to attack the axis, by dropping her bombs on a submarine off the Northeast Brazilian coast. The B-25 has the standard U.S. camouflage of Olive Drab over Neutral Grey. The serial number on the vertical tail has been painted over and the number 10 and the name "Lero-Lero" are painted yellow on her nose. The roundel on a white disc is in six positions.
(Christopher A. Ebdon, Collection Wim Nijenhuis)

The numbers 5053 and 5054 in flight. Both airplanes are natural aluminium finished and the roundels in six positions. The FAB serial number is vertically applied to the vertical stabilisers. The B-25J-15 airplanes were delivered in 1944 and have the serial numbers 44-29008 and 44-290009 respectively.

(Plastimodelismo Santos)

"O Coyote", number 5064 is a B-25J-20, s/n 44-29494. On the vertical stabilisers in small characters the aircraft identification CB-25J with below the full serial number 5064. "O Coyote" is a fictional character created in 1943 by the Spanish writer José Mallorquí Figuerola (1913-1972), inspired by the character of Johnston McCulley's Zorro. The character is popular in Spain, having been adapted to movies, comic books and radio programmes. The Spanish author ended up writing 192 titles until 1953. The Coyote stories have been released in Brazil between the late 1950s and early 1960. *(Plastimodelismo Santos)*

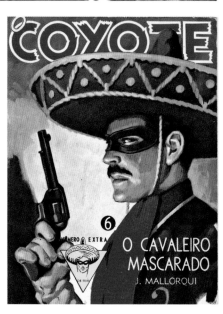

The cover of "O Coyote" Extra Nº 6 of "O Cavaleiro Mascarado" from 1962.

(Collection Wim Nijenhuis)

No. 5068 "El Macho" is another airplane from Natal Air Base. This is also a B-25J-20, s/n 44-29498.

(Plastimodelismo Santos)

Detail of the insignia on one of the ships of 5° Grupo de Aviação. (FAB)

Number 5070 in Olive Drab/ Neutral Grey scheme. This B-25J-20 with serial number 44-29500 was delivered in 1944 under Lend-Lease and received the FAB number 5070. It was operated by the 1°/10° Grupo de Aviação. The Olive Drab/Neutral Grey ship has the roundels without white disc. The airplane is currently preserved at the Museum Eduardo André Matarazzo at Bebeduoro. (FAB)

The same ship after a crash landing. The paint has been removed and the ship was transferred to 5° Grupo de Aviação. The insignia of this group is applied to the nose. At right, she is photographed during a flight over sea. Note that the top turret now has been replaced by an astrodome and she has only the national marking on the left wing and no marking on the fuselage. *(FAB)*

Right: *Airplane no. 5070 is preserved at the Museu Eduardo A. Matarazzo at Bebedouro, São Paulo. There is little colour left.*
(Marco Antônio)

No. 5071 was a B-25J-20, s/n 44-29501. She was based at Natal and nicknamed "Maria Boa". During the Second World War, Maria Boa was an influential woman at Natal. Actually, Maria Boa was just a nickname, her baptismal name was Maria Oliveira Barros (1920-1997). She was the owner of the most famous and busiest nightclub in the city of Natal. Many young American soldiers, who served at Natal, loved to spend the nights in the city along with the girls of Maria Boa. The site provided good music, beautiful women and the best drinks, cigarettes and music were there. *(Aero & Nauta)*

A fully armed number 5085 takes off for a new mission.
(FAB)

Below: *Aircraft No. 5092 was based at Recife and went later to the Escola de Especilistas de Aeronáutica (EEAR).*
(Collection Wim Nijenhuis)

A picture of No. 5097 before she was painted in bright national Brazilian colours. This B-25 was configured for freight and pas-senger transport. For this configuration, all weapons were removed and the fuselage and instruments were modified. She was painted green, yellow, blue, white and black. The airplane was called "Super Maconha". At right, the colourful airplane after the conversion.
(FAB)

No.5111 at Base Aérea de Natal. This B-25J had a little nose art on her nose. (FAB)

Centre: An example of the nose art on Brazilian B-25s in the 1970s. This is a CB-25J
number 5127 called "O Macacão". The airplane
with U.S. serial number 44-30069 flew with
the maintenance unit Parque de Aeronáutica de
São Paulo. This maintenance unit was formed
in 1936 as Parque Aeronáutica of the 2° Regi-
mento de Aviação. It became an independent
unit as Parque de Aeronáutica de São Paulo in
May 1941 and got its current name Parque de
Material Aeronáutico - São Paulo (PAMA-SP)
in January 1974. This ship is overall polished
aluminium with a white fuselage top, and the
lower areas of the engine nacelles and cowling rings are black. The wingtips are Day-Glo.
The airplane is now on display at the Museum
Aerospacial at Campos dos Afonsos Air Force
Base, Rio de Janeiro. *(FAB)*

Above: No. 5118 of 5°
Grupo de Aviação at Natal
in the final for the landing.
The ship is unarmed. *(FAB)*

This B-25J-25, s/n 44-30245, is Olive Drab/Neutral Grey and
has a small number FAB5133 painted on the nose. The airplane
belonged to 1° Grupo de Bombardeio Médio, 5° Grupo de Aviação
and is nowadays displayed at the Praca das Velhas Águias at Natal
Air Force Base. *(FAB)*

No. 27 is taxiing in Sao Paulo. On the nose the insignia of Parque
de Aeronáutica de São Paulo. The insignia of the current name
Parque de Material Aeronáutico - São Paulo (PAMA SP) is
slightly different but the clown has been retained. *(FAB)*

Left:
A nice action shot of a camouflaged B-25J No. 5141, with all the guns removed. (Plastimodelismo Santos)

Number 27 in action in a paint-ing from the Museu Aeroespacial at Rio de Janeiro. (Museu Aeroespacial)

A picture of number 5136, a B-25J model delivered in 1947. The airplane was based at Natal. The insignia of the Base Aérea de Natal (BANT) is added on her nose. The engine cowling rings are yellow.

(Plastimodelismo Santos)

A part of the Brazilian Air Force B-25 strength. Here are ten B-25Js at the flight line. The two airplanes in front on the right are 5126 and 5143. (Collection Wim Nijenhuis)

No. 5143 at Natal Air Base. On the nose is written "Comigo a pisada é essa!", meaning "This is the foot-step with me!". The airplane crashed in Recreio dos Bandeirantes, Rio de Janeiro on 31 October, 1968, killing the entire crew of the EEAR. (FAB).

These two colourful ships of the EEAR are B-25J-20, s/n 44-29495, registered as number 5065 and again number 5143. Both seem to be camouflaged overall grey. The natural aluminium finished or grey trainers of the EEAR often had black engine nacelles and Day-Glo bands around the rear fuselage and nose as well as Day-Glo wing tips. (FAB)

A post-war formation of Brazilian B-25s. The airplanes are overall natural aluminium finished with green/yellow rudders. The engine nacelles are painted black.

(Defesa Aérea & Naval)

CHILE

The Chilean Air Force received 12 B-25s. On 21 March, 1930, the Air Force became an independent service and was called Fuerza Aérea de Chile (FACh). During the 1930s, the FACh received aircraft from Great Britain, Germany and Italy. In 1941, the FACh received larger quantities of training aircraft and also some combat aircraft through Lend-Lease agreements during the next years. The history of the B-25 in the FACh began in July 1946, when at Base Aérea de Quintero activities were started for two instruction courses: one for the twin-engine B-25J bomber and another for the single-engine P-47 fighter. In 1946, the country received 12 B-25J bombers. These aircraft which were almost new initially belonged to the USAAF. In October 1946, one of the B-25s suffered an accident at the base and was removed from the inventory, leaving only 11 operational B-25s. In January 1947, the FACh had a number of officers graduated as B-25 pilots, bombardiers and mechanics for the maintenance of the new twin-engine bombers.

After the air and ground crew instruction, the U.S. Government offered the bombers to the FACh, however, the Chilean High Command did not contemplate the acquisition of these aircraft, which is why they rejected this offer. The B-25s were parked in the open air without flight activity and maintenance and pending the decision of

Number 803 with six other ships of the Fuerza Aérea de Chile with crew members of Grupo de Aviación 8. (FACh)

the U.S. Government either to persuade the FACh to acquire them as yet, or to assign them according to the American Republics Projects programme to another South American country. In March 1947, the High Command again confirmed the initial decision not to acquire these planes. From that moment began a long period of discussions and in the beginning of July 1947, negotiations seemed to end well. It was not until early October that the 11 Mitchells were incorporated into the FACh. Their U.S. serial numbers were: 44-30252, 30272, 30373, 30274, 30392, 30401, 30412, 30413, 30416, 30445 and 30465. Then retraing began of staff that had followed the courses at the end of 1946 and inspection of each of the aircraft. In this way, the B-25 began to operate effectively in the FACh from November

1947. The airplanes got the Chilean serial numbers 801 to 811, reserved for the bombers.

The aircraft at Quintero served as the basis for the formation of Grupo de Aviación 8. This unit was formed on 19 May, 1948, as Grupo de Bombardeo Pesado N° 1 and was renamed Grupo de Aviación 8 in 1949. They began to develop manoeuvres in support of the army and the navy, as well as other activities such as logistics, air photography, instrument flight training and training of air gunners. The busy summer of 1948 would start with the normal development of instruction for new crews, carrying out patrols and training exercises and activities of combat. The constant movement at the air base of Quintero, whose facilities accommodated a large number and diversity of aircraft, gave an atmosphere like an air war. Mid 1948, one of the B-25s had several technical problems and the number of operational aircraft dropped to ten. In November 1948, the B-25s of the group took part in the manoeuvres that were held in the Antofagasta area. In December 1949, the B-25s conducted exercises of high-level bombing and took part in exercises combined between the army and the FACh carried out near Los Vilos in the Province of Choapa. In 1949, there remained a monthly average of only five aircraft at the flight line, reflecting the increasing and high wear of the ten airplanes of the group. By June 1952, two of the B-25s were removed from the inventory, leaving a total of eight. The remaining B-25s were given a new lease of life by being approved for MDAP Grant Aid spares and maintenance support, as well as for special depot maintenance tools and equipment.

COLOURS AND MARKINGS

All B-25s supplied to Chile were delivered in natural metal finish with a black anti-glare panel applied to the fuselage in front of the cockpit. The wing tips were painted Day-Glo. The national markings consisted of a white star on both sides of the bright blue painted rudders. The Chilean roundels were on the upper right wing and the lower left wing. The serial numbers were painted in black on both sides of the rear fuselage, the upper left and the lower right wing.

The Chilean B-25s had no further nose art or inscriptions. At the time the B-25s were at Cerro Moreno, they had a unique emblem, which consisted of a condor holding a bomb in attitude of bite. This new emblem of the Grupo N° 8 was the emblem that the unit adopted in Cerro Moreno. So this emblem became to the first logo of the Grupo N° 8.

FACh roundel

White star on both sides on blue rudders

The eight airplanes were combat ready at the end of September 1953 and remained at Quintero until the end of 1954. In November, 1954, they would move to a new destination. At that time, the High Command considered it necessary to establish a group of information in the southern region Punta Arenas. So three B-25s that were in the best airworthy condition (Nos. 806, 809 and 811) received a colour and for the first time the top of the engine nacelles was painted entirely gloss black. In January 1955, they finally were transferred to Base Aérea Cerro Moreno, leaving the rest at Quintero. The last FACh B-25 that flew in Chile was number 806. It made an emergency landing at Cerro Moreno in May 1956, meaning the end of service of the B-25 in Chile.

This is a well-known picture of airplane number 801. The same ship is seen in a beautiful painting.

(Collection Wim Nijenhuis, Museo Nacional Aeronáutico y del Espacio)

Number 803 of the Grupo de Bombardeo Pesado Nº 1, later renamed Grupo de Aviación 8. The pennant on the fuselage nose was used only on number 803, since it carried the commander of the unit. The parts of the pennant that are darker were yellow. A black number 3 is applied on the front of the nose glazing below the machine gun.
(Museo Nacional Aeronáutico y del Espacio, Collection Danilo Villarroel Canga)

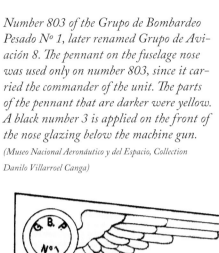

Three B-25s in flight. These are the last three numbers of the Chilean B-25s. Number 810 made a crash landing in April 1950, reducing the number of FACh B-25s to nine at the time.
(Museo Nacional Aeronáutico y del Espacio)

The three B-25Js with the numbers 806, 809 and 811 look like new before they move to Cerro Moreno. Note the top of the engine nacelles are painted gloss black. These three B-25s were the last in service of the FACh and were removed from the inventory in 1956.
(Museo Nacional Aeronáutico y del Espacio)

More than half of the Chilean B-25 fleet can be seen in this picture. Number 804 and six other B-25Js of the Fuerza Aérea de Chile. The airplanes are seen at Quintero Air Base in August 1949. They served with the Grupo de Aviación 8. (FACh)

Emblem of Grupo N° 8 on the nose of number 811 at the time it was stationed at Cerro Moreno. This emblem, which consisted of a condor holding a bomb in attitude of bite, became the first emblem of Grupo N° 8. The condor, the most significant bird of prey from the Andes, is a recurring theme in Chilean arms insignia.
(Collection Danilo Villarroel Canga)

Engine maintenance on number 811, one of the three B-25s at Cerro Moreno.
(Collection Wim Nijenhuis)

COLOMBIA

During the Second World War, Colombia received modern American trainers, although they could also be used for combat duty. Except for anti-submarine patrols there were few wartime engagements. On 15 July, 1942 the Air Force became an independent service and was named Fuerza Aérea Nacional (FAN). Only two years later, on 31 December, 1944, the service was renamed Fuerza Aérea Colombiana (FAC). Soon after the war, the FAC acquired notable amounts of surplus American equipment including P-47 Thunderbolts and A-26 Invaders. In 1949 and 1950, the FAC operated three groups with three operational squadrons each. Despite tensions with neighbours, internal political upheavals and economic uncertainty, the FAC grew and evolved with, and took advantage of all the latest aerospace technologies. Its main combat missions were dealing with FARC guerrillas and narcotic traffickers.

In October 1946, the Fuerza Aérea Colombiana received three B-25Js under the American Republics Projects programme. Because of long negotiations, the airplanes were formally handed over to the FAC on 21 July, 1947. Their U.S. serials were 44-30358, 30397 and 30408. The three airplanes were all B-25J-25 models. They were assigned the FAC serials 657, 658 and 659, although not necessarily in the order of their USAAF serials. The B-25s were assigned to 1° Escuadrón de Bombardeo Ligero. This unit was formed in 1947, when the B-25s arrived. Between 1947 and 1953 they were stationed at the Base Aérea Capitán Germán Olano Moreno. This base is located in Palanquero, near Puerto Salgar, in the Cundinamarca department of Colombia.

Around March 1949, the B-25s flew a number of patrol missions over the Leticia region, at the border triangle of Colombia, Peru and Brazil. Airplane number 657 crashed in April 1949. By May 1950, the two airplanes remained operational but were no longer assigned to the tactical unit. They were assigned to the Maintenance and Supply Depot at Germán Olano Moreno at Palenquero. In 1952, the two airplanes were given a new lease of life by being approved for MDAP Grant Aid spares and maintenance support. By February 1953, they were assigned again to the 1° Escuadrón de Bombardeo Ligero. By January 1956, only one remained in the active FAC inventory. The B-25 disappeared from the FAC inventory in October, 1958.

One of the three post-war B-25J-25s of the Fuerza Aérea Colombiana. This is number 657. In this picture, the colours of the fin flash have not been applied on the rudders. (FAC)

COLOUR AND MARKINGS

The three Colombian B-25s were clean machines and delivered in natural metal finish with a black anti-glare panel applied to the fuselage in front of the cockpit. The national markings consisted of the Colombian roundel on the upper left wing and the lower right wing. At the time, the FAC had two versions. One until 1953 with a nine pointed white star and one with a five pointed white star since 1953. Probably both versions were used on the B-25s.

The Colombian serial numbers were painted in black on both sides of the rear fuselage and repeated in small figures on the nose. The numbers were also applied in large figures on the upper right and the lower left wing. The letters FAC and the serial number were applied on the outside of the vertical stabilisers. The Columbian fin flash was fully painted over both sides of the rudders. The engine cowlings were painted yellow.

An excellent in flight computer animation of number 658 that show the colours of the Colombian Air Force.
(Jota05/warthunder.com)

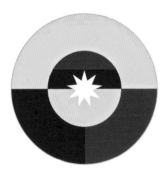

FAC roundel until 1953

FAC roundel since 1953

Fin flash

A poor but interesting picture. A colourized picture of number 658. At right, another picture of 658. Her number is missing on the fuselage. (FAC, Fotos de Colombianos)

B-25 number 659 in flight and with full armament on the ground.
(FAC, Javier Ordoñez J.)

CUBA

The Cuban Air Force received six B-25s. One batch of four and a batch of two. Unfortunately, information about Cuban Mitchells as well as photos, are very rare. In 1913, the Cuerpo de Aviación del Ejército de Cuba (CAEC) was created. In 1934, the service was divided into the Cuerpo de Aviación del Ejército de Cuba and the Aviación Naval. In April 1952, a reorganisation combined both army and naval aviation elements in a semi-autonomous force with the titel Fuerza Aérea del Ejército de Cuba (FAEC).

Early in 1947, many U.S. surplus aircraft were delivered to the Cuban Air Force under the American Republics Projects programme. In July 1947, four B-25Js were purchased from the ARP programme. Three were B-25J-25 models with U.S. serial numbers 44-30095, 30326 and 30348. They received the Cuban serial numbers 303, 304 and 305 respectively. The fourth airplane was a B-25J-15 model with s/n 44-28848 and was assigned number 302. In October 1947, the CAEC acquired two more B-25s via the revolutionary Fuerza del aire de Liberacion del Caribe when they surrendered to the Cuban government. These were a B-25H-5 with s/n 43-4536 and Cuban registration 300 and a B-25G-1 with s/n 42-32385 with number 301. Actually, the latter was a B-25C-15 model and was one of the five C-15s which were modified by North American Aviation into a canon nose B-25G-1 model.

Pictures of Cuban B-25s are very rare. These three airplanes were purchased from the ARP programme and are the B-25J-25 models with the numbers 303, 304 and 305. The picture was taken prior to 1953. (Dan Hagedorn)

The B-25 bomber unit was simply called Escadrón de Bombardero. The unit was formed in 1939 as Escuadrón de Observación y Bombardeo. During the 1950s, the unit was renamed Escuadrón de Bombardero. During 1953 the name 2. Escuadrón de Bombardero was adopted for a short while, but later changed to Escuadrón de Bombardero again. By January 1954 the operating unit was redisignated as Escuadrón de Bombardero "4. de Septiembre". The unit was based at Base Aérea Campo Columbia at Havana. This air base became operational in 1935.

By November 1948, the old B-25C was withdrawn from service and was used for spare parts. In 1950, three B-25s were refurbished with the aid of the USAF Mission and the fourth via the USAF Mobile Air Depot at Brookley Air Force Base, Mobile, Alabama. By 1953, the B-25s were mainly demilitarised and by August 1953, special USAF teams from San Bernadino Air Material Area (SBAMA) at Norton Air Force Base, California, re-installed the necessary parts and equipment making the airplanes combat-ready. The top turrets were deleted as well as the canon of the B-25H. Early in 1957, the three B-25Js and the B-25H ended their activities in Cuba and were returned to the USAF and subsequently assigned to Urugay. The Cuban B-25s were used for transition training, coastal patrols, and against revolutionary activities.

COLOUR AND MARKINGS

Left: National marking until 1955

Centre: National marking 1955-1959

Right: Fin flash

Number 303 is lined up in front of the headquarters building at Campo Columbia near Havana, in the 1950s. Camp Columbia was built by the U.S. military in the 1890s. When the U.S. left Cuba in 1909 it became the headquarters for the Cuban Military. Campo Columbia was located west of Havana in the area known as Marianao. The base was renamed Campo Libertad in 1961. (Dan Hagedorn)

The Cuban B-25s were overall natural metal finished. Until 1955, the national marking was applied in four positions, above and below each wing. This marking used by the Cuban military aviation, then Cuerpo de Aviacion del Ejercito de Cuba, was a blue disc, with an inscribed red triangle pointing downwards and a white star within the triangle. From 1955 to 1959, the roundel used by the then named Fuerza Aérea del Ejército de Cuba (FAEC) was a white star with red border and blue side bars. This marking was displayed in six positions, above and below each wing and on each side of the rear fuselage. It is not certain whether the B-25s have flown with this marking. In 1959 and 1962, after the disappearance of the B-25s in Cuba, the marking was changed again.

The Cuban national flag was used as a fin flash. It was painted on both sides of the whole rudders.

The Cuban serial numbers began with number 1 and were used in chronological order as aircraft arrived in the Air Force. From 1928 on serials started again with 1 as most of the present aircraft were destroyed during a cyclone. The six B-25s had the Cuban serial numbers 300 to 305 applied on the rear fuselage in large black figures.

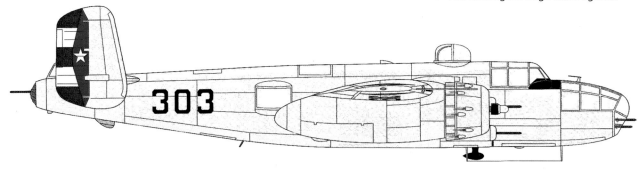

Natural aluminium finished B-25 of the Escuadrón de Bombardero in the early 1950s. The B-25J-25 with U.S. serial number 44-30095, received the Cuban serial number 303.

DOMINICAN REPUBLIC

B-25H-1, s/n 43-4106, still in the U.S. and stored as surplus at Searcy Field, Stillwater, Oklahoma in 1946. The airplane arrived in the Dominican Republic in October 1950 and was already withdrawn from use due to lack of spares by November 1950. (Woody Harris)

In 1949, dictator Rafael Trujillo was looking for airplanes for his air force including B-25s. He used the services of George C. Stamets, technical advisor to the Dominican Air Force. During World War Two, Stamets served as a Marine Corps torpedo pilot in the Pacific. After the war, he served as executive officer of the U.S. Naval Mission in the

Between 1950 and 1952, five B-25s were delivered to the Aviación Militar Dominicana of the Dominican Republic. El Arma de Aviación del Ejército Nacional was formed in 1932 as part of the Dominican Army. The service was renamed Compañia de Aviación del Ejército Nacional in October, 1942. During World War Two, the Dominican Republic received limited quantities of Lend-Lease military equipment and in 1947, it received again large quantities of aircraft as fighter-bombers and trainers from the United States. In the process the Compañia de Aviación expanded and became an independent service in February 1948, and was renamed Cuerpo de Aviación Militar Dominicana. The Air Force underwent several name changes during the 1950s. It was being known as the Aviación Militar Dominicana (AMD) during 1952 to 1955 and 1957 to 1962, and as the Fuerza Aérea Dominicana (FAD) during 1955 to 1957. In 1962, it came to be known again as the Fuerza Aérea Dominicana. By 1956 the FAD had about 240 aircraft. During the next years,

Ex FAD 2502, the B-25H-10, with s/n 43-4999, withdrawn from use and derelict at Mercer County Airport, West Trenton, New Jersey, during 1957 to 1960. She is seen here sitting derelict at the airfield in the late 1960s. (Collection Gary Fitton)

most of the post-war equipment was at the end of its useful life. After the assassination of President Trujillo in 1961, funds for the Air Force decreased and in 1963, the FAD had only 110 aircraft.

Dominican Republic to develop an air force and set up a pilot's training program. Mid 1949, Stamets was negotiating for three B-25s in the U.S. and, although they were purchased, the first airplane actually arrived only in April 1950.

Number 2501, an overall natural aluminium finished B-25J with a strafer gun nose near Ciudad Trujillo (now Santo Domingo) in 1950 or 1951. The engine nacelles are black. (Dan Hagedorn)

The first of the three B-25s was a B-25H-10 with s/n 43-4999 and the second was a de-militarised B-25J-10 with s/n 43-36075. The third was a demilitarised B-25H-1 with s/n *43-4106* and a fourth airplane joined them and was a B-25C-1 with s/n 41-13251. The third and fourth airplanes arrived only in October 1950. Finally in 1951, a fifth B-25 was acquired in the U.S. and was a B-25G-10 with s/n *42-65168*. The B-25s served for a very short time. By July 1952, three of the airplanes had been traded in and were in Miami for further sale. These were the B-25C, the B-25J and the B-25H-10. The H-1 s/n *43-4106* was already withdrawn from use due to lack of spares by November 1950 and the fifth, the G model, was the last operational B-25 until September 1969 when it was sold to a Florida firm. This airplane was probably converted into a VIP transport.

The B-25s were assigned to Escuadrón de Caza-Bombardeos "Leonidas" based at Base Aérea Trujillo. This was the major air base in the country, constructed east of Santo Domingo. It was originally called Base Aérea Trujillo, but after the dictator's assassination in 1961, it was renamed San Isidro.

COLOUR AND MARKINGS

As far as known, the Dominican B-25s were natural aluminium finished. The engine nacelles were fully or partially painted black. The national marking was displayed in two positions on the rear fuselage sides of the airplane and on the upper left wing and lower right wing. The fin flash was displayed on the outside of the rudders. The Dominican serial number was black and displayed on the rear fuselage sides and on the upper right wing and lower left wing. The airplanes were given the serials 2501 to 2505. Different sources give different numbers for the B-25s. Therefore, it is not entirely clear which airplane had which Dominican number.

National marking

Fin flash

Crew members in front of number 2501.
(FAD)

Centre: *The B-25J at West Trenton. The airplane still has some remnants of the Dominican national markings and the airplane number is still faintly visible. The airplane was struck off charge in 1952 and went to the civil market registered as N3969C. She was reported derelict at West Trenton from 1958 to 1969. In 1969, she was broken-up and scrapped.*
(Collection Gary Fitton)

It looks like the same B-25J, but this airplane has the post-war modified engines with the larger boxy air intake scoops made by the U.S. companies Hughes and Hayes in the mid 1950s. The airplane still has some remnants of the Dominican national markings. So the question is whether this is the same B-25J or is it another modified airplane?
(Dan Hagedorn)

ECUADOR

The Air Force of Ecuador acquired only a single B-25J. This airplane served in the USAF until 1959, when it was sold as surplus. It was a B-25J-30 with s/n *44-86866*, operated with the civil registration N9069Z in the U.S. and was used in Latin American cargo operations. The airplane was impounded for carrying contraband cargo at Guayaquil, Ecuador in 1965. It was transferred to the Fuerza Aérea Equatoriana (FAE) in 1970, although it never flew with the FAE. In the middle of the 1970s, it was displayed at the Museo Aeronáutico de la Fuerza Aérea Ecuatoriana at Quito. The museum was founded in April 1972 and from October 1986 located at the former Air Base of Mariscal Sucre of Quito.

This picture was probably taken late 1980s or early 1990s. (Dan Hagedorn)

COLOUR AND MARKINGS

The B-25 was initially painted in fictional colours of the FAE. It was painted light grey and it had the Ecuadorian flag as a fin flash on the rudders. There were no national markings on the wings and fuselage and it had a red nose front and red engine cowling rings. For a time, it had the letters FAE painted in black on the nose. Curiously, in 2012 it was repainted in the colours of "Apache Princess", a B-25 that flew with the 501st Bomb Squadron of the "Air Apaches", the 345th Bomb Group of the USAAF.

At left, another picture of the airplane taken in March 2010. Time has taken its toll, there is little more colour left. At right in 2012, now with a new paint and nose art displayed as "Apache Princess" of the famous 345th Bomb Group "Air Apaches" of the U.S. Army Air Forces.
(Javier Franco "Topper")

HAITI

Haiti had only one B-25. The bomber was purchased by the "Haitian Coalition", one of the opposition groups to Duvalier's regime based in New York. The Corps d'Aviation d'Haiti was formed in 1943 with some airplanes from the United States. Its main task was transport and communication. Headquarters were at Bowen Field, Port-au-Prince, a former U.S. military airfield, which was the main air base of the Haitian Air Force until 1994. In 1965, the airport opened as François Duvalier International Airport, named after then Haitian president François "Papa Doc" Duvalier and in 1986, the airport was renamed Port-au-Prince International Airport. During the 1940s, Haiti received small quantities of training aircraft. The first combat aircraft arrived in the country in 1950. In 1958, the name of Haiti's military was changed to Forces Armées d'Haïti (FAd'H).

The B-25 was an ex USAF B-25J-25 with serial number *44-30484*. It was delivered to the Royal Canadian Air Force in 1952 and numbered 5250. It was sold to the civil market in 1961 and registered as N92882. In 1963, it went to A&A Enterprises at Bozeman, Montana. Later, the B-25 was purchased from the Hamilton Aircraft Group in Tucson, Arizona and subsequently moved to Ft. Lauderdale, Florida. On 20 May, 1968, the B-25 took off from the Bahamas towards Haiti. It had on board ten bombs to be dropped over strate-

gic military points in Haiti. A few hours later, the B-25 dropped as planned five bombs over the National Palace, but none of the bombs exploded. The airplane continued towards Bowen Field and dropped another bomb, which again did not explode. The airplane went back to the Bahamas, leaving nevertheless a general panic in Port-au-Prince. In the afternoon, the B-25 (with a DC-3 and a Cessna) was getting ready to

take off for the second phase of the operation. The Cessna landed first in Cap-Haïtien International Airport, followed by the DC-3 and the B-25. But the operation was a total failure, and gave greater incentive to Duvalier to extend his wave of terror towards the whole area. The members of the commando were hunted down by Duvalier's troops; some of them were killed, and several heads were brought in buckets to Du-

The only B-25 of the Forces Armées d'Haïti. In 1968, this B-25J-25, with U.S. serial number N92882, tried to bomb the National Palace in Port-au-Prince and did not make it out of the country. Although the colours are weathered, the B-25 is still painted in the RCAF scheme. (Larry Johnson)

Despite the poor quality, these are very rare pictures of the Haitian B-25 at François Duvalier International Airport, formerly called Bowen Field. The airplane has no national markings on her fuselage.
(www.servicepals.com)

valier in the National Palace. A few were arrested, tortured and imprisoned for years. The B-25 stayed behind and the Haitian Air Force now had one good B-25 which they have repaired and flown to Port-au-Prince weeks later at the order of Francois Duvalier, who personally went to the airport to oversee the operation. Later, the B-25 was left parked for years by the taxi way and reported derelict there in 1976.

COLOUR AND MARKINGS

The B-25 in Haiti still had her RCAF scheme. She was natural aluminium finished with a white fuselage top and a red lightning bolt on the fuselage. It is not known if she had the national roundels or an airplane number.

Another rare picture of the Haitian B-25 taken in March 1972 at Port-au-Prince. The aircraft is accompanied by an F-51D and T-28S Fennec. (aviadejavu.ru)

Mexico

In the post-war period the Fuerza Aérea Mexicana (FAM) went through a number of changes, being re-equipped with the majority of the Lend-Lease aircraft it had received during the war years. It had a large number of combat aircraft. In March and May 1945, three B-25Js were delivered to the FAM. These planes did not come through the Lend-Lease Programme but via the USAAF Demonstration Flight Project. The three B-25s were all J-30 models with the U.S. serial numbers *44-86712*, *44-86717* and *44-86718*. They actually arrived in Mexico in December 1945. These aircraft were assigned to the Escuadrón Bombardero Ligero, a Mexico City-based light bomber squadron.

The B-25s received the letter code BMM, which stood for Bombardero Mediano Mitchell, and a four digit number. Number 44-86712 received the letter/number code BMM3501, *44-86717* became BMM3502 and *44-86718* became BMM3503. In January 1949, the three B-25s were assigned to Escuadrón Aéro 206 part of 4/o Grupo Aéreo at Cozumel, Quintana Roo. After 1954, BMM3502 and BMM3503 were transferred to the mechanics training school near Mexico City and were finally scrapped. So, by June 1957, only one B-25 was still on strength. The B-25s were employed from 1945 for patrol missions over the Mexican waters in the Gulf of Mexico and Caribbean Sea and the last one is believed to have served until the 1960s.

Two of the three B-25s intended for the Mexican Air Force but still with the USAAF markings. Above is number 44–86718 which received the Mexican serial number BMM3503.
(Aviacion Militar Mexicana)

One of the three B-25s of the Fuerza Aérea Mexicana in natural aluminium finish. This is BMM3501, a B-25J-30 with s/n 44-86712. It is seen here in 1946 or 1947 at Guatemala City Air Base, now La Aurora International Airport, in Guatemala.
(Collection Wim Nijenhuis)

COLOUR AND MARKINGS

National marking

Fin flash

The B-25s arrived in natural aluminium not wearing any other colour. The anti-glare panels in front of the cockpit and the inner side of the engine nacelles were dark green. After assignment to Escuadrón Aéro 206, they were quite colourful. They received red paint on the engine cowlings, and the engine nacelles were also painted, but here there is no absolute certainty. The fuselages upper surfaces were painted light grey and the under surfaces off-white. The name Fuerza Aerea Mexicana was spelled in black full over the top fuselage above the wings area. The final scheme was light grey upper surfaces with off- white lower surfaces, blue engine nacelles and red engine cowlings and wing tips. But also is mentioned a natural metal finished upper fuselage with light grey lower fuselage.

The Mexican national marking, the red-white-green triangle, was carried in six positions, two on the rear fuselage and four on both wings. The rudder markings consisted of green-white-red stripes on both sides. The serials were added in black on the vertical stabilisers. BMM3503 carried a personal crew insignia consisting of a tiger in a white circle. Later, she carried the head of an Aztec Eagle Warrior in a circle. This was later modified with the same insignia surrounded by the text "Bombardero Ligero B-25".

BMM3502 is also a B-25J-30, s/n 44-86717. All the machine guns have been removed.
(FAM)

BMM3503 carried a personal crew insignia consisting of a tiger in a white circle. Thereafter, the airplane was provided with the feathered head of an Aztec Eagle Warrior in a circle. This was later modified with the same insignia surrounded by the text "Bombardero Ligero B-25".

(Aviacion Militar Mexicana)

Aztec Eagle Warriors

A painting of an Aztec Eagle Warrior created by the Mexican painter Jesús Helguera (1910-1971). The Aztec Eagle Warriors were without doubt some of the most skilled and feared fighting forces of the Aztec empire. Adorned in feathers, with clothing and shrouds for the head, what mimic the visage of their namesake, the Eagle warriors were surely a splendour to behold. The Aztec empire flourished between the 14th and the 16th century.

(Collection Wim Nijenhuis)

BMM3503 in new colours. After assignment to Escuadrón Aéro 206, it received red paint on the engine cowlings, and the engine nacelles were also painted red, but here there is no absolute certainty. The fuselage and wings have light grey upper surfaces with off-white undersurfaces. The name Fuerza Aerea Mexicanan was spelled full over the top fuselage above the wings area. It has the modified Aztec Eagle Warrior in a circle and on the nose is a unique artwork.

(Aviacion Militar Mexicana, Alfredo Macias Narro)

She looks like new from the factory. The final scheme of BMM3503 was light grey upper surfaces with off-white lower surfaces, blue engine nacelles and red engine cowlings and wing tips. Some sources mention natural metal finished upper surfaces and light grey lower surfaces. But the picture points more in the direction of light grey and white.

(Aviacion Militar Mexicana)

Again BMM3503 but probably at a later stage. The machine guns below the cockpit have been removed as well as the top turret.

(Aviacion Militar Mexicana)

PERU

One of the eight B–25Js of the Fuerza Aérea del Perú in 1947. A clean machine with the red/white/red flag painted on both sides of the rudders. The black serial number on the rear fuselage is probably 461.
(Dan Hagedorn)

The Cuerpo de Aviación del Perú (CAP), in 1950 renamed Fuerza Aérea del Perú (FAP), acquired eight surplus B-25Js in 1947 under American Republics Projects. By November 1946, the formalities for transfer to the CAP of a large batch of aircraft, including eight B-25s as well as maintenance and support equipment, spare parts, tools and ammunition necessary for their operation began. Given the fact that the airplanes were all second-hand from surplus stocks of war, it required quite a lot of work in Peru before they could be delivered fully operationally in their new operator's conditions. So, the U.S. government scheduled delivery of the airplanes by May of the next year. On 21 July, 1947, with the delivery of the aircraft acquired through the ARP programme, the CAP was finally able to replace the material that it had received between 1943 and 1945. The ceremony took place at the El Pato air base in Talara. Civilian and military representatives of the Peruvian and U.S. governments taking part in the ceremony for the formal final delivery of the first aircraft including the eight B-25J Mitchells. These were all B-25J-25 block models with the U.S. serial numbers 44-29912, 44-30296, 30360, 30361, 30384, 30398, 30403 and 30418. They were assigned to the Escuadrón de Bombardeo Nº 21 at Base Aérea El Pato at Talara. This unit was formed as part of 1° Agrupamiento Aéreo, in 1947 at Talara.

By June 1950, seven B-25s were inoperable because of a lack of spare parts. The unit was then based at Base Aérea Teniente Coronel Pedro Ruiz Gallo at Chiclayo. In 1952, only six B-25s were still operational and by February 1953, of the six B-25s, only two flew regularly. By June 1954, the six airplanes were still on strength. In 1955, only five of the ships were airworthy and the unit was joined by eight B-26 Invaders. By June 1958, the five were still on strength. In 1960, the squadron became Escuadrón de Bombardero Liviano Nº 21 and moved her Invaders to Base Aérea Capitán Guillermo Concha Iberico at Piura. It is not exactly known for how long, the B-25s have been in service. Some sources say that one or two B-25s have flown until the 1960s.

As far as known the only nose art on a Peruvian B-25. The picture was taken in the early 1950s.
(Collection Oscar Gagliardi, Jr.)

COLOUR AND MARKINGS

The eight Peruvian B-25s were natural aluminium finished with probably black anti-glare panels in front of the cockpit and on the inner side of the engine nacelles. The national marking was applied on top of the left wing, under the right wing and on both sides of the rear fuselage. They had a black three-digit serial number in the 400 series. This number was displayed in four positions. Above the right wing and below the left wing and on each side of the rear fuselage. The airplanes had the Peruvian flag as a fin flash on both sides of the rudders. In the 1950s the fin-flash was replaced with a large black letter.

National marking

Fin flash

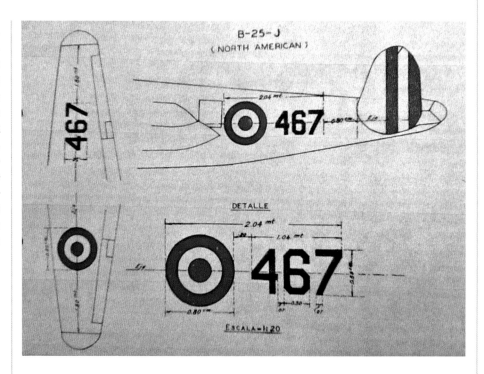

A document from the Fuerza Aérea del Perú showing the national markings, the fin flash and the Peruvian serial numbers on the B-25. (Collection Oscar Gagliardi, Jr.)

A picture of poor quality but rare and probably taken at Chiclayo Air Base. A row of three B-25Js of the Fuerza Aérea del Perú. In front is number 486 with a remarkable band around the fuselage behind the cockpit. (FF.AA Peru)

Below: *Natural aluminium finished B-25 of the Escuadrón de Bombardeo Nº 21 in the 1950s.*

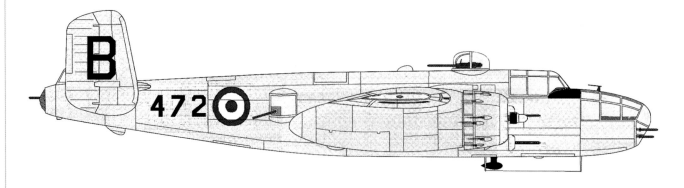

URUGUAY

The Uruguayan Air Force received a total of 15 B-25s. Eleven B-25s were delivered to the Fuerza Aérea Uruguaya (FAU) in 1950 under American Republics Projects. In 1958 a further three B-25Js and one B-25H were delivered. The B-25s carried out transport flights, reconnaissance and photography missions and were used for dropping food and supplies. In January 1949, negotiations were announced to acquire B-25 bombers for the Uruguayan Air Force. At the time the air force was named Aeronáutica Militar. It was renamed Fuerza Aérea Uruguaya (FAU) in December 1953.

The B-25s were acquired by the ARP programme and 11 were delivered. The B-25s were stored at Pyote, Texas and were nearly brand new. After the war, the renamed Pyote Air Force Base was transferred from the 2nd Air Force to the San Antonio Air Tech Service Command and became an aircraft-storage depot. During this time, the base served as a storage facility for as many as 2,000 aircraft including B-25s. In December 1949, members of a Uruguayan Commission made preparations for transfer

of the B-25s from Texas to the Grand Central Airport Company, Glendale, California. The airplanes were to be overhauled here. After the war, thousands of P-51s, C-47s, B-25s and other aircraft transitioned through Grand Central Airport for updating and refurbishment.

After overhaul in California, the airplanes were flown to Uruguay by crews of the Aeronáutica Militar. The delivery flight from California to San Antonio, Texas to Tampa, Florida, and then via Cuba, Puerto Rico, British Guyana and Brazil, took about two

Uruguayan B-25s in the Californian desert, where their crew members received instruction. Rare colour pictures of nine B-25s of the FAU. The nearest airplanes are G3-152 and G3-153.
(FAU)

and a half weeks and the airplanes arrived on 9 June, 1950. The B-25s flew 8,000 miles from Los Angeles to Montevideo, of which more than half were over water, and about 2000 over jungle area. The airplanes were numbered 150 to 160. This ferry flight was divided into three groups called Esquadrilla A, B and C. The A was commanded by airplane 160 and included the numbers 152, 153, 154 and 157. The B was commanded by number 159 and included 150 and 156. The third Esquadrilla C was commanded by airplane number 158 and flew with the numbers 151 and 155.

On 22 May, 1950, the long journey to Uruguay started. On 23 May, a stop was made at San Antonio, Texas, and one day later at Tampa, Florida. Upon reaching this city, the formation was surprised by a severe storm, forcing it to split up and land at MacDill Air Force Base and Drew Field Municipal Airport. But, they managed to land the airplanes and were highly praised by the local press. On 28 May, after a three days' inspecting of the airplanes, they went to Cuba and the next day to Puerto Rico. On 31 May, they left for British Guyana. In the first days of June, they flew to Brazil and on 9 June they began the last stage of the ferry flight to Uruguay.

After their arrival, the 11 B-25s were assigned to the Grupo de Aviación Nº 3 (Bom-

A clean shiny Mitchell, s/n 44-30593, with Uruguayan number G3-153 of the ferry flight A in 1950. The national marking is applied in four positions on the wings and the ship is unarmed. (FAU)

bardeo) at Base Aérea Gral. Cesáreo Berisso at Carrasco. During 1952, the number of hours of the B-25s had greatly reduced due to the lack of spare parts. One thing was to have aircraft and another to keep them in

the air. The situation was slightly improved, mainly thanks to the inventiveness and initiative of the officers of the group, friendly contacts and good will of some airline pilots, who combined to "import" informally some parts. This situation improved greatly by the Agreement on Military Assistance (MDAP) in 1953.

A first accident with a Uruguayan B-25 occurred on 30 September, 1952. Number G3-155 crashed and broke off the wings, killing the entire crew. By January 1954, the B-25 unit status was nearly zero because of the Uruguayan financial situation and the ten B-25s were grounded. By mid 1954, a U.S. Mission made six B-25s combat-ready again. In 1956, six B-25s were grounded again because of problems with the supply of cylinder exhaust stacks. In 1958, the Government provided funding to overhaul the B-25s and to get four new B-25s. These four new airplanes were received from the Cuban Air Force which replaced its B-25s

Maintenance of airplane number G3-150 during the ferry flight in 1950. This is a B-25J-25 with serial number 44-30269. (FAU)

Airplane G3-157 in April 1950 at the Grand Central Air Terminal, California, during the final stages of its overhaul before the delivery flight in May. This was a B-25J-25 with s/n 44-30735. (Dan Hagedorn)

Centre:
The airplanes number G3-157 and G3-158 during the ferry flight in 1950. Number 158 had the U.S. serial number 44-30743 and was the commanding airplane of the third ferry flight Esquadrilla C. The national markings are clearly visible on the wings. (FAU)

with B-26s. They were overhauled in the U.S. for resupply to Uruguay. The four airplanes were a B-25H model and three B-25J models. They received the Uruguayan serial numbers 161 to 164. Number 161 was delivered in November 1957 and the other three in January 1958. By March 1959, the four new B-25s were being flown and the other old ones were grounded awaiting a major overhaul.

A second accident occurred on 10 July, 1959. Airplane number 161 impacted the ground after a bombing mission, killing five crew members. In 1962, the B-25s were grounded because of the fact that corrosion was found in the central beams of various machines and for most B-25s this corrosion was crucial to their final destination. They were scrapped in 1962.

COLOUR AND MARKINGS

Upon delivery, the B-25s were natural aluminium finished with Uruguayan serial numbers G3-150 to G3-160. G3 was the prefix for the Grupo de Aviación Nº 3 (Bombardeo). From 1941 prefixes for unit identification were used. But in the mid 1950s, this practice was discontinued. The numbers 100 to 199 were used for bombers and crew trainers. With the renumbering the engine nacelles were painted black.

The main national marking was displayed at first in four positions on both wings. From 1953, this was changed and one marking was applied above the left wing and one below the right wing. The inscription "FAU" was usually displayed in two positions,

National marking

Fin Flash, the red band can slant forwards or backwards.

Fully armed B-25s of the FAU. A shot of G3-155 and G3-158. The ship with the number G3-155 is a B-25J-25, s/n 44-30723.
(Collection Wim Nijenhuis)

above the right wing and below the left wing. The fin flash was displayed on both sides of the rudders. Noteworthy is that the red band of the fin-flash can slant both forwards and backwards. Both versions can be seen on the rudders of the B-25s. Some airplanes also had black lower sections on the vertical tails. The serial number was displayed in black on the rear fuselage of the airplane and with small figures also on both sides of the fuselage nose.

In the last years of their service some B-25s had some modest nose art. They had a relatively large shield placed on the left side of the nose. This shield showed a young Indian sitting on a bomb. On front of the shield the name of a tribe or Indian chief was applied. It has been established that the airplane number 150 was "Guenoa", number 151 was "Yaro", number 156 was "Charrúa", number 158 was "Tabaré", number 162 was "Chana", number 163 was "Arachán" and number 164 was "Boanes".

On their way to Uruguay. G3-159 is leading Esquadrilla B which included number 150 in the background and number 156 with the running propeller in the foreground. (FAU)

Some of the airplanes on a stopover during the ferry flight in 1950. Number 160 had the U.S. serial number 44-31190 and was the commanding airplane of Esquadrilla A during the ferry flight to Uruguay. (FAU)

Again number 160 still with the registration G3-160 but now fully unarmed. (FAU)

The FAU was established on 4 December, 1953. This is a phone card of Uruguay's Administración Nacional de Telecomunicaciones (ANTEL) from 2003 to mark the 50th anniversary of the FAU. It shows ship No. 160 in flight. On the back side a picture of number 163.

(Collection Wim Nijenhuis)

Carrasco, 1962. From 1953, the national marking was applied in two positions supplemented by the inscription "FAU" on the wings. The engine nacelles are black. This is a B-25J-25 with s/n 44-30273. The airplane has been completely stripped of her armament, but the top turret is still present. (FAU)

The ex-Cuban Air Force B-25H in her final stage. She had the Uruguayan number 164 and the U.S. serial number 43-4536. Note the difference in the slant of the red bands on the vertical tail surfaces of the ships. (Dan Hagedorn)

The B-25s of the Grupo de Aviación Nº 3 (Bombardeo) carried special insignia and nicknames by the early 1960s. Number 156, which was named "Charrúa", is seen here during service in the 1960s. On the colour pictures, the airplane with a weathered insignia photographed in August 2012 at the Museo Aeronáutico, Montevideo, Uruguay.

(Collection Wim Nijenhuis, Robert Domandl)

Charrúa

Charrúa were South American Indians who inhabited the grasslands north of the Río de la Plata in a territory somewhat larger than modern Uruguay. The Charrúa were hunters and gatherers, and after the introduction of the horse they lived by catching wild cattle. They were fierce in war, using the skulls of their fallen foes as ceremonial drinking cups. It is thought that the Charrúa were driven south into present-day Uruguay by the Guaraní people around 4,000 years ago.

(Collection Wim Nijenhuis)

Left:
23 August, 1961, a great picture of seven B-25s of the Grupo de Aviación Nº 3 (Bombardeo) flying over the Base Aérea Gral. Cesáreo Berisso at Carrasco. We see from left to right the numbers 162, 158, 163, 156, 150 and 164. The seventh airplane is number 151 and is flying next to number 158. (FAU)

VENEZUELA

After the Brazilian Air Force, the Air Force of Venezuela was the largest user of the B-25 in Latin America. It had operated the B-25 between 1947 and 1973. However, there is much uncertainty about the Venezuelan Mitchells. The birth of the Air Force can be traced back to 10 December, 1920. On that date, the Escuela de Aviación Militar Venezolana was formed. After the Second World War, the Air Force was reorganised with American aid, eventually leading to the formal inception of the Fuerza Aérea Venezolana (FAV) on 22 June, 1946.

The first B-25s arrived in Venezuela as part of the ARP agreement between the U.S. and Venezuela. In total, the Venezuelan Air Force received over 40 B-25 medium bombers. The first batch of B-25s arrived in Venezuela during the years 1947 to 1949, and a final batch comprising nine B-25Js arrived in 1963. The FAV was designated to receive three B-25s through the ARP programme on 8 May, 1946. However, they were actually handed over on 28 August, 1947. By May 1948, all three were still in service and the FAV was negotiating for a batch of 12 B-25s stored at Pyote Air Force Base, Texas. They were all B-25J-25 models. These 12 airplanes were officially handed over to the FAV on 4 April, 1949. By October 1949, 15 B-25s were actually on hand, but 7 were inoperable for a number of reasons and one was pending delivery from the U.S. All air-

B-25s of the Escuadrillas A and B of Escuadrón de Bombardeo 40. Two B-25Js with the squadron codes 1-A-40 and 5-B-40. The numbers are applied on the nose and vertical stabilisers. The roundels are of the early type whitout side bars, which means that this picture was taken before 1953. (Collection Omar Quintero)

planes were then assigned to Grupo Mixto de Bombardeo y Transporte No. 0 at Maracay. By January 1950, a total of 16 B-25s was reported and by June of that year, 8 were still out of service.

In 1951, the FAV was reorganised and comprised airplane type specific squadrons. All B-25s were incorporated in an unnumbered Escuadrón de Bombardeo. In the middle of 1952, a second squadron with 10 new B-25s was formed. These 10 airplanes were bought from the U.S. They were mostly ex-Canadian Air Force airplanes and all were

overhauled by L.B. Smith. This company was based at Miami, Florida, and was specialised in conversions of C-46 and C-82 airplanes as well as producing airliner interior components. It was founded in 1947 by company president L.B. Smith, and quickly became one of the foremost aircraft conversion, overhaul and modification centres in the United States. About at the same time one B-25 was bought from the Charles Babb Company in Miami. This was an ex-Dominican Republic airplane and most likely a B-25H model. At the end of 1952 and early in 1953, these new B-25s led to the operation-

Airplane 3-A-40 with full armament during an aeronautical exhibition at Air Base Generalissimo Francisco de Miranda at Caracas, but mostly referred to as La Carlota Air Base. The airplane was B-25J-25 s/n 44-30627, and belonged to Escuadrilla A of Escuadrón de Bombardeo 40. (Collection Antonio Berrizbeitia)

al unit Escuadrón de Bombardeo 40. This had two subordinate squadrons, "A" and "B". Escuadrón de Bombardeo 40 was formed, when the Escuadrón de Bombardeo 3 and Escuadrón de Bombardeo 7 merged in 1952. It was based at Campo de Aviación at Maracay until 1964. After a reorganisation in 1961, the squadron became part of Grupo Aéreo de Bombardeo 13 and was based at Base Aérea Teniente Vicente Landaeta Gil at Barquisimeto. In December 1971, the unit moved to the Base Aérea Teniente Luis Del Valle García at Barcelona.

In 1954, a further 5 B-25s were acquired through the Foreign Military Sales (FMS) provisions of the Military Assistance Programme. By December 1954, the service counted 16 operational B-25Js and one B-25H. In 1956, this was reduced to 15 airplanes. In 1956/1957, 9 of the 15 B-25s were overhauled by L.B. Smith in Miami. In October 1958, 9 B-25s of Escuadrón de Bombardeo 40 were stationed at the Aeropuerto Internacional de Maiquetía. This international airport is located at Maiquetía, about 21 kilometres from downtown Caracas, and is now known as Simón Bolívar International Airport. This detachment was caused by the tensions with the Dominican Republic. The airplanes were present in anti-guerrilla operations and flew four- to six-hour patrol missions.

In December 1963, Venezuela finally acquired 9 low-time ex-Canadian Air Force B-25s. Prior to delivery, they were also overhauled in Miami. In the middle of 1971, a few B-25s were assigned to the Headquarters of the new Grupo 13 at Base Aérea Teniente Luis Del Valle García. The others remained in service with Escuadrón de Bombardeo 40. By November 1973, a few of the still airworthy B-25s joined the headquarters of Grupo 13. From then, the last B-25s were used in a transport role and were gradually withdrawn from service.

The FAV B-25s were operated in actions against the "Porteñazo" and "Carupanazo". These were two unsynchronised military rebellion groups during the presidency of Romulo Betancourt (1959-1964). The B-25s were also utilised in surveillance missions over the Los Monjes islands. These aircraft were used for border surveillance and anti-guerrilla operations. The B-25s ended their

Four B–25Js of the Fuerza Aérea Venezolana in Miami in 1957. From left to right: airplane No. 3–A–40, 5–B–40 and number 3–B–40 of Escuadrón de Bombardeo 40 following completion of overhaul. In 1957, nine B–25s were extensively overhauled by L.B. Smith Aircraft Corporation in Miami. (Dan Hagedorn)

service life in 1973 at Base Aérea Teniente Vicente Landaeta Gil at Barquisimeto, when they were replaced with the North American Bronco OV-10E.

Centre: National marking to 1953

National marking after 1953

COLOUR AND MARKINGS

The B-25s were basically natural aluminium finished with black anti-glare panels on the fuselage nose and inner quarter of the engine cowlings. However, the first B-25s until 1950 had the anti-glare panels probably painted Olive Drab. After 1950, the engine nacelles were painted black. Until about 1953, the national marking was a roundel without side bars and was displayed in six positions, four on the wings and two on the rear fuselage. After 1953, it was a roundel with side bars and displayed in four positions, above the left wing, below the right wing and on each side of the rear fuselage. The fin flash was displayed on both sides of the rudders. The letters FAV were painted in black below the left wing and on the upper right wing.

Right:
Again airplane 5–B–40. It was the former USAAF B–25-J–25 s/n 44-30630. The ship is now unarmed and the top turret has been removed. (FAV)

Less is known about the serial numbers of the first B-25s around 1949. From the early 1930s until the late 1940s, the Venezuelan airplane serials began with number 1 and were assigned in chronological order as airplanes were incorporated in the FAV. From the late 1940s, there was a code system which provided an immediate identification of an airplane's Escuadrilla and Escuadrón. The codes consisted of a plane-in-flight number, an Escuadrilla letter and the Escuadrón number. Thus, for example airplane 5-B-40 was the fifth airplane of Es-

Fin flash

cuadrilla B of Escuadrón de Bombardeo 40. Late in 1966, the FAV changed its aircraft/unit codes into a four digit code. Until 1953, the serial number was displayed in black figures in four positions, on the fuselage nose

This airplane, originally delivered on 4 April, 1949, was a B-25J-25 with U.S. serial number 44-30467. Number 6-A-40 was overhauled by the L.B. Smith Aircraft Corporation at Miami, Florida. Note that by this time the operating unit insignia had been added under the pilot's window. (Dan Hagedorn)

and on the vertical stabilisers. On some airplanes the first digit of the airplane code on the nose was red coloured. After 1953, the codes were applied above the right wing, below the left wing and on each side of the fuselage nose.

The four digit code was applied on the vertical stabilisers. In later years, the insignia of Escuadrón de Bombardeo 40 was located on the left side of the fuselage below the cockpit.

Left:
A clean and shiny machine. Another picture of 6–A-40 with the letters FAV applied on the upper right wing. (FAV)

Number 14-A-40 with two other B-25Js. They were overhauled by L.B. Smith when delivered in the late 1950s. The dorsal turret has been replaced with a small observation dome, and the glass noses have been extensively modified. The national markings on the fuselages have not yet been applied. (Dan Hagedorn)

A nice picture, but unfortunately of poor quality. Five B-25s in a row. From left to right: airplane number 10-A-40, 4-B-40, 9-A-40, 2-B-40 and 10-B-40. Three of the airplanes have the squadron emblem on the nose. Ship 10-B-40 in front has no top turret. *(FAV)*

Nose detail of number 2-B-40 of the Museo Aeronáutico Luis Hernán Paredes, better known as Museo Aeronáutico de Maracay. However, it was originally registered as 15-A-40, became then number 3741 and is seen here representing 2-B-40 with the squadron insignia of Escuadrón de Bombardeo 40.

(Museo Aeronáutico de Maracay)

Believed to be the last two airworthy B-25s of the FAV. The airplanes made a flypast at Maracay before retirement.

(Dan Hagedorn)

The FAV even had this ex-Canadian B-25 with the former strafer nose. Number 11-A-40 has the post-war engine modification and no national marking on the rear fuselage. *(FAV)*

By 1966, the surviving Venezuelan B-25s had
received four-digit random number serials. This
B-25J-5, photographed in 1976, had the U.S. s/n
43-28096. It had the Venezuelan number 3741 and
a faded unit insignia below the bombardier's station.
This ship was one of the last operational examples of
the FAV. At right, a badge of the squadron.

(Dan Hagedorn, Collection Wim Nijenhuis)

Four B-25s of
Escuadrilla B
of Escuadrón de
Bombardeo 40 in
flight. (FAV)

Left:
A B-25 of the Fuerza Aérea
Venezolana in her aftermath
and photographed in 1968 at
the Aeropuerto Internacional
de Maiquetía. She has no serial
number or aircraft code.

(Collection David Lawrence)

Spectacular pictures of B-25s of the Fuerza Aérea Venezolana in action. However, it looks more like an early form of photoshopping. A Venezuelan military retrospective of the ARV Zulia D-21 with four B-25s in 1954. The ARV Zulia D-21 was a Venezuelan destroyer. Named for the Venezuelan state of Zulia, it was the leader of the 2nd Destroyer Division and the second ship of the Nueva Esparta class. The ship was built for the Venezuelan naval forces in the early 1950s by Vickers Shipbuilding and Engineering, Ltd. This was a shipbuilding company based at Barrow-in-Furness, Cumbria in northwest England that built warships, civilian ships, submarines and armaments. The other picture is showing three of the four B-25s in formation with four P-47s and another P-47D Thunderbolt making a very low pass over a Lockheed L12A of the FAV. *(Museo Aeronáutico de la Aviación)*

Two Venezuelan B-25s at the end of their service waiting for their final destination. *(Dan Hagedorn)*

FINAL WORD

Both during and after the Second World War, many countries have had B-25s in their armed forces' inventories. These were either or not provided with camouflage or special paint jobs. Also these countries introduced new certain forms of nose art. The military forces of some countries flew the B-25 until the late 70s of the last century. The majority of the aircraft were scrapped after retirement from the service, putting an end to an illustrious career of the military role of the B-25. However, some B-25s also performed a new role. After the war, many airplanes of the military were bought for private use. This was also the case with the B-25. Several private firms used the B-25 for their business purposes. Also these ships were sometimes embellished with the most beautiful colour schemes. The B-25 also became known for its use in the film industry. Fortunately, nowadays there are dozens of B-25s preserved and on display in various museums worldwide. And today, there are many more to be seen in airworthy condition as a warbird with sometimes beautiful nose art. So, the phenomenon of nose art on old airplanes still exists today. Mostly those are derived from the original art displayed by their counterparts in World War II. Therefore, a further study into the civilian B-25s would be in place. In the future, I hope to be able to encapsulate it in a final volume 3 of "Mitchell Masterpieces" about the civil use of the B-25.

Post-war B-25s as aerial fire fighters in Canada.

Page left:
Warbird "Yankee Warrior" in April 2017 at the B-25 gathering at Grimes Field, Ohio, for the 75th Anniversary of the Doolittle Raid.
(Wim Nijenhuis)

INDEX

BIBLIOGRAPHY

Mitchell Masterpieces Vol. 1 - Wim Nijenhuis
ISBN 978-90-8616-236-9. 2017, Lanasta, Emmen

Operácie sovietskeho dial'kového letectva nad Slovenskom v rokoch 1944/45, Cast 1 – Mitchelly - Stana Bursa
ISBN 978-80-971891-2-9, 2017, Spolok Slovákov v Pol'sku

Squadrons No. 16 The North American Mitchell -
Phil H. Listermann
ISBN 978-2918590-98-9, 2016

B-25 Factory Times - Wim Nijenhuis
ISBN 978-90-8616-304-5, 2013, Media Primair Modelbouw B.V.

Allied Wings No. 9, The B-25 in RAAF service - Phil H. Listemann
ISBN 978-2-9532544-4-0, 2011, Phil H. Listemann

Warpaint Series No. 73 - Key Darling
Warpaint Books Ltd.

B-25 Mitchell The Ulimate Look - William Wolf
ISBN 978-0-7643-2930-2, 2008, Schiffer Publishing Ltd.

U.S. Aircraft in the Soviet Union and Russia - Yefim Gordon & Sergey Komissarov with Dmitriy Komissarov
ISBN 1-85780-308-2, 2008, Midland Publishing

De vliegtuigen van 320 squadron - Nico Geldhof
ISBN 90-672-0397-1, 2006, Uitgeverij Geromy B.V.

De operaties van 320 squadron - Nico Geldhof
ISBN 90-672-0396-3, 2006, Uitgeverij Geromy B.V.

Monografie Lotnicze 82
ISBN 83-7237-125-3, 2003, A-J Press

North American B-25 Mitchell - Jerry Scutts
ISBN 1-86126-394-5, 2001, The Crowood Press Ltd.

De Nederlandse Mitchells - G.J. Tornij
ISBN 90-9013058-6, 1999. All Media Productions

B-25 Mitchell, The Magnificent Medium - Norman L. Avery
ISBN 0-9625860-5-6, 1992, Phalanx Publishing Co., Ltd.

B-25 Mitchell At War - Jerry Scutts
ISBN 0-7110-1219-9, 1983, Motorbooks International Publishers and Wholesalers

2nd Tactical Air Force - Christopher Shores
ISBN 85045-030-6, 1970, Osprey Publications Ltd.

Mitchell Masterpieces

Volume 1 focuses on the B-25s which have flown in military US units all over the world.

Expected

Mitchell Masterpieces Volume 3. The third and final volume about the North American B-25 Mitchell in service. In this book many B-25s will be described which operated in civil service in all different countries. This book should serve as a general view of the companies, organisations and owners and the B-25s they flew. Moreover, much attention is paid to the civilian B-25s in the various museums and the warbird circuit. All this is described in detail and supported by more than 900 pictures, many of which are in full colour.